Love Never
From Heaven my

First Edition Design Publishing

Love Never Dies: From Heaven My Sister Speaks
Copyright ©2014 Angela Dawn

ISBN 978-1622-873-05-0 PRINT
ISBN 978-1622-873-06-7 EBOOK

LCCN 2014946337

September 2014

Published and Distributed by
First Edition Design Publishing, Inc.
P.O. Box 20217, Sarasota, FL 34276-3217
www.firsteditiondesignpublishing.com

Acknowledgments

This book is dedicated to the memory of
my dear mother and sister: to a love that never dies.

A note from the Author

I am not afraid of death ever since I lost my lovely Mum and, shortly thereafter, my sister and best friend, Linda. I know that one day we will be reunited in Heaven. I look forward to that wonderful day. Please don't misunderstand this as a "death wish," nor as meaning that my life is unhappy; it is not. My life is significantly different without the daily comfort of those whom I love. I miss them both immensely. Events since my mother's death have impacted my life profoundly to the point that, now, I share my story with you in hope that it may be of comfort to those who grieve for their loved ones and struggle to live in a world without them.

Introduction

No one can prepare you for the death of a loved one. There comes a time in your life when you will lose someone you love. Whatever your religious beliefs are, you probably have an opinion on the existence of life after death. Many people believe that you go to Heaven after you die, but what and where is Heaven? Seeking the truth became a big part of my life when, suddenly, in a short period of time, I lost my dear Mum and sister to a place I call Heaven.

My journey began initially when I lost my mother, but in reality it began with the loss of Linda, my sister and best friend. Grief stricken, I set off on a journey to discover the truth: Where did they go? Is there life after death? Is there a place called Heaven? Is that where God has taken them? In desperation, I wanted to find them and discover the place called Heaven. I thought that there must be a way, and I was determined to find it. I had nothing to lose; my loved ones had already gone. This distraught state of mind led me on a journey that soothed my pain and gave me the courage not to be afraid of death.

I discovered a world, a Heaven, where I found my mother and sister—I did not lose them. I came across the ability to communicate with my mother and sister through "inspired writing" at times least expected. To my surprise, it came so easily and naturally that my sister told me that together "we" would write a book to help other people. My sister's personality comes through her writings where she brings her great sense of humor, creating lively meditations, and in her words "*to put some humor in the book.*" Other times she talks to me in a stern voice while giving me sisterly advice. She refers to Heaven as *"this side"* and not "the other side" as I call it—she often corrects me! Linda says that her side is *"normal to them"* just as we see our world as "normal to us."

This book is based on my experiences during meditation and silent prayer, writing down what I saw on my spiritual voyages to Heaven, where I travel through realms of consciousness, going deep within where I could see Heaven, the afterlife. It is a narrative of my spiritual experiences, the story telling of my meditation sessions where I communicate with Heaven.

In this book, I talk about the love that bonded us together, a love that continues from the grave to Heaven, the afterlife, and a love that never dies. I began my journey to discover the truth and, in turn, it helped soothe my pain. I wish to share my experiences with you in hope that it will comfort you in your time of grief and help you discover your path in life. If my story plants a seed and encourages just a small number of people to discover their journey, then this book will have served its purpose. I ask only that you open your mind.

My mother and sister have given me much guidance in writing this book and, for the clarification of the reader, I have used *italics* when writing in a meditative state. The meditation sessions are full of life's lessons, life's purpose with examples and analogies, which give insight to the meaning of life and how to live happily. This book is an on-going dialogue with Heaven.

Love Never Dies:
From Heaven my Sister Speaks
By
Angela Dawn

Chapter 1: Life Changes

I have always believed in Heaven. I know that is where God has taken my mother and sister. Although I did not grow up in a particularly religious family, we believed in God. As children, we were all christened in a local church, in a small town located north of London, England. The choice of church was not based on any particular denomination, but, rather, on the location; closest to home was the best criteria. Even more conveniently located was the weekly Sunday school at the local school hall, which we were all encouraged to attend. Again, this was not based on any religious beliefs; instead, it gave my mother and father a small break on Sundays to prepare the family dinner without children "under their feet."

My twin sister, Louise, and I were sandwiched in between Linda, our elder sister, and Scott, our younger brother. We all got along so well as children and this continued into our adult lives. There were many fun and happy "teasing" times. We bonded together through the trauma of our parents' divorce when Mum became both "mother and father" to us.

I took a natural likening to Sunday school and continued to attend well into my late teens. My siblings happily abandoned Sunday school many years earlier, as soon as they were able to find a "better use" of this time by "having fun" with friends. Linda was always the funny one, with her quick wit and good sense of humor. She used to say that going to Sunday school gave me "Jesus points in the bank," and that, when I was older, I could "draw them out." At the time, I had no idea what she meant by this, but later, throughout our lives, if ever good fortune came my way, Linda would remind me that I was using my "Jesus points."

Being five years older than "the twins" as we were called, Linda was like a second mother to us, especially during the time that our real mother, after her divorce, suffered from severe depression and could not cope with life, nor her family. Linda took us to school, prepared our meals, and helped us with our homework. On Sunday mornings, Linda took us for walks and played a game with us in which we had to memorize all the street names so "you can always find your way home," she'd say. By the time Linda was 21, she set off on her journey "to see the world." When she came home, we sat and listened with great joy to all her adventures.

I, too, left home and moved to San Francisco to begin a new life with my husband. San Francisco is one of the most beautiful cities in the world, and my family visited me often. My brother, Scott, moved to Australia to experience life "down under," and Louise remained close by to Mum, living in our hometown with her husband and two small children. Mum enjoyed being a grandmother and spending time with her grandchildren. Although the family was "scattered around the world," we visited each other often and as much as possible.

Linda was in her early thirties when she moved to America to be close to me. I had settled in a small town outside of Washington D.C. called Charlottesville, not long after my marriage had dissolved. Linda enrolled at the local college and immediately made many friends. She loved the idyllic town with panoramic views of the Blue Ridge Mountains of Virginia. Most of all she loved Harvey, an older cat whom she adopted from the S.P.C.A.. It was not long before Harvey became diabetic, and Linda lovingly administered his daily insulin shots. When he passed away a few years later, Linda was heartbroken and decided to return home to England to be closer to mother and the family.

Linda adjusted back into British society and was thrilled to work for an American Company she said was like having a piece of America and the best of both worlds. Everyone was pleased to have Linda home, especially mother. Linda would pop in to visit Mum on her way home from work and to take her out on Sunday afternoons. Mother never learned how to drive, so she enjoyed their weekly rides out to the countryside, stopping at garden centers along the way. Also, Linda reunited with her childhood sweetheart, Jimmy, and happily settled into her new life.

Although I lived in America and my family lived in England, distance was never an obstacle when it came to our special family bond. I traveled several times a year to visit them, and there wasn't a year that went by that one of my family members did not visit me. They loved America, and they especially loved New York. Mother used to say how she felt "alive" there, and in her experience as a world traveler, "there was no place like New York." On her 60th Birthday, I took her to the Windows of the World, a restaurant located at the top of the Twin Towers. She sat in the restaurant looking over the city of New York and exclaimed "at sixty years of age I am sitting on top of the world!" She was so excited. She even took a photograph inside the elevator of a display panel of the buttons for each floor. She always appreciated traveling to new places and never missed an opportunity to live in the moment. She saw the goodness in everyone and appreciated every adventure.

Despite the distance, we were a close family. I was fortunate to have an excellent deal on my mobile phone with a low cost international calling plan, which meant I could call Mum every morning at eight o'clock on my way to work. With the five hour time difference between the two countries, it would have been one o'clock in the afternoon in England, just late enough in the day for Mum to have the latest news on family, friends, and neighbors. One day I called and she was crying. "What is the matter mother?" I asked thinking she was fine just yesterday. "It's Mrs. Prichard," my mother cried. "She passed away this morning." "Mrs. Prichard?" I said puzzled. "I thought you didn't like one another?" Mrs. Prichard was a neighbor mother had quarreled with over 30 years prior and had never spoken to since. "I know," she said still crying. "But it was nice knowing she was there." I told her that I understood completely because, for better or worse, people are part of your lives. Sometimes I wonder if they met in Heaven when mother crossed over.

Our phone calls were like a daily soap opera, my news then her news, and I looked forward to them. Just two months before she passed away, my mobile phone stopped working. I went to the mobile shop to replace it, but the new phones did not have international coverage, and the sales associate suggested that I wait a couple of months until a new model came out. I started calling mother on the weekends from my landline instead. I was disappointed that I could not talk to Mum everyday as I missed our daily conversations, and reluctantly, I adjusted to our weekend phone calls instead. When Mum passed away I felt that somehow I had been weaned off the daily calls, like a baby weaned off her mother, and somehow, I was saved from this further loss of our daily contact.

Our mother's death came as a shock to all of us. Before she died, I did not think about death. Death only happened to the elderly or people who had serious illnesses. Relatives on my mother's side lived long lives, well into their 80s. My maternal grandmother at 89 years old was still alive when mother died and lived until she was 93 years old. It came as a complete shock when, at 66 years of age, mother passed away suddenly in her sleep; it was a cardiac arrest, the doctor said. How could she be dead? She had a long life ahead of her. She had plans. We all agonized over these questions as we tried to climb out from the depths of despair and the agony of our grief.

ANGELA DAWN

The Day Mother Died

I remember the day my mother died. It was the day that changed my life. I woke up to find the world a different place from the life I once knew. I was awakened to find a life that I did not want, a life I did not choose, a life without all the things I had ever known. The phone call came at 7:00 a.m.. *Why is England calling so early?* I thought. England was my home country, where I grew up, but that was a long time ago. My family still lived there and, with the time change, they were five hours ahead. They knew it was still early in the U.S., so why were they calling this early?

I was tired. I had flown on an all-night flight from San Francisco, after visiting with my friend, Kate, and immediately went home to sleep. When the phone rang I had only been asleep for a short time, less than one hour. I heard the speakerphone built into the telephone announce "Out of area," which I knew meant England was calling. Who could it be? My mother? My sister? Don't they know it is only 7:00 a.m. here? I picked up the receiver and was about to say "It's only 7:00 a.m. here," when I heard Linda's voice say "Come home Angie, come home. You've got to come home." Linda was crying. I could hear the tremor in her voice, I could sense her fear, I could feel her pain, and I knew that something was wrong. "What's wrong? What is the matter?" I said, knowing something awful must have happened. "Why are you saying I must come home?" In a daze I heard the words, "It's mother. She's dead." The words spun around in my head. I tried to make sense of what I was hearing. "What are you saying? Don't say that Linda. Why are you saying that?" I screamed down the phone. "She's dead Angie. Mother's dead. You've got to come home." Linda repeated. With these words echoing in my ear, I dropped the phone and fell to the floor. My knees hit the ground and my body fell on top. "No, no, it can't be true, not my mother, not my lovely mother," I cried out. She was only 66 years old and had been in the hospital with pneumonia and was supposed to be going home today. How could she be dead? There must have been some mistake. I picked up the phone off the floor and heard my sister crying. Linda managed to tell me that Mum's heart had stopped beating and there was nothing they could do. I felt my body get heavier and heavier. I could not move. Was this a bad dream? Would I wake up soon? It had to be; it couldn't be real.

That evening I caught a flight back to England. Linda, my twin sister, Louise, and my younger brother, Scott, were all there to meet me. We stood in the arrival hall at the airport crying and holding one another. We could not believe our lovely mother was gone. We were four children who loved their mother so dearly. We stood there, lost, clinging to one another, clinging for any strength we could find to help us through this nightmare: a nightmare that we knew would never end.

There had been some confusion at the hospital, Linda explained. According to the doctor, Mum had a bad heart, a leaky valve. They were going to do more tests on her heart, but before they could do them, they wanted to give her some antibiotics to control the pneumonia, which she had contracted within the last few weeks. Then, on Friday, the doctor announced good news: the pneumonia was better; mother could have the tests done on Monday for her heart, and then she could go home. How could our mother be dead when she was supposed to be discharged today?

We didn't want to tell anyone that our lovely mother was gone. We did not have the courage to face it or to talk about it. All we could do, all we wanted to do, was sit in her house, in her living room, on her settee, just to be with Mum. How could our mother be dead? How could we tell anyone when we couldn't believe it ourselves?

Visit To Spiritualist Church

In England there are many Spiritualist Churches that have a philosophy that life continues after death. After a death, most people I know go to a Spiritualist church to see if they can get a message from the loved one whom has passed. It was as natural as going to the pub. When famous actors die, you watch the reruns of the actor's movies on TV. When music artists die, you listen to the artist's songs played on the radio. This was my world growing up and remains the same today. Spiritualist churches are also known to give healing. If you have pain or discomfort, or you are not feeling well, then you can always go to healing night at the church, where healers place hands on your body giving you healing energy. Over her lifetime, mother was a regular at the church on healing nights, always exclaiming how much better she felt after each visit.

The following day after she passed, all four children went to the Spiritualist church in a desperate hope to get a message from her. At the time, we did not know that the person giving the message was called a medium. We had no idea how the messages came through, only that it was comforting when you received one. Linda, Louise, Scott, and I sat holding hands, hoping the medium would come to us with a message. Her name was Babbs, and we liked her straight away. To our relief, Babbs turned to us and said that she "sensed a lady, who she believed to be our mother, who had passed suddenly, very recently, and her passing was to do with her heart." She said, "Mother was around us, giving a rose to each of us, and that mother had a message for us: 'Always see the good in people, and always do the best you can.'" We were amazed at Babbs's accuracy and found comfort knowing our beloved Mum was still around us, not gone forever. We spent the next several weeks attending as many Spiritual church services as possible in the hopes of receiving any communication, any contact from our mother.

I found refuge in the church and was comforted by the thought that life continues to exist after death. My mother lived-on in Heaven and that made me happy. In a repeat of our childhood days together, my sisters and brother quickly dropped out of attending church, while I attended as often as possible. They did, however, like to hear about the messages I received from mother. Linda often became upset when I told her about the messages—not because they were sad, they were not. It was exactly the opposite; they were always messages of love and hope. Linda was upset because she could not talk to Mum in person. Linda wanted mother back and did not want the only communication with her to be through a third party, a stranger, a medium. Mother's death was more than she could bear.

After Mother's Death

Life changed after mother died. There was a big hole in everyone's heart. She was indeed the matriarch of the family, and our lives centered around her. She was special; she was loved. We loved her. I can honestly say that I never knew what love was until that day. I was forty-four years old. I knew about love and thought I had even been in love, after all, I had a large circle of family and friends, been engaged, and even married. I had had plenty of love in my life, or so I thought.

The day my mother died, the moment I received the phone call from Linda, was the first time I understood the meaning of love. Love is a state of being, a connection you have to another person, animal, place, or thing. For me, the measurement of that love can only be found once that person, animal, place, or thing is taken away from you. The pain you feel is the equivalent, the exact opposite, of the love that you felt. The deeper the love, the greater the pain. It was this great pain that I had the instant I heard my mother had suddenly, and without warning, died.

I knew I loved my mother. I knew we were friends. I knew I loved to talk to her every day. I knew all these things. What I did not know was just how much I loved her or what love really meant. It was only through her death that I discovered the depth of my love for her, and in a short time, I also gained my love for humanity. I found that death brings to you a life's lesson in humanity, and with this thought I became inspired to write:

Death comes like a messenger in the night and leaves with the soul of your loved ones. Often it is not invited, and it is not wanted, but nonetheless, its power comes with strength that you cannot defeat, and once it has gone, once it has the heart and soul of your loved one, there is nothing, absolutely nothing you can do. You are powerless. Death is a strong force that moves in an instant, when everything you have ever known, your whole world, is taken from you. It is then, when you are left to pick up the pieces of your broken soul, that the pain begins.

Chapter 2: Picking up the Pieces

Linda could not accept mother's death. She suffered with pain from the guilt of not being there when mother died. She lived with the guilt and it made her ill, taking control of her life. Although all four children struggled with mother's death, my eldest sister Linda could not cope with her grief. She often said, "I just want my mother back." My brother Scott sought counseling and, twelve months later after weekly meetings, he seemed to be doing well. My sister Louise spent more time with her family dealing with her grief the best she could. I lived thousands of miles away on another continent and pretended in my mind that mother was on holiday, in another place.

Linda and I talked every Saturday morning. She lived with Jimmy just a few miles from our hometown in England. Jimmy used to look at the time and around one o'clock in the afternoon he would say, "America will be waking up soon." Then, when the phone rang at two o'clock Jimmy added, "America calling." With a five-hour time difference it was only 9:00 a.m. on the East Coast. Linda and I looked forward to our weekly calls.

We each dealt with mother's death in a different way. As I mentioned, Scott was in weekly therapy, Louise occupied herself with her family, and I wrote down how I felt each day and read my journal to Linda on the weekends. Sometimes she would stop me and say it was "too upsetting" and did not want to hear any more. Linda cried often and said, "If the doctor told me I had a terminal illness with only three months to live, then that would be alright with me because I would be with mother sooner." I told her I understood completely, and at first, that thought had crossed my mind initially but only for an instant, then it was gone.

Linda often talked about the last few weeks of mother's life, remembering how ill Mum was and said how guilty she felt that she and Jimmy went on vacation. "How selfish was I?" she exclaimed. "Mother needed me, and I wasn't there to take care of her." Although Louise and Scott were there taking care of mother, it didn't change how Linda felt. As

Linda sat in her new conservatory, she cried because mother was never able to see it.

The following year offered some good news for the family. Our niece, Susan, gave birth to her daughter Macy, ten months to the day of mother's passing. We believed that Macy was a gift from mother, and we were delighted. Life slowly seemed to be joyous again. As much as the new baby brought joy to our lives, Linda was upset that mother was not here to see her.

More heartache was to strike Linda. Jimmy was diagnosed with terminal cancer. She immediately took time off work to care for Jimmy since, in her mind, she had not taken care of mother. The weeks and months went by, and the effects of Jimmy's illness became more and more apparent. There were many doctors' appointments and, occasionally, there was some good news that Jimmy's body had responded well to a medication or a treatment: a small light of hope in a desperate situation. It was during this time that Linda complained of headaches and "not feeling well." At the time, this seemed natural and understandable based on the circumstances.

The Omen

My family believes in old wives tales, superstitions, and especially omens. Growing up, we knew about all of the common superstitions such as, "If you break a mirror it will bring you seven years of bad luck." It was bad luck to walk under a ladder, or to open an umbrella indoors. There were many more, all taken with great heed. Being children, we found them to be fun and sometimes scary. I remember the time, when I was approximately ten years old, that I experienced my first omen. One afternoon, while riding upstairs on a double-decker bus, a bird flew by and hit the window of the bus. Immediately it flew away. Instantly, I heard two elderly ladies on the bus exclaim, "Oh, dear! It is an omen, a sign of death." A few days later the elderly lady, across the street, passed away. I was convinced that omens were real.

It was Christmastime, just a few months before Linda died, that a bird hit the window. I was leaving America that evening to catch a flight to England for my annual Christmas visit with my family. I was anxiously delivering last minute Christmas cards to my neighbors. With a Christmas card in my hand, I approached the letterbox of my next-door neighbor. Suddenly, a bird flew out of the bush just two feet away and violently hit the neighbor's glass front door, directly in front of me. Without any distress, or apparent injury, it calmly flew up and away. I knew in an instant it was an omen, a sign of death. I froze in terror. Memories of my childhood and my experience on the bus came flooding back.

Immediately, I thought of my family members. Are any of them ill? Is someone going to die? I thought of my niece Susan who was pregnant with her second child: is something wrong with her or the baby? With these thoughts rushing through my mind, I slowly composed myself and ran back to my house, quickly closing the front door and securing the lock, as if the door was my protection from the messenger of death.

In shock, I called Linda and told her of the incident. Although Linda was not as superstitious as me, she was aware of the old wives tales and omens, just as most people we knew were. Since Jimmy had been diagnosed with terminal cancer just a few months before, she assured me it was probably an omen about his death and not our niece, Susan, or the baby. I listened to Linda's words, and they calmed me down. It made sense that the omen was for Jimmy; after all, he was terminally ill. I felt a small sense of relief, although I was not completely convinced. I also felt a sense of knowing that the omen was not for Jimmy and prayed that it was just a silly superstitious belief of mine. Later, when Susan had a healthy baby girl, I breathed a huge sigh of relief. It was not to last.

During my Christmas visit home I had not noticed anything unusual about Linda. Occasionally she mentioned she had a headache and wanted to rest, but that was only natural since she was concerned about Jimmy, and taking care of him was beginning to take a toll on her health. She was heartbroken over his prognosis, and after losing Mum just a year before, Linda never thought she would experience another loss so soon. As Jimmy's health deteriorated, Linda spent most of the time at the hospital, sleeping upright in the only chair next to his bed. She began to have more headaches, which she put down to not enough sleep and the stress she was under.

The Wedding

Although Jimmy and Linda were once childhood sweethearts, they never married. Linda had traveled the world during their time apart, and they had only been reunited for seven years. They planned their wedding day for February 14, Valentine's Day, with a wedding reception at the village hall to be held in the spring time, "when the weather was nicer," they said. Since I worked in the airline industry, I was fortunate to have employee travel benefits. Traveling back and forth across the pond for the past twenty years had become quite normal to me. I caught a flight from the U.S. to England to attend the wedding.

I knew it was a lifelong dream of Linda's to marry, and finally her dream was coming true. Her happiness was our happiness, and since we had known Jimmy since he was a teenager, he was already part of the family. My brother Scott picked me up that morning from the airport, and as we drove the short journey home, he said that the wedding was postponed. I was very surprised to hear this and said, "What do you mean postponed? Has Jimmy's health deteriorated? I spoke to Linda a few days ago and she said Jimmy was doing okay."

"No Angie," he replied. "It is not Jimmy; it is Linda. She's not feeling well and is seeing a doctor tonight. Jimmy has been taken into a hospice because Linda is too ill to take care of him." I could not comprehend what Scott was saying. How ill could Linda be? Surely she couldn't be so ill that she had to postpone her wedding? Scott explained about the headaches, the pain in her head, and how she did not say very much, and that she was slow walking around the house. This sounded strange to me. Could her headaches be so bad that they incapacitated her this way?

When we arrived at mother's house, there was a note on the cupboard from Linda, welcoming Scott and I home. She signed it: "Your single sis, for not too much longer." That evening I took Linda to the family doctor. We sat there, in the waiting room, for nearly one hour; all the while, Linda was slumped over the chair with her coat over her head shielding out the noise and the light. I went into the examination room with Linda. The doctor had been the family doctor for many years. She examined Linda and flashed a small light into her eyes, felt around her neck, took her pulse and then her temperature. The doctor concluded Linda had severe migraines and a sinus infection and wrote a prescription, with an additional note requiring two weeks off work. We immediately went to the pharmacy to fill the prescription, in hopes of a speedy recovery, and brought Linda home to mother's house, where Scott and I were staying.

We fed her chicken soup, soft-boiled eggs, and slices of bread and butter—the usual family staple for a recovery diet—in hopes of bringing her strength back. A few days rest in bed usually did the trick when anyone in the family was under the weather, and we all thought Linda would be as fit as a fiddle in no time. We knew that Jimmy's illness had taken a toll on her mentally and physically, and now all she needed was complete rest and a chance for her medications to get into her system. However, just three days later, Linda wanted to go home. I drove Linda to hospice and, together, we picked Jimmy up and drove to their home. Jimmy's body was frail, and Linda and I held his arms as we walked slowly to the front door. The door had a big step up into the house, and

Jimmy tripped over the step and fell to the ground. "I am okay," he said, as he fumbled to grab onto my arm. "It is just my weak legs," he said, as I helped him to stand up. My eyes filled with tears as I could see the deterioration of his body that the cancer had caused in less than six months from the time of his diagnosis. I stayed with Linda and Jimmy, prepared meals, and administered medications. They decided to reschedule the wedding for the following week. Linda never mentioned the pain in her head. The medications must have been working, I thought.

On the morning of the wedding, Linda and Jimmy were excited about their big day and discussed the last minute details. I drove over to Mum's house to pick up the wedding decorations. Since Jimmy was very ill, and on oxygen at the time, they decided to get married in the living room of their home, next to the fireplace—just a small family affair. Linda said she was going to take a bath while I was gone. Two hours later, when Scott and I returned, we were shocked to find Linda still in the bathtub. I knocked on the door and said, "Linda are you okay? Everyone will be here in less than an hour." Linda answered softly, "Yes," then asked, "What took you so long? I've been waiting." When Linda finally got out of the bathtub, to my surprise she said, "It took me a while to get out of the bath. I was stuck." I thought this was an unusual thing to say because I could not imagine how she could be stuck in a bathtub. I knew Linda had gained a few pounds in weight, but she was by no means too large to get stuck. With only one hour until the ceremony, I did not give this comment a second thought since we were getting ready for Jimmy and Linda's big day.

It was a lovely ceremony, although Linda had some difficulty repeating her vows. She seemed to forget the words that she was supposed to repeat. Still, this did not raise any alarm bells. We all thought that, at 50 years old, after waiting her whole life for this day, that she was naturally nervous and had wedding jitters. Looking back on the day, I remember that, after the ceremony, Jimmy took a rest, and Linda went into the conservatory and sat on the settee talking to one of the guests. She remained there for several hours. At the time, most of the guests were in the kitchen and dining room area, where Linda usually would have been. I wondered why Linda was not socializing in the kitchen area with everyone, since she enjoyed parties and celebrations and this was her big day. Now I understand that Linda was not well. Her symptoms had made it difficult for her to stand and move about the house. She needed to rest and to sit down.

It was not the idyllic wedding that a girl dreams of and looks forward to all of her life. There was no village church, no white wedding dress, no bridesmaids, no reception hall, and no professional photographs to put in the wedding album. Jimmy was terminally ill, and later we were to discover that Linda was too. But on that day—their wedding day—after they were pronounced man and wife, their love was sealed on earth and as it is Heaven. The following day when Jimmy opened his eyes, I heard him say to Linda, "Good morning, wife," and on cue she replied, "Good morning, husband," and so they were husband and wife.

Chapter 3: Linda's Diagnosis

After the wedding, I returned home to America. Louise lived close by Linda and checked in on her and Jimmy every day. Louise prepared meals and took care of day-to-day needs. She called me daily with an update. I found it hard to concentrate on daily life, and I was worried about Linda's health. Sadness filled my heart. I wanted to be with Linda. As the days passed by, Linda's health deteriorated; the pain in her head increased, and her ability to walk decreased. Linda had no sense of time, taking thirty minutes or more to make a simple cup of tea. Louise was concerned. She made a follow up appointment with the family doctor. This time, the doctor diagnosed Linda with severe depression, stating that it was "quite understandable with the news of Jimmy's diagnosis so shortly after losing her mother." This time, the doctor prescribed anti-depressant tablets as treatment.

Louise had the prescription filled, and Linda started the new treatment. The medication made Linda more lethargic, and she spoke and moved even less. She became unable to take care of herself or Jimmy. Louise tried to talk Linda out of depression and arranged for family and friends to visit her. At meal times, when Louise called Linda to come downstairs, it took Linda over thirty minutes or more to make her way. One time, Louise came upstairs to see what was taking Linda so long. She found Linda standing in the bathroom picking hairs out of a hairbrush, mesmerized as if she had all the time in the world. Louise thought she must have been depressed, just like the doctor had said.

Linda was spending more and more time in her bed, stating that she was not hungry, and she no longer came downstairs; Louise was concerned. What else could she do for Linda? Alarmed, she called for an ambulance. The paramedics came and Louise took them upstairs to Linda's room. "Do something," she said, with desperation in her voice. "My sister is not well." The paramedics asked Linda to get out of bed and walk across the room. They wanted to test her physical ability. Immediately, Linda got out of bed and walked across the room, turned around, and with a big smile on her face showed the world that she was normal. With that smile, and the fact Linda could get out of bed, the paramedics were convinced it was psychological and left.

Linda continued to stay in bed and ate less and less. Louise realized that Linda was seriously ill and was alarmed. She drove Linda to the emergency room at the local hospital. "Help her!" she screamed. "She is not well." The hospital staff performed an assessment and determined that Linda was clinically depressed and admitted her into the hospital's psychiatric ward.

Linda Is Admitted To The Psychiatric Ward.

It was eleven o'clock at night when Linda was admitted to the psychiatric ward. Louise watched as her lovely elder sister, who had been so strong and independent all her life, was at the mercy of doctors and nurses who had committed Linda to a small room with a square glass window in the center of the door. Louise was tormented: "How could I do this to my sister? How could I leave her there? Would Linda leave me there?" Louise went home praying that Linda would get well again. After all, she was finally under the twenty-four hour care and supervision of a medical team.

Louise visited Linda morning, evening, and every moment she could around her day job. Linda's health was getting worse. The simple task of going to the bathroom took Linda almost an hour. Concerned, Louise called me and said, "Linda's getting worse, not better." *What was happening to Linda*, I thought. Immediately, I caught the next flight home to be with her.

The nurses and staff at the psychiatric center took an instant liking to Linda and tried to make her as comfortable as possible. It was heart breaking to see her confined to a small room, with a glass window in the door, where the nurses looked through to monitor the patient, my sister. How could our sister, who was always so strong, always in control, be reduced to being a patient in the psychiatric ward?

After two weeks in the hospital Linda was permitted to visit her husband at their home. It was a Sunday afternoon visit, and I arrived at the hospital thirty minutes late. Linda was sitting by the door. She was slightly annoyed and pointed out that I was late. As guilty as I felt, I was pleased to see that Linda was annoyed as this was the first emotion I had seen in a long time.

When we arrived at the house, I helped Linda into the living room, and she sat in the armchair across from her husband. Jimmy sat in his Queen Ann reading chair by the fireplace, the same chair in which he was married. They both smiled and looked lovingly at one another, and Linda commented on the blanket covering his legs. Although I could not hear clearly the mumbled words Linda had spoken, Jimmy immediately explained to me that Linda "did not like that blanket because it had a cigarette burn on it." They were so in tune with one another that they knew instantly what the other one was thinking and saying. They looked so natural together. It was heartbreaking at the same time, knowing Jimmy only had only months to live and Linda, severely depressed, was unable to deal with the situation. *Is this really happening?* I thought.

Curfew at the hospital was five o'clock. Since Linda had not been eating much, I suggested we go to McDonald's for a hamburger. A big smile came on her face. All our lives I had told Linda to eat properly and healthily, which she did for my benefit but only in my presence. Often, she would order a pizza when I was not around then quickly hide the evidence—the pizza box—so I could not see it. We drove up to the drive-thru window, and I proudly ordered two hamburgers. Her eyes lit up and a little smile came upon her face. We parked the car at the front of McDonald's and watched the cars as they drove by. I ate my hamburger in just a few minutes, and I noticed that Linda had only taken a couple of bites. Usually it was Linda who took only minutes to eat a hamburger, and now it took all her ability and coordination just to eat so little. I wanted to cry.

It was five-thirty in the evening when we arrived back at the hospital. I was thirty minutes late. The staff were concerned and commented on the time. I explained that it was my idea to take Linda to McDonald's and promised not to break the rules again. I knew that they only had Linda's best interest at heart and had been concerned for her whereabouts. I found it difficult to abide by a curfew for my sister, who was a grown woman.

On Wednesday afternoon, after two months of treatment for migraines, sinus infection, and severe depression, the psychiatric doctor made an appointment for Linda to have a CT-scan. Since Linda could not walk without the help of a walking stick and the assistance of a person's arm, a member of staff drove Linda and I to the CT-scan department at the hospital. We all got lost in the building and walked through many wards before we came to the right location. Linda tried her best to focus on her steps, and each time we stopped to enter an elevator, turn a corner, or open a door, she braced herself to move. Linda did her best to smile and never complained about the difficulty or the pain that she suffered while walking.

The staff in the CT-scan theater room was very kind and helped Linda onto the bed. All of Linda's life she had been claustrophobic, and they assured her that the machine was only going over her head and that, if she panicked, she could press a buzzer, which they placed in her hand. I waited outside. After twenty minutes, I began to wonder why it was taking such a long time. I had been monitoring other patients who had examinations, and they seemed to be finished much more quickly than Linda, or was it my imagination?

I noticed the technicians were talking amongst themselves, and then I saw the light above the theater door switch on again; it said, "Do Not Enter. In Service." They were taking another test. Finally, when the door opened, Linda smiled at me as if to say, "See Angie, I am doing everything they want me to do." Her eyes said, "I will get better soon; don't worry."

Jimmy's Last Hours

When we arrived back at the psychiatric ward, there was a message for Linda that Jimmy's health was quickly deteriorating, and it was only a matter of twenty-four hours, or less, before he would pass. The psychiatrist told Linda of her husband's condition and asked if she felt well enough to travel to see him. "Yes, of course," Linda said. "I want to be with my husband." The hospital staff droved Linda and I over to hospice to be with Jimmy.

When we arrived, we went directly to Jimmy's room. I was shocked to see the deterioration in his health since Sunday, the last time we had seen him, just a few days before. Linda sat in the chair and held his hand. The doctor informed us that, "It would be less than 24 hours." The head nurse at the hospice contacted the psychiatric ward and arranged for Linda to stay at the hospice with Jimmy. Linda sat by his bed, holding his hand. They did not talk very much. Jimmy was dying.

Linda asked for a pen and paper and wrote her last love note to Jimmy "Will meet you in Heaven, all my love your darling wife, your baby." She folded the piece of paper in half and placed it under his hand. That night, Jimmy passed peacefully away, with his wife by his side.

The Diagnosis

Two days later, I returned to America, and Linda returned to the psychiatric ward under the care of the medical staff. Just twenty-four hours later the phone rang. I heard Louise's voice saying "Angie, Angie, is that you?" "Yes, Louise, of course it is me," I said immediately recognizing her voice. "It's not good, Angie; it's not good" Louise repeated. "What do you mean, it's not good, Louise? What is not good?" I said with confusion and dread in my voice. Louise blurted out "We have the results of Linda's CT-scan, and it's not good Angie. She has a brain tumor. Linda has a tumor, and they can't do anything for her." She proceeded to describe the kind of tumor that Linda had. All I remember is hearing something about grade IV, inoperable, with months to live. I sat there in the chair listening to the pain in my sister's voice. I wondered how much worse life could be. *Are we really going to lose our lovely sister? This cannot be happening.* With my bags still packed, within hours of arriving back in America, I turned around and flew home to be with my family and my dear, dear sister, Linda.

Scott picked me up from the airport, a repeat of just a few weeks earlier, when I had arrived for the joy of a wedding. We cried most of the way to the hospital. Scott explained that Linda had been told of her CT-scan results and was aware of her prognosis. All I could wonder was how had Linda taken the news of her own mortality?

Linda, Louise, Scott, and I met with the neurologist, the oncologist, and a nurse in a large, cold room at the end of the ward. Linda was sitting in a wheel chair as she was finding it difficult to walk. The neurologist explained the type of tumor she had, all the reasons why it was inoperable, and confirmed that, "At best she had a few months to live." We refused to believe that there was nothing that could be done to save Linda and asked whether she could have chemotherapy or radiation, not knowing exactly how each one worked. The oncologist instantly dismissed chemotherapy, and we were told radiation-therapy might have been be an option. Linda smiled at this ray of hope. It gave us all hope. The oncologist agreed to try the radiotherapy, which he explained would not cure the brain tumor but would increase her life's expectancy by a few months. A few days later, Linda was fitted for a radiation-therapy mask. We remained hopeful.

More bad news quickly followed. It was Easter weekend, and the hospital had limited staff coverage for the holiday; therefore, the radiation-therapy was now scheduled for the following week. Meanwhile, on Easter Sunday, Linda suffered a brain hemorrhage caused by the effect of the tumor. It destroyed a large amount of her motor skills and speech. Although she could feel and move her arms and legs while lying in the hospital bed, she could not sit up by herself or turn over from one side to another. After the Easter weekend, the specialist came into Linda's room and asked if he could speak to Louise, Scott, and I. He took us into a small side room where the nurses kept their personal belongings. There was a small desk in the corner with a chair squeezed neatly underneath. He reiterated that Linda had an aggressive tumor, which was growing at the rate of one centimeter per week. He said the bleed had caused much deterioration, and he explained that Linda was not well enough to benefit from the radiation-therapy, and, therefore, decided not to perform the treatment.

Louise, Scott, and I sat there listening to the words of this specialist. "But this is our sister!" we exclaimed. "How can you decide not to perform the very treatment that would extend her life?" "We do *not* want to lose our sister!" I remember the specialist giving some long explanation, adding that, "any radiation at this point may have severe side effects for Linda." "How much time does Linda have left?" we asked. "A few weeks, maybe a couple of months at best," he said. He added that he was sorry for the situation and from this point onwards all they could give Linda was palliative care and with that statement he left the room.

How do you tell someone, the person you love, that the one thing that could help them, the radiotherapy treatment, was no longer going to be an option, that there was no hope, and that she was going to die? How do you tell someone that? When we walked back into Linda's room, she was smiling and asked where the porters were to wheel her bed down to the theater. We sat by her bed, holding her hands, holding her head, and looked at her. We all cried. Linda looked down to the floor and said, "I'm not going to get better am I?" "No," we said, hardly able to believe it ourselves. We repeated the conversation we had with the specialist. We squeezed one another's hands, and we cried.

For the next five weeks, we sat by Linda's bed, helpless. Linda's husband Jimmy had passed away just a few weeks before and never knew that his wife had anything but severe depression. As the days passed by, the image of the bird, the omen of death went through my mind. I thought how violently the bird had thrown its body against the window, how it sat in wait for me in the bush, just like the tumor had sat in wait for Linda and had struck her so violently and was soon to take her life.

The Last Few Weeks

It is hard to watch your loved one die. I think it is important to talk about what it was like during the last few weeks of Linda's life. I can only imagine how difficult it was for Linda to face her own mortality, and suffer with the pain that riddled her body. Each awakening hour she looked at her family sitting around her bed; knowing and feeling the loss, the pain, the grief they were experiencing and knowing that soon she would be gone. I wondered what thoughts went through her mind. What was she thinking? I wanted to ask her but I could not. Is it fair to ask her? It is selfish of me to ask her? If she wanted me to know, then she would tell me, I reasoned. Did she think about her death? Was she frightened of dying? She never said, and I never asked.

I told her that mother would be waiting for her on the other side in Heaven. Mother would be there to take her by the hand and welcome her. I told her not to be afraid because we were all here on this side, taking good care of her, and mother would take care of her once she passed over. As I stroked her hair, I asked, "Linda, am I taking good care of you?" I was not expecting a response because she hardly spoke at all anymore; it was more of a rhetorical question. To my surprise she answered, "Am I being recorded?" I put my face close to her so we could look into each other's eyes. She then exclaimed, "You've got a pudgy nose!" Throughout her illness, Linda never lost her sense of humor!

We held her hand until the very end singing "You are my sunshine, my only sunshine" over and over again as the minutes went gently by. When the moment came a big smile came over her face, and the pain was gone. At 50 years of age, just five weeks after her diagnosis, our lovely sister, Linda, passed away quietly to Heaven.

Chapter 4: The Journey Begins

The funeral was lovely, as lovely as it could have been without actually wanting a funeral for your loved one in the first place. You want them to be alive and well, not dead, never to see them again. My family and I struggled through the day the best we could. It was as though we were watching a movie of someone else's loved one, not ours, especially since God had taken our mother just a few years before. How could God be so cruel to take our sister too? Wasn't it enough that he took our mother? Now we had lost both of them! How does God expect you to live your life without those you love most in the world? I was left in a daze and angry at God.

I had to know where they were. I had to know why they went. I had to know. I could not accept that they were taken from me. It wasn't fair! I loved them so much. I could not let them or our love go. I could not accept that a lifetime of love and memories could disappear in an instant, and, furthermore, I refused to believe I lost them forever, never to see or hear them again. I knew they were in Heaven—the spirit world—and that there was a spirit world because I grew up in a society that believed this. It was this belief that led me on my quest for the truth. Is there life after death? What and where is Heaven? Have they gone forever?

All these questions floated around in my mind. Scott immediately went back into therapy, and Louise spent all her time with her young grandchildren, feeling sad because they would never know Aunty Linda. In desperation, I turned to the comfort of the church.

Spiritualist Church

After the funeral, I stayed in England with my family for several weeks before returning to the states. It was where I needed to be as the family struggled through the realty of Linda's death. In my grief, I went to my local Spiritualist church in hopes of a message, a repeat of when mother died. I was not to be disappointed. Sensing I needed a message, the medium came to me straight away. She gave accurate information about Linda, acknowledging that she had passed over very recently. She described her age, height, build, and said my sister wanted to thank me for taking care of her the weeks before she died. Accurately, she described the pain in Linda's head, leading to the cause of her illness and subsequent death. The medium added that both sister and mother were together and very happy. I found comfort with this message.

The weeks following Linda's death, I visited many other Spiritualist churches, including those out of town, in hopes of receiving more messages. Most of the time I did receive a message, and I would like to share a few examples with you:

"Man and woman passed within weeks of each other. They were broken hearted but are happy together now. They look after her mother and not the other way around. Mother is saying that she left flowers pressed inside pages of books, which I did not know were there, and I should keep them."

Obviously, the man and woman are Linda and Jimmy, and I did find pressed flowers inside mother's books!

"A recent passing of a woman, weight loss at the end and pain in her head: she will help you get through this period of sadness. Seeing the names "Peter, John" around this person."

At first we could not place both names, but my niece reminded that Linda's funeral was at St Peter's Church with Reverend Minister named John Howes.

These messages helped soothe my broken heart, giving me solace when I needed it most. It also convinced me that I needed to find out more: Where did they go? How did the mediums communicate with my mother and sister?

Quest For The Truth

All that love between us, did it just end or disappear? Where did it go? I had known about Spiritualist churches my whole life, and I knew the answers would be found there: but how do you discover the truth? I did not want to go through another medium to communicate with Mum and Linda. In fact, that is what made it hard for Linda when Mum died. She said she did not want to communicate through another person to speak to mother. Yet, in reality, it was the only option left. I was aware that certain people contacted the dead: mediums at churches, famous mediums on TV, such as John Edward in the USA and Colin Fry in the U.K.. I wondered: how did they do this? Is there a secret to it? Is it a gift? Are they born with it? Can anyone learn how to do it? Can I learn how to do it?

Arthur Findlay College

The local Spiritualist churches are full of information about the religion of Spiritualism. There are seven principles that outline the philosophy of the religion, and yes, they do believe in God. Most of the churches belong to the "Spiritualists National Union," which is affiliated with the Arthur Findlay College at Stansted, near London. On the walls of the church you can find a great deal of information about Spiritualism, and it was on one of these notice boards that I found a picture of Arthur Findlay College. It was a beautiful picture that immediately caught my attention of an old stately home, a manor home, with a vivid blue sky and lush, green grass.

The college is described as a "residential centre where students can study Spiritualist philosophy and religious practice, Spiritualist healing and awareness, spiritual and psychic unfoldment and kindred disciplines. Courses, lectures and demonstrations are all offered by leading exponents, together with the additional features of a library, museum, lake, magnificent grounds, recreational facilities and full board accommodation." This seemed exactly what I was looking for. I hoped to find answers about the world my mother and sister now lived, and how mediums could communicate with them. For the first time since their deaths, I felt in control again. I felt a determination and strength to go forward. I no longer felt helpless; I felt happy.

A beginner's course with a suitable title "searching your soul" appealed to me. I eagerly signed up. This was a weeklong introductory course for students new to Spiritualism. *Perfect for me*, I thought. The classes took place from 9:00 am until 9:30 pm, beginning on Sunday afternoon and finishing the following Saturday morning. The course explained the history of modern day Spiritualism and that Spiritualism is the seventh largest religion in the United Kingdom. The philosophy of the religion is contained within the "Seven Principles of Spiritualism and followers are called 'Spiritualists.'"

I had heard wonderful things about the college, which is home to many world renowned mediums. It has its own library and museum with a vast collection of artifacts about Spiritualism. One of the most famous Spiritualists is Sir Arthur Conan Doyle, known to the world as the author of the famous detective character Sherlock Holmes. Although most people are not aware, Sir Arthur Conan Doyle was a Spiritualist, and he wrote several books on Spiritualism, as well.

The tutors explained the different types and levels of mediumship, the importance of commitment and responsibility to the religion, and the importance of respect when communicating with spirit, each of whom are highly intelligent beings. In the opening class, the tutors took the time to discover and evaluate each person's interest in Spiritualism, what they hoped to learn, and, depending on ability, they opened our minds to the aspects of mediumship. I sat there absorbing the information that came my way, and with it came great theories and practices. I was like a sponge, wanting to absorb every little drop of information I could. The more I absorbed, the sooner I would discover the truth.

Daily Meditation

Each day began and ended with a meditation. At first, no matter how hard I tried, I could not concentrate and only thought about all the other things in life I had to do, such as *Did I remember to pay the phone bill?* I did everything other than meditate. During one meditation, the tutor asked the students if we could see a certain color. This brought my mind back to the room. *Oh yes*, I thought. *Yes, I can see a pinkish, reddish color.* Encouraged, I started to concentrate on the colors I saw. I saw a whole rainbow of colors and eventually the beautiful colors of a peacock. I was thrilled. I was excited. I could do this!

The tutor suggested we pick one color that was most vivid to us. I saw a beautiful array of colored gemstones. They were magnificent. I liked all of them. It was hard to pick one from another. After I scanned the colors, not wanting to take my eyes off them, my mind kept returning to the emerald green colored stone. Emerald green was my mother's favorite color, so I stayed with that one. The tutor told us the purpose of this exercise was to pick a color, and the color we picked was one that was important to us at that time. It was a color that we needed at this time. I understood exactly what she meant by this: I needed my mother. She also suggested, for those people who couldn't sleep at night, to repeat this exercise. When you pick your color, start thinking what this color means to you; think of as many things as possible. As you focus on the color, you will drift off to sleep. I have always been a sound sleeper, so I haven't practiced this yet, but maybe one day.

Attunement

I learned about attunement and how we can attune our mind to the spirit world. The tutors guided the students through this process so we could experience this practice. For a class exercise, we broke up into small groups and practiced attunement in order to make a link, a connection with the spirit world.

I was very nervous as I did not know what to expect. The tutor led the class through a visualization of a candle flame that flickered in front of our eyes and built up into a ball of energy. We were told to imagine this ball of energy moving behind us to the back of our heads. We were to say whether or not we could feel a presence of a man or a woman. I wondered to myself: *How will I know if I am sensing someone? What if I do not sense a presence? What if nobody is there?* We all took turns standing up in front of our small groups practicing. Soon it was my turn; I felt nervous. I told myself to *'just stand up and see what happens!'* I decided that if I followed exactly what I had been told to do, then at least I could say I did my best. I stood up and the tutor repeated the process. She asked me if I felt a presence?

I felt a slight panic: *Oh no, now is the moment.* I checked my senses. *Can I feel a presence?* I waited for something to happen, anything at all. Amazingly, to the right of me, I could sense something. I was so excited! I did not know who or what, but I could definitely sense a presence. Confidently, I replied to the tutor "Yes, I can sense a presence to the right of me." "Very good," she said encouragingly. "Is it a man or a woman?" I thought about this next question, and asked myself how can you tell if it is a man or woman, but instantly, I just knew it was a man. The best way to describe it is as if you had a blindfold on and someone stood next to you and, without looking at that person, or talking to that person, you can sense if it is a man or a woman. I felt very strongly that it was a man standing next to me, so I answered, "It is a man."

Then, the tutor asked me to see if I could sense his height, his build, and his age. His height was easy to sense, because I felt he was just a couple inches taller than I am. So, I said, "He is about 5'7", medium build and he reminded me of my father who is in his 70s, so I put this gentleman in his 70s also." So far, so good I thought.

The next step was to ask this person to place something in my hand. I held my right arm out in front of me with my hand facing upwards and waited for something to happen. I thought to myself: *This will be interesting. How is he going to put something in my hand?* No sooner had this thought entered my head that I felt a heavy ball in my hand. With this sudden weight, my hand immediately fell toward the floor. I quickly used my left hand to support underneath my right arm. Then, I tried to figure out in my head what kind of a heavy ball it was.

The tutor asked me to describe the size and weight of the ball. I went through a list of all the balls I could think of: basketball, no too big, a cricket ball or baseball, no too small. A bowling bowl? Yes, that was exactly what it felt like, and somehow I knew that was correct. During this time, the tutor told me to recap the information I had provided to the rest of the group. "A man who passed over who is about 75 years old, 5'7" and gave me a bowling bowl." The tutor instructed me to ask for a memory. Again, following directions, I asked for a memory. In my mind's eye I could see the beach and seven children who were playing ball and having a nice time; this is how it appeared to me. I explained this scene to the group.

The next part of the process was to ask people in my group if any of this information meant anything to them. Immediately, Tina, a lady in the group, told me that her father passed away, age 75 years, who was a member of the local bowling team and lived by the sea where he used to play ball on the beach with his seven grandchildren. I was amazed. *Wow*, I thought, so this is how the mediums do this! What an amazing experience I had.

Although, I knew mediums could connect with the spirit world, it wasn't until I had made my own communication that I knew for certain it was real. Any doubts I may have had vanished at that moment. The link with the spirit world came very easily since there was a lot of energy in the room. I knew at that moment the key to finding out more about where my Mum and sister were right there inside of me, and all I would have to do is tap into my own thoughts and ability. Yes, ability. This is what I need to develop and work on. As a child, my mother always told me that I could do anything and be anything I wanted, just like those other children who had their daddies living at home. Just because my daddy no longer lived with us did not mean that I was any different from those other children. Mum made sure she built up our confidence the only way she knew how, and it worked.

This was the time in my life to put this belief into practice because I needed to communicate with my Mum just like other mediums could, and I knew with all my heart, with all my being, that Mum would not let me down. She had never let me down. Now was not any different just because she was on the other side. In fact, I had a feeling that because she was on the other side she would help me even more. Nothing could change our love. I knew it was still there, stronger than ever, and could not be broken.

LOVE NEVER DIES: FROM HEAVEN MY SISTER SPEAKS

Cooperation With Spirit

One important aspect of mediumship that the college explained is that communication with spirit is all about cooperation between you and the spirit world. The energies between you and a spirit blend your conscious thoughts together. It can be as little as 10% spirit energy and 90% you, and through practice and experience these percentages can change, if you allow it to. Some of the experienced and well-trained mediums are capable of blending up to 90% spirit and only 10% of their own minds. The tutors pointed out that at no time is it ever 100% spirit; you are never fully possessed. It is about cooperation on both sides that can easily be ended at any time. Spirits are intelligent beings and only want to communicate for the good of mankind. They want humans to live a fulfilled life while on earth with the knowledge that the soul continues after death and that we are all part of the one Great Spirit, one God.

The College

Arthur Findlay College has an excellent reputation for the study of spiritualism. It is a great way to immerse yourself with as much knowledge as possible in a short period of time. Although my class was a beginner's class, there are many intense courses available for the advanced. It far exceeded my expectations. I should add (for the benefit of future students) that the quality of the actual accommodation for students was low in comparison. Although it is a beautiful, stately manor, with its grand staircase, library, and ornate décor of times gone by, the bedrooms are dorm-style with mostly two or three people to a room. They do have a hand basin in the room, but many of the bathrooms are down the hall, two per floor. With this inadequate number, I found myself often waiting at least ten minutes each morning for my turn in the shower room. The college does have some single rooms with en-suite, but good luck trying to get one; they are booked at least six months in advance. I was assigned a room with two very nice ladies from the Netherlands. Their English was excellent, and we all got along very well, which was a good thing because we had seven nights together.

The college has a great family style dining room with lovely home cooked dishes. They even have a full bar, so at the end of the night you can have a little drink if you want to. The saying at the bar is "From one spirit to another!" I would like to share with you a funny story about my first visit there. I was sitting next to a gentleman, approximately 73 years old, who told me he had been to the college many times before and had been a medium most of his life. He also told me that students could not give readings to each other as this was against college rules. However, after a few drinks he seemed happy to give me a message! He said that my Mum was there with me, and she was very pleased that I was at the college. This very kind man also gave me evidence that my mother had been around me lately and he said she was showing him a place with lots of books on the shelf. I confirmed that I had been in the library doing research the week before. He stated that mother had watched me trying to lock a door that I was having difficulty with. Again, this was true; the lock on my back door was sticking, and I was having problems with it. He added, "Your mother is giving me the name Macy." I was amazed how accurate this man was, especially as we were in the middle of a bar. This was my first night at the college, and I knew I was in the right place. I also knew that if this man could communicate with my Mum, and that I had already communicated with a student's father in spirit, then surely, one day, I would be able to communicate with my own mother.

I left the college with a better understanding of the meaning of life after death and came away with a sense of knowing that mother and Linda lived on in the spirit world, in Heaven, and that their souls, their spirits are alive and well. The week at Arthur Findlay College had been invaluable to me. Contented, I returned home to America to pick up my life again.

Chapter 5: First Communication

When I returned home to America, after being in England for three months, I decided to visit my friend, Kate, who lived in San Francisco. It was Kate whom I had visited the day before my mother had died. We had been friends for over twenty years; we were hired in the same stewardess training class for a local California airline. She knew my sister Linda during the time Linda visited me while I lived in San Francisco. There is comfort being around friends who know you and your loved ones; they typically understand your pain, and Kate certainly did.

The following morning, I awoke early and came downstairs. I sat on the settee in her cozy living room, listening to the ticking sound of the grandfather clock. With each tick of the clock, I felt a warm, comforting feeling fill my body; mesmerized, my mind wondered. Thoughts of mother and Linda flooded into my mind. I thought about all the sad people in the world who had lost their loved ones. "Now I know how they feel," I said to myself. At that moment, I realized I belonged to a secret club, a club for people riddled with pain caused by the loss of a loved one. I had a membership to a club that I was forced to join. A membership I did not want.

Grief Stricken

I thought about my pain and all the other people in the world who were experiencing their own pain. *How can I help them and in return help myself? What words of comfort will heal their grief, and in turn heal my grief?* Suddenly, I felt compelled to write, and the following words flowed onto the page:

Talk to them about their loved ones, their lives, and their legacies. They did not pass in vain: What were they like? What did they do? What do you remember most about them? What was the most important thing they did? If they were here now, what would you say to them? What would you want to say to them, when you meet them again in Heaven? Will you laugh about something you did today when they say to you, "I watched you do that. What were you thinking?"

Wow, I thought, as I wrote these words. Where did they come from? They certainly did not sound like words or ideas that I would say. However, they did seem like very appropriate words to say to someone who has lost a loved one. In my short experience, I know that talking about Mum and Linda to people certainly helps me. It helps me to talk about Linda's illness, her misdiagnosis, and her death because it helps me to understand and accept that it happened. I continued to write as more thoughts entered my mind:

> *Hold their hand and help them through the pain. Let them know you care and that you know how the pain feels and what to expect. It is the love that you have for your loved one, and your loved one's love for you, which will bring you through this grief. It will make you stronger and more compassionate. It will make your life worthwhile going forward because you have this compassion, this depth of compassion for mankind that you never had before.*

I can honestly say that I truly understood the meaning of compassion, to have compassion and to feel compassion. I felt compassion for people whom I did not know. I wondered if they, too, may have lost a loved one and whether we shared a special bond. For the first time since I lost Mum and Linda, I found that I wanted to write about the pain I felt. I had never experienced this depth of pain. At first, I felt numbness when Linda passed away because I had known for several weeks that her death was coming, and I had resigned myself to the situation. It was only after she died and when the reality came that she was gone, that the pain resurfaced from Mum's death and combined with the deeper pain from losing Linda.

The Depths Of Pain

> *It is a deep pain that feels like a knife going through your body that twists and turns. It rips the inside of your body in half, then into quarters, then slices it up with more pain. It travels all through your body reaching all your senses, distorting your face. It stops your breath and you gasp for air. You cannot breathe, and there is nothing in the world that will make the pain go away. You cannot stop it, only "love, love, love." The love that caused the pain will soothe the pain. Love will bring you through this.*

These words captured how I felt inside. My heart was bleeding. Tears flowed uncontrollably at any time of the day or night, and at other times, I felt numb. This pain described above was exactly how my pain felt to me. I was amazed to see the words fill up the pages. Although I was holding the pen, it felt like it was being guided by a strong force of power. As the words appeared in my mind, they also appeared on the page instantaneously—one word after another, as fast as the pen could go.

I realize that I cannot compare my pain to your pain because we each have our own pain, and no one can measure the degree of someone else's pain, only the person who feels the pain. We can relate to another person's pain because the symptoms are the same: the loss, the loneliness, the missing them, the longing to see them, wishing they were here so we can love them, throw our arms around them and hold them tight again, and protect them from death. But we cannot. All the love, all the wishing, all the hoping in the world will not bring them back. We are left alone with our pain.

There is no magic answer and nothing that I, or anyone else, can say or do will ever make the pain go away. All we can do is learn to live with it, control, and manage the pain to the best we can because we have our own lives to live and family and friends who need us. We have to be strong for them and ourselves. We are still alive and have lives to live. We need to learn how to do that all over again. There are other times in our lives when we have to learn to live again. Sometimes it is a new job, a new partner, a new house, and we have to learn to live our lives in a new way.

Learning To Live Again

The loss of a loved one makes you live your life in a new way. We need to adjust and try and fill the void the best we can. It is not easy, but we have to take control and learn to manage our grief and our sorrow. The way we move forward, the way we choose to move forward, will determine our path for the rest of our lives. How do we want to spend the rest of our lives? What is important to us? We may think that nothing is important, that nothing matters, but we are wrong. All the more, things matter to us, things are important to us, and how we choose to live our lives without our loved ones will be a test of our souls.

What are the reasons for being alive? Why do we have a soul if our soul makes you suffer this way? It makes our souls evolve, makes us mature, makes us grow up. Some people grow up very early when a loved one is lost at an early age in life, and some people make it into their 40s, 50s, or beyond without experiencing this loss.

In my case, I was in my 40s when I experienced my first pain. The grief, which was so overwhelming, felt like a knife in my heart that was never going to come out. It stayed there, stuck, adding to the pain with every twist it made, releasing floods of tears that came up through my body making my lungs feel as if they were filling up, and I, when this occurs, I choke. It feels like a balloon is blowing up inside and taking all the air out. I gasp for breath and let out a yelp, like a trodden on dog.

When does the pain decrease? Does it ever go away? Will I ever feel normal again? All these questions were swimming around in my mind. I look at other people who are happy and ask myself "Who are they to be happy? Shouldn't they feel my pain? Shouldn't they feel any pain? How does life go on? What is the point? What is the purpose? We don't want to live a life without our loved ones, but what can we do? What must we do?

We have to learn to live again. Learn to live a life without them. That does not mean we stop thinking about them or wishing they were still here, but it does mean accepting that we cannot bring them back. We must fill the gap in our hearts with the memories of them, our experiences of life shared. Remember how we felt when we recall a special time or event when you went shopping or watched a movie. These times were all so special because that's what makes the pain so deep now.

Without all the love you shared, you would not be feeling the pain you have now. It is the depth of this love, the loss of this love that causes pain in your soul. I say soul because soul is your whole body, not just a pain in your heart. That is where the pain starts, then it travels down your legs and arms from top to toe. It's a ripple of pain from the heart, and it keep rippling, rippling until you curl up and hold yourself until it stops.

The pain stops but the ache is still there, at first with jolts of pain. Your arms feel heavy, your legs feel like crumbling, and your breath, each breath, is a labor of energy to suck in the air, slowly, deeply, until your head feels light and dizzy. It feels like it is coming off, floating to another world. It becomes lighter as it leaves and sucks all the heaviness out of your body and floats away. You feel exhausted; it feels as if all life has been sucked out of you. You feel you are falling into a deep sleep, a place where the pain has gone and is no more. You do not dream because there is nothing to dream about. You do not want to dream. All the memories of your loved one remains in the distance like a fog. You sleep, and the pain goes away.

The words flowed from my pen reflecting how I felt inside. Faster and faster they came, filling up the pages, almost out of control. I had been inspired to write, but how? At this point during this remarkable writing, I asked myself: How long will this pain go on? I could not bear to feel this way anymore. All my energy and my zest for life had gone. Will I suffer this pain for the rest of my days? Can you help me Mum? Can you help me Linda? I need you to help me. I need to know that you are okay and that you are with me. Tears rolled down my face and fell onto the paper as I wrote. I needed my mother and sister, more than ever, to comfort me and to let me know they were there, with me.

Linda Communicates With Me.

As I sat in this emotional state, my thoughts in a fog, the sound of my sister's voice came into my head as if I was attached to a telephone line and she was speaking at one end and I was listening at the other. As I felt her presence, the inspiration to write again became stronger with an urgent sense to write immediately. I reached for my pen and started to write down the words I heard.

Linda: "Yes, we are with you." I heard these words as clear as if Linda was sitting there talking to me. These words caught my attention: what is happening to me? Linda is dead. How can she be talking to me! The voice, the words were loud and clear. I continued to write:

We are helping you write this because it will help you, and it will help others who have lost their loved ones. You can help others; you are strong. You were always the strongest one, emotionally and spiritually, out of all of us kids. You brought a lot of love to me, and I am so grateful and thankful that you were in my life. You made my life a beautiful life. I was so happy. My life ended so quickly that I did not have time to say the things I wanted to say, but you knew what I was thinking—didn't you? I could tell by the way you held my hand and comforted me. Every day you were so kind. Mum was watching and she was so proud of you. She knows you will take care of Louise and Scott.

We will help you to help others. I know you want to ask questions. I can only give you advice or steer you in the right direction. You can do it; just keep doing what you are doing. When you need me, just sit quietly, and I will come. Just like I did today! Trust me! I will never leave you! Everyone wants to help you on both sides, not just this side—Ha! Ha!

(I heard a little laughter in Linda's voice, just like she used to laugh on earth.)

Go and enjoy your life. Yes, it is without me, and you did have a nice life with me—I must say!! But now, it is up to you, and you and I both know that we are still together. Just because I am not in a physical form, do not think I am any different. I know you so well, Angie, probably better than you do yourself. There is so much that I want to tell you, and we will have plenty of time to communicate.

I am so happy you are choosing this spiritual life. Mum is so pleased also. I am with her now. I spend most of my days with her. I am so happy! You have no idea. You will only know when you join us, but don't worry that is a long way off. I cannot give you the fate of you or anyone; that would not be fair. It is for people to figure out. You will get it though. You always did, going to Sunday school and collecting all those Jesus points! As long as you speak from your heart, that is all that matters.

This is easy, isn't it Angie? I am so excited for you. Have more faith in yourself. I always did. I may have been good at English writing, but that is all. You are good, too, if only you write from your heart and let the words flow. My death was not in vain. It was my time to go. My life is here with Mum. I am with her every day and it makes me so happy. I love her just as I love you, Louise, and Scott. I will watch over you all every day. I am with Jimmy and, we are very happy together. It was our time to go. He says "Hi."

The moment Linda mentioned that she was with her husband, Jimmy; I heard the sound of Jimmy's voice:

You will be amazed at what we do over here. Always work to be done—I never worked so hard before! You have to talk to many people, have meetings, discuss people's lives on earth, and make sure they are on the right track. It is like managing a group of kids—it is the same up here. Please be happy for Linda; she is so happy here. She feels bad for leaving all of you behind because she knows how much you all loved her, and she loved you and still does. She wanted to take care of you but now she can take care of you from this side, watch over you all at once. It is like looking in all the rooms in a house at one time. She can zoom in and out any time she wants to and she does! She likes the fact you were at Arthur Findlay College! She likes the old manor house. Nice people there—"like your type," she is saying. That is enough for now. Check in anytime with us. Your Mum says she will come next time.

I could see them waving good-bye and, just like that, they were gone, and so was my trance-like state. I was wide awake. I felt as if I had just hung up the telephone after talking with Linda for an hour or more. When I looked at the clock, two hours had passed by. I felt comforted and at peace for the first time since Linda's death. However, I was left with many questions: What just happened to me? Was it really Linda and Jimmy talking to me? How could this be?

Coincidences

I was eager to share my writing and thoughts with Kate, who listened intently with encouraging comments on the whole experience. She suggested we go to the bookstore and look up some books that discussed meditation. *What a good idea!* I thought. I knew I wanted to do something after this meditation, and the bookstore sounded like the ideal place, and they sold coffee. While I was in the new age section, Kate looked in the travel section for a book on vacation destinations.

The new age section was full of all types of books for mind, body, and spirit. I picked up the first book that caught my eye *Sacred Symbols* with its red and gold colorful cover. I flicked through the book and became engrossed in a paragraph about "Coincidences and Signs." I looked for a vacant chair in another part of the bookstore since both seats were taken in this popular section and found a cozy nook in the business section. Obviously, the business section was not quite as popular as the new age section on this Sunday morning. The book explained how there are no such things as coincidences, even the fact that I picked up this book in the first place was apparently not a coincidence either!

The author talked about how she had sat in a book shop, searching for a book in the self-help section and accidentally came across a book about starting a new career at midlife, which was exactly what she wanted to do. She did not believe this was a coincidence, that the book had been put there for her to find. It was at that moment when I heard a small thump sound, which brought my attention back to my surroundings. I noticed a book had fallen onto the floor; the title was *How to Build a Website.* My first thought was that somebody had accidentally knocked the book off the shelf, but as I looked around the section, there was nobody there but me! *Very strange,* I thought. I picked the book up off the floor and looked for an open spot on the shelf to place it. I noticed a space on the top shelf: "Perfect," I said to myself. As I reached up to put the computer book on the shelf, I noticed a book next to the empty space with the title *Blogging.* It caught my attention.

I was very familiar with blogs since they had become very popular in the last ten years. I liked the idea of blogging, and I eagerly took the book off the shelf and flicked through the pages. A page with a subtitle called "Ideas for Blogs" caught my attention. I wondered if there were any ideas that would appeal to me. I began to read the list with excitement. The book recommended that you write about "something that is of interest to you and that you are knowledgeable about." Instantly, an idea came into my mind: there was one thing in my life that I was very much interested in and that was my quest for the truth. The blog could reflect my journey along the way, a place where I could post all my notes. I even thought of a title for my blog "Spirits in the Sky," which was the title of Linda's favorite song that we played at her funeral service. I left San Francisco with a renewed spirit and a determination to seek the truth.

Chapter 6: Lily Dale

After my experience at Kate's house, I was convinced that I needed to know more. I had many questions and I wanted many answers. What had happened to me? It was as if I had an actual telephone conversation with Linda: How could this be? Was it really her speaking to me, guiding me as I wrote? How did she communicate with me? I needed to know. I knew from an early age that spirits can communicate from the other side; I had believed that my entire life. I thought back to my childhood days, when as a family, we had played with the Ouija board. Often we received messages without understanding meaning or purpose. Whether the glass moved around the table by either spirits or by our physical touch, it only added to the spooky fun of the night.

Louise and Scott found some comfort in hearing about my communication with Linda. They were curious and asked "how could I be sure that it was really her?" - A question that I had asked of myself. The answer, for me, lies in what you believe, and in my grief it was exactly what I believed. I knew from my recent experience at Arthur Findlay College that I could communicate with spirits, but did I really communicate with my own sister, or was it just wishful thinking on my part? Could it happen again? How do I make it happen again? I was anxious to find out more about how spirit communication worked, so I continued on my quest for the truth.

Lily Dale

I had read about Lily Dale, New York, in a new age magazine I picked up while having breakfast in a local coffee shop. The article stated that Lily Dale is the world's largest center for spiritual development and for the practice of the Spiritualist religion. Established in 1879, it is the center of modern day Spiritualism.

The history of Spiritualism is very interesting. Modern day Spiritualism was founded by the Fox sisters in Hydesville, N.Y. in 1848. The Fox sisters were two young children who had heard rappings in their home and started clapping to the sound. They started a game where if they clapped then the rappings mimicked the sounds back, so they devised a simple system of "yes" and "no," then an alphabet system to communicate with the sounds. The message they received was from a peddler called John who communicated to them that he had been murdered, and gave the name of his murderer. Approximately 50 years later, the body of John, the peddler, was found buried in the walls of the basement where he was murdered. From the rappings of the Fox sisters a new movement and religion called Spiritualism which spread throughout parts of the world. In 1916 the Fox sister's home was moved to Lily Dale.

I was pleased to discover that Lily Dale was in driving distance of my home in New York. I knew that, in order to learn more about the spirit world, Lily Dale would be the place to go. The summer season is open to workshops, seminars, and other events. Eagerly, I signed up for several classes over the summer months and set off on my journey.

The Town

The first time I went to Lily Dale I felt I had stepped back in time, into a time when life was simple without modern day stress. It is a quaint Victorian style town, and I could already imagine a Dickens-style Christmas. Immediately, I felt comfortable and at home.

It is a community with approximately two hundred homes and even has a post office. It also has a small beach area next to a lake and a campsite for family vacations. You can choose from the lovely Bed and Breakfasts or one of the two hotels, which to me looked like they were haunted. There are a couple of cafeteria-style restaurants, a coffee bar, and picnic tables with scenic views of the lake.

A small population of people live all year round at Lily Dale, but in the summertime, like all resort spots in the world, the town becomes flooded with tourists who go there for their summer vacations. What makes Lily Dale different is that it is a town for Spiritualists where they can meet and congregate with like-minded people. It is unique in that aspect. There are many Spiritualist centers, such as the Arthur Findlay College, the Omega Institute at Rhinebeck, NY and many more; however, there is only one town where there are permanent residents, shops, and a post office.

I was surprised to see how lively the town was especially as I had only just discovered it! Everyone seemed friendly, relaxed and knew their way around. They knew which classes to take, which cafes to go to etc. I had a lot of catching up to do. There were many new people, first timers, like myself, but there were many old timers who came every year. People, from all over the world, flock to this small idyllic town. I met people from as far away as Australia.

There were many seminars and workshops to choose from. The classes are staggered throughout the town in various halls, rooms, and churches, some in the outdoor amphitheater or arena. The classes vary in size from small and intimate with 10-15 people to upwards of hundreds of people in the large auditorium. Lily Dale has many morning, afternoon, all day, evening, and weekend classes, with a broad range of topics to choose from, such as how to develop mediumship and intuition, along with astrology, healing, and dream classes. The guest speakers come from all over the world, including the U.S., Canada, U.K., and Europe. Famous mediums and authors attend and teach at Lily Dale, as well. I found several fun classes that interested me, along with more intense development classes. I decided to book a variety of classes, as many as possible, to get the full flavor of Lily Dale.

<u>Classes And Seminars</u>

My first class was called "Mirror Gazing," which I found to be very informative and interesting. It is an excellent, relaxation technique in which you can tap into your creative abilities. Unfortunately, over the centuries it has been classed as "evil" but, in reality, it is just another tool to induce a slight light-trance, similar to those you experience while staring out of a window, not knowing time has ticked by.

Mirror gazing is one of the many tools that come under the heading scrying. You can also use a candle, water bowl, or any object that you can stare into. In Biblical times they used stones, and in Genesis: 44:15 Joseph interpreted dreams and scryed using a silver cup. It is known that Michel de Nostredame used a bowl of water for scrying and wrote his predictions. More recently, J.K. Rowlings is known to have sat on a train, on a rainy day, and, apparently while looking out of the window, she saw the entire story to her famous Harry Potter books. It was difficult to practice this technique in the classroom with the distractions of people talking amongst themselves, and people talking outside as they walked by the open window. Therefore, when I looked in my mirror, I could not see any spirits. I could only see the reflection of the red exit sign hanging at the back of the room. However, I found the class to be a lot of fun.

I signed up for a class called "Perception and Development," which was an interesting course to help one to "discover your energy and the energy that surrounds you." We can use our sensory perception, which is when all our senses come into play when we make a decision. I understood this to be our gut feeling: when we know something feels right or not. Everything is made up of energy and it affects you. When people sit next to, you can smell their perfumes, you can sense if they are happy or sad. This was a great workshop for feeling and sensing energy, something we all do naturally, without even thinking about it.

The "Psychometry" class was a hands-on experience that I found fascinating. As the previous class had mentioned, everything is made up of energy, and this was reiterated for the purpose of this class. We were taught that "psychometry is the ability to hold a personal object and receive impressions from the energy that is held by the object." In this class we took turns holding each other's objects, such as car keys, key rings, watches, rings, etc., and describing to the person any information that came into our minds. I had never done this before, and it certainly sounded like a lot of fun. I sat holding the car keys belonging to the lady sitting across from me. I could see a hospital building and a silver tray with surgical tools. I also saw big ships on the water and the sun shining brightly. The lady said that it did not apply to her, since she worked in a small office and in the Midwest, with no water or ships close by. I was beginning to doubt the process when suddenly she exclaimed, "Wait, my sister was visiting me last week from Fort Lauderdale. She is a surgical nurse at the hospital, and there are cruise ships nearby, and she did drive my car last week!" We were both amazed at this! *It works*, I thought!

If you like astrology, Lily Dale has weekly Astrology Roundtables that are very educational. I have always struggled with astrology beyond naming the planets and knowing the astrological signs. However, I do enjoy reading my daily horoscope. There was a large turnout for this class; people were actually standing at the back of the hall, so I know many people are interested in astrology and particularly enjoyed this class. For me, I will stay with my daily horoscope.

When I saw a class entitled "Platform Mediumship," I definitely added this to my list. I was not to be disappointed. This class discussed how a sprit communicates with a medium and how that information is passed along to the recipient in the audience. We were taught that mediumship is an act of compassion, one of the kindest things we can do for our fellow man. Mediums are instruments of service and cooperation. "Energy is the consciousness of humanity," the speaker said. I like this statement. From my limited experience, I know that we can communicate with the spirit world through our thoughts, our consciousness, and that consciousness is energy, everything is energy. This is what I was beginning to understand about the spirit world.

I also learned from this class that we have gatekeepers who work with us. Together we decide how we are going to work together. Our consciousness blends together when we communicate with them, similar to how our energy blends when we talk to a person sitting next to us, except that we work at a different vibratory rate. We listen to the gatekeeper, establish evidence to identify the spirit of the loved one present, and then give the recipient in the audience a message from them. We were also reminded that as mediums we want to help people who are grieving receive messages from their loved ones, and we want to educate people about the spirit world. This sums up, quite nicely, my own interpretation and views of mediumship.

In addition to the workshops and seminars, there are open events throughout the day and evening. Some of them are free such as the daily Message Circles at the Stump. This is a small outdoor amphitheater style arena with benches set up to the left and right with a center aisle. At the front there is a large tree stump, where the mediums stand and give out messages to the audience from loved ones in spirit. The message circle at the stump is hosted twice a day by the local mediums that rotate. These events are very interesting to attend, especially when one of the famous mediums take the stage. There is also a weekly ghost walk at 10:30 pm at night—fun for all the family. Although we didn't see any actual ghosts, we did see orbs, which are spirit light on film. We saw when guests took photographs on their digital cameras. Not surprisingly, most of the orbs on the photographs were the ones taken in the museum, home to artifacts of past mediums.

As you may tell, I enjoyed my time at Lily Dale. The town and all the people I met were very nice. I came away with a wealth of information and a better understanding of how to communicate with the Spirit World.

What Did I Learn?

I attended several workshops over the course of the summer season. I learned that psychics are not mediums, and only mediums communicate with spirit guides or teachers. In each of us there is an inner knowing or hunch that is part of your connection with your spirit guide. As humans, we live on a different energy level than the spirit world, and it is our spirit guides who balance the energy fields between us allowing the flow of communication, the blending of energy and consciousness.

When we pass over into the afterlife our consciousness, our soul, is woken up, and we become conscious beings in the spirit world. We also retain our personalities, which is why, when spirits communicate with their loved ones, the mediums can sense if they are a happy or jolly soul or if are sad. We can all expand our awareness of the spirit world, through meditation, through our prayers and through our dreams.

After understanding that communication with the spirit world can take place through meditation, I now understood that I was in a slight meditative state in San Francisco when I experienced my first communication with Linda. I also learned that this was called inspired writing, which is one of the many forms of Mental Mediumship.

Types Of Mediumship

At Lily Dale and Arthur Findlay College aspects of mediumship are discussed. There are many books that explain these forms in detail. The summary below is intended to give you a basic overview to clarify some of the different types of spirit communication.

There are two forms of mediumship: mental and physical. Mental mediumship is subjective while physical mediumship is objective. In both physical and mental mediumship, mediums obtain and relay information from spirit.

Mental mediumship comes through the mind of the medium. The medium becomes aware of the communication with spirit, within his or her mind. Then the medium relays the information to the recipient. The medium receives the information through clairvoyance, clairaudience, clairsentience, spirit writings, and spiritual drawings, to name just a few. Spirit can also move closer to the medium where energies blend on a deeper level. This is called a "trance-state."

Physical mediumship was the first form of mediumship beginning with the Hydesville Rappings in 1848 (discussed above). In physical mediumship everyone can hear and see the same thing. Physical mediumship includes levitation, spirit photography, transfiguration, direct voice, and materialism, again, to list just a few.

It was explained that some phenomenon may fall under both mental and physical mediumship, such as automatic writing. It is mental mediumship because it comes through the mind of the medium, and it is physical because spirit controls the hand. From my understanding, this would depend on the energy level of Spirit.

This is very interesting to me. When I experienced my communication with Linda through writing, I was convinced that the physical action of writing was controlled by some energy force. My hand felt as though it was being moved which could be classed at physical mediumship. Yet, thoughts and sounds in my mind appeared as Linda's voice and Linda's words, which is classed as mental mediumship.

Chapter 7: Judge's Approval

It has been several weeks since I received my first communication with Linda. I attended classes at Lily Dale, N.Y. and absorbed as much information as possible. I kept a notebook of my experiences and added them to my new blog "Spirits in the Sky." I was beginning to understand how communication with the spirit world worked and became more comfortable that I was on the right track in my quest for the truth. After understanding that my meditations were truly communication with spirit world and not my imagination, I felt encouraged to continue on with my newly discovered journey.

I longed to feel Linda's presence again. I decided to experiment and see if I could repeat my experience that I had in San Francisco. I made certain the phones were switched off, the windows were closed, and the doors were locked. I did not want to be interrupted. I made myself a comfortable position on the settee and sat there with my notepad and pen in hand. I said out loud that I wanted Linda and Mum to visit me again if they could, and then I waited.

As the minutes went by, nothing happened. I did not sense or feel anything. I could not focus. My mind was distracted by the noise of the lawnmower across the street and the sound of cars as they passed by. I became annoyed at the unknown operator of the lawn mower—why can't he hurry up and finish? My mind shifted from any hopes of meditating to wishing the lawnmower would breakdown.

Tutors at Arthur Findlay College teach you to block out any distracting sounds during meditation because you cannot always expect to have complete silence. I decided this was a good time to try this technique. I acknowledged the noises outside and told myself that they were not going to interrupt my meditation. Again, I sat and waited. Nothing happened. What if my communication with Linda was a onetime experience? What if I was just in a distraught state of mind and was not actually communicating with Linda? Again, I thought back to my week at Arthur Findlay College and the meditation techniques I learned. Can they work here in my home? I decided to choose the simplest one and the one I liked the best:

Picture a staircase in front of you. Describe it in your mind. What does it look like? What shape is it? Imagine yourself walking up the staircase, counting each step you take. When you arrive at the top, what do you see?

I liked to imagine a big, grand staircase like those seen in the great Hollywood movies. Each time, as I ascend each step, I imagined myself to be Scarlet O'Hara, in the movie *Gone with the Wind*. The first time I reached the top of the stairs I did not see anything, just darkness. So in my mind I went back down the stairs then, one by one, I climbed them again (another technique the College teaches). This time, as I reached the top of the staircase, I saw the image of my mother. It worked! I felt a rush of excitement throughout my body. She was smiling at me! In an instant I could hear her voice just like I had heard Linda's. I could hear her voice loud and clear! We were connected! Her voice sounded the same as if we were having a telephone conversation. I was so excited!

First Communication With Mum!

Yes love, Mum is here. Mum is always here! Remember that. Just because you can't see my physical body, know I am here. I am always here. You had a lovely time at Lily Dale, and I was with you all the time. Stop asking for proof. Just believe. Be secure in your decisions and judgments. Help others when you can. That is what life is about, helping others. You are not the second eldest child by accident. You are the family's guardian angel. You don't have to be on this side of the world to be an angel. I get tired just like I did on earth and have to take my naps. So I will go now. Linda sends her love.

It was a short message from Mum, more like a quick hello. I hoped that she would have had more to say, since it had been nearly three years since she passed over. Nonetheless, I was so happy to hear from her. I knew she would come through. I always assumed that she was around me, just as any mother would want to be around their child. As soon as Mum mentioned Linda's name, an image of Linda came into my mind. Simultaneously, Linda began to communicate with me.

Linda Tells Me To Write A Book!

"Mum and I are with you all the time," Linda said as if validating what mother had said. *"You are the only one that can communicate with us. Scott tries. I mean, he talks to us but it is not the same as you."*

I understood what Linda meant by this. Scott often talked to them while he was out walking or alone in his house. It was a one-way conversation because, although they could see and hear Scott, he could not see or hear them.

"If you like, Mum and I will help you write a book! Linda said to my amazement. She continued: *You know I was a good writer and so was Mum with her poetry. We can help you. The book will help you and, most importantly, it would help others. I think the best way is to write it down like you are doing now. Buy lots of paper because you will need it to write everything down!"*

Linda always had to tell me what to do, whether I needed her help or not. *Some things never change*, I thought. Linda continued on with her instructions for me. It brought back memories of when we were children, her taking charge, helping us with schoolwork, etc.

"I will help you. Keep a log of all our conversations and it will help you. You can mention that we talk this way and that we decided together what would be best to write in the book, but at the end of the day, the book will be yours with a little help from your loving sister."

I was laughing to myself at this point. Her phrase "we decided together" was just the way it used to be. Linda often decided something and then made you think it was your idea and that she was just helping you! Linda switched from talking about the book to a personal thank you for taking care of her in her final weeks:

"I want to thank you for taking good care of me. So much love you gave. We are very lucky to have each other. I will never leave you, although I have work to do on this side. It is just like being on earth, you meet people, you talk, and you have group meetings, committees, and places to go to meet people."

Linda switched topics again, from words of gratitude to all the work she has to do on her side! She changes from serious to funny all in one sentence. Very similar to how she was on earth.

"Still waiting for Mum ha! ha! She takes so long to get ready! Just like she used to on earth! She rests when she gets tired. She laughs the same way too! (Mum used to have this loud infectious laugh.) *I take her places with me. We go together just like we used to! It is nice, Angie. Well, I must go. You can talk to me anytime— you know how to do it! T.T.F.N. Love Linda."*

T.T.F.N. (ta-ta for now) was one of her favorite sayings. I do not hear many other people say this, but Linda did and often. It was nice to hear her say it again and it brought a smile to my face. *She's just the same*, I thought. *She hasn't changed.*

I was so happy to hear from both Mum and Linda, although Mum's message seemed so short. I reread the part where Linda told me to write a book. I thought that it was a crazy idea, since she knows that writing was never my favorite thing to do. I often struggled with it, writing papers, rewrites, edits, etc. Linda was the writer in the family. Words used to flow from her pen with ease. She used to check my school papers for grammatical errors then could not believe it if one of my professors found one that she had missed. How was I going to write a book? Surely she must have forgotten my limited writing skills!

The following day I sat and meditated again. This time I had no problem blocking out distracting noises and concentrating on my meditation. To my delight, Linda came through with a very long communication.

"I am here, Angie. I am always here. I am near you. Can you feel my presence? No, it does not wear me out because I want to be with you. I love you so much that I can help you all you want. Scott and Louise don't do this, only you, so I can talk to you anytime like this."

Linda was referencing things I had wondered about. Was I interfering in her development? Did her visits take too much of her energy? Was it exhausting for Mum to visit me?

"Now look at Scott with his new dog. I am glad he likes it. Scott needs him to help him get through this difficult time."

Scott did have a new dog, Archie, from the local animal shelter. Archie is a beagle and just the perfect size for Scott's small home. Scott lives just minutes away from the ocean, and they spend many days walking on the beach.

> *"You all need something new to help you, since I know you are all dealing with my loss. I am helping as much as I can. I miss you all terribly, but I am here. I am here, if only Louise and Scott would get it into their minds, like you, that they can communicate with me. It is no secret that we can communicate from this side over there."*

Linda suddenly changes from loving thoughts of comfort to giving stern advice on my life.

> *"Stop trying to get your ducks in a row. Life is not like that. You have to do things for today. Please don't wait for the future and say, "I'll wait until then." Life passes by so quickly, and you of all people should know that."*

Linda is also referring to my idea on remodeling my house. This week, I had looked at new kitchen cabinets and decided against buying them because, one day, I hoped to move and live by the ocean. When Linda advised me not to wait for the future, she was referring to Mum, who for the last twenty years of her life did not remodel the family home because she hoped to move one day, especially since several psychics had told her so. Mother never did move home.

> *"Start living your life today. Be confident in your decisions. Keep going in that direction. It is the right way to go. Always waiting for something to happen stops you from living your life. How many times have we said that! Haven't you learned enough from Mum's life? Where did it get her? Always waiting for something to happen. When things happen, they will happen; that's all there is to it and all the thinking and waiting won't make it happen any sooner. Instead, you will miss out on all the things in life you are meant to learn and enjoy. I feel strongly about this. Don't make the same mistakes. Go with what you feel instead of analyzing what you should do. Intuition is your soul telling you what to do, just like I am doing now. It is your soul that lives on because it is part of all the souls of mankind, whether on*

earth or in this world, the spirit world, it is really the same thing. We are all energy."

(This reminded me of the philosophy I heard at Lily Dale: we are all energy and connected to one force of energy in this world and in spirit.)

"Some souls are able to take on a physical form. When it is time for them to learn something, they choose to come down to earth level. Please tell everyone you know about this so they can learn about the evolution of the soul and can find happiness in their lives.

A Meaningful Life

Live every day the best you can by helping others. Ask yourself: have I helped anyone today? If you have then you are doing the right thing. Learn your lesson on earth; you can't learn everything in the spirit world because that would be too easy. Life lessons have to be learned on earth in the physical form because that is the true test. Make your life happy, and you will make other people happy. Life is all about making other people happy, which brings you happiness.

This sounds like a sermon, doesn't it? Yes, it is supposed to! It is sad that people do not get the meaning of life on that side. Only when we pass over do we really understand why we were put on earth. I can help you understand that now, Angie. You don't have to wait until you get on this side because it is important that you and everyone else understand it now. I never really got it while I was there. I lived life how I wanted to, never really gave it a second thought. Love and happiness go together. You can't have one without the other.

You have to give love to be happy. That is what life is about. It is so simple, yet people do not get it. Love is all that matters; love is all there is. All you have to do is listen and love one another. "All you need is love," just like the song. Many songs are written by spirit; however, people don't realize it. The Beatles have many songs about love that are meaningful. I chose The Beatles to remind you of Britain—ha! ha! But really, listen to the words of the songs. Go and start your life from today. Don't look back.

Goodbye for now, with all my love, Niecee."

"Niecee" was the nickname for Linda growing up. No one called her that name after she became a teenager. I was surprised to hear her use this. It felt good to hear her say it. I found this meditation very interesting because of the philosophy that came through. *My! My!* I thought. *Linda has certainly evolved into a religious soul with such words of wisdom.* Linda was a kind, loving person, who everybody loved. She had a smiling, happy face, the type that invited strangers to speak to her. Often, while out shopping, strangers would approach her and ask her advice on an item they were intending to buy, whether it was a new dress or an item at the food shop. All the while, I would be standing by her side and was never approached in this way by a stranger. Linda often said that I had the don't talk to me face; meanwhile, she had the I am very friendly and helpful face. It was true. As these memories flashed through my mind in an instant, I felt the strong presence of Mum again. She began to speak.

"This is Mum now. I know you want to see me and I wish I was there. But I am there; I am always there; just tune in any time. You will get better at this. Look for a feather today on the pavement. It is just me saying hello. (I actually found two feathers in close proximity of each other.) *Don't get hung up on all the details. Go with the flow. Energy moves you along in the right direction so don't fight it. Go with what feels right.* (Interesting: another mention of the word "energy.") *We are all souls and have the same spirit. Some of us are old souls, and some are new, just starting out. Souls need to learn new life lessons. They can learn them up here, which is the easy way. Or they can come down to earth. Some actually like coming down there. They come of their own free choice. Don't worry about all that now; it will come later, one thing at a time. You are just getting acclimated to everything and need to practice to get more confident, so we will give you dribs and drabs to get along with."*

Linda interrupted Mum and said:

"We are always here, Angie. We are like Tweedle Dee & Tweedle Dum. (Laughing) Not saying who is who. We have a laugh up here, Angie. Yes, sometimes we look-in at everyone and have a laugh. We know all that is going on. We have front row seats. Just remember that sometimes! We will never leave you or

*the family. The children are coming along very nicely. They bring lots of joy." (*Referring to our great-nieces)

Mum returns:

"Well, goodbye, and I will love and leave you for now. Linda is yelling 'bye' to you. She goes here, there, and everywhere, just like she did down there. Me, just going for a rest. God bless. Mum."

What a great comfort it was hearing their voices again. Was it necessary to have proof that it was their voices? As long as the communication came, I continued to meditate and listen. A few days later, I had a meditation that was clearly memorable to me, which I would like to share with the reader. I began the meditation by picturing a staircase and began to climb the stairs very slowly. With a few steps left to climb, suddenly I saw my mother who took me by my left hand, and pulled me up the remaining stairs. From behind, I saw Linda as she pushed me up the stairs. I could feel her hands on my back! In no time at all, I was standing in a room, in front of a committee, with a judge-like figure of a man with a smaller hammer in his hand.

I listened as Mum said to him, "This is Angie. She is ready to join us." She laughed, and then said, "You know what I mean! Not literally to join us on this side!" The judge said, "We are here to discuss how we can develop you." I stood there and wondered: what was happening here? Mum said to the judge, "Angie is good at public speaking," then Linda said, "and she presents herself well." With those words, the hammer came down and hit the pad. The judge announced "very well then!"

The scene disappeared and my meditation abruptly finished. I felt some disappointment because I was unable to ask the judge what he meant when he said "very well then."

Chapter 8: Talk of Heaven

I began to meditate daily, first thing in the morning. It became a wonderful obsession. The more I meditated the easier it became. I found I could meditate up to two hours a day! The lawn mowers, leaf blowers, cars passing by, even the phone ringing did not affect me anymore. I could be in a deep meditative state within minutes without having to picture a staircase or a walk through a beautiful garden. It felt so natural and I loved it. Of course, Louise and Scott thought I was being obsessive and suggested I slow down and limit my daily sessions. But I couldn't. I enjoyed them too much. I found it fascinating that my mind could actually do this. If people want to call it my imagination, that is fine with me, but I never had such a great imagination. I had never been so inspired to write and never been able to write so philosophically. It was a journey I wanted to stay on. I wanted to learn more, I wanted to go further, and I wanted see where it took me.

In the beginning when I first meditated I was very cautious of being by myself, at home, all alone. I never meditated at night. I had seen too many Hollywood movies, and I never liked the dark. I developed my own technique for meditating. At the beginning of my meditation, I opened with a short prayer. I asked that God's love surround and protect me, then asked if my mother and sister could visit me. This seemed to work very nicely!

I had been meditating for approximately two months, and I was very fortunate to always be able to communicate with Mum and Linda. On this day, when I began my meditation, I did not see Linda or mother; however, inspired thoughts came into my mind, similar to how they appeared in San Francisco. I thought this was strange but continued to write down all the inspirational thoughts as quickly as I received them.

Love Is A Verb

A wonderful world awaits you on the other side. Once you know and understand it, it changes your life so much, that you are not afraid of anything—not even death. You can call it Heaven if you like, whatever you imagine Heaven to be; that is what the world is like when you pass over. It is a place full of love. It is a place where you continue to learn and develop love.

Love is a verb, an act of doing: I love, you love, we all should love; all should love one another. That is all. That is all there is to learn in this life and in the afterlife. Learn to love one another and you will live the greatest life of all. Jesus, Gandhi, Mohamed, Mother Theresa, all preached love, and they are here in the afterlife teaching love, just like they did on earth. You don't change your thoughts or philosophy when you cross over. You take these with you. Some have more to learn when they cross over because they did not learn it when they were there. They continue to grow and evolve as a spirit.

Sometimes it may mean you have to come down back to earth again and learn that lesson again.

Sometimes you can learn them up here, but the greatest challenges and learning experiences come from your time on earth because you have obstacles such as temptations, lust, greed, etc. to overcome. These temptations are not here in the afterlife because they are only relevant to the physical body, which of course you lose when you pass over. Love is the essential or essence of life in your world and the after world. It is such a simple word, yet its meaning is ten-fold. Love is a verb; love one another. The act of loving, forgiveness, understanding, caring, and nurturing are all the words that represent and mean all what is good in life.

Discover your soul's journey; discover your own journey. It is the most exciting thing in the world. It will become part of you and your life. By that I mean, everything you do will have a purpose, a meaning. Your whole existence will make sense once you discover the meaning of your life. It is the same meaning for everyone. Your life's purpose on this earth: we are here to love and be loved.

Love everyone, not just your family and friends, which is the easy piece. But to love everyone, people who come into your daily life, even if it is only for a moment, make that moment special and show your love. A one second smile at a stranger can brighten that person's day. A genuine thank you to someone goes a long way and will make them feel special. Here you will find that they have helped you in more ways than you know. By saying a special thank you to them, or a 'good morning' to a stranger, it will leave you with a feeling of love and warmth that you made someone else's day brighter, and there is no more reward greater than that.

Life is so simple if only people didn't complicate it by making assessments of others. Assessing others is the mirror of the depth of the pain that is within your own self. You are projecting outward what is inside of you, making that pain inflict itself onto another person for a short-term fix of making you feel better. It is a cop out, as the expression goes. Instead, learn to love that other person and see the good in them, for it is you who put the bad in others by verbally bringing it out in your words and actions. So I say to you, as the great teachers such as Jesus, Mohamed, Gandhi and Mother Theresa, love one another for there is no greater gift on earth than love.

Thank you for today's sermon. I hope you have enjoyed it and that it has given you food for thought for your journey ahead. God bless each and every one of you.

As this sermon came to an end, I listened for a sound or an image to appear of either Linda or mother. It did not feel like Mum or Linda communicating with me. I sensed a male energy, and an image of a monk came into my mind. I felt very comfortable and at ease with this new energy. When I came out of the meditation, and said my closing prayer, I thanked the kind spirit who came that day and gave me this inspirational writing.

What Is Heaven Like?

What is Heaven like? I wondered. Like most people, this thought had crossed my mind many times. Since losing my loved ones, I was curious about Heaven. Could Linda tell me? Would she? I am certain that Linda, in her human body, would want to know. My idyllic view of Heaven is a perfect place full of love and kindness. People often use the words "Heaven" and 'Heavenly" to describe something that tastes, feels, or looks wonderful. For example, if you eat something delicious, you may say, "It tastes like Heaven." Heaven is a place where everything is more "Heavenly."

Could it be possible that Mum or Linda could describe Heaven to me? Or, was it off limits? I closed my eyes and prepared to meditate. I saw Linda's face appear and almost immediately she started talking about Heaven. She had been listening to my thoughts.

ANGELA DAWN

Linda: It is like a balcony: people hover over it looking down at earth waiting to see if they have been called in. There are classrooms off the hallways that you have to go into and learn. Some of them are like classrooms on the earth, like most classes with desks they want you to sit in them. Some of the advanced souls get to go to executive-style rooms with a conference room, and then beyond that, it is like something out of the Roman days where they sit around and talk about philosophy. On days when many are learning for want of a better word, their souls link, into something of a universal system, and they learn as one.

In between sessions you can come and look over the balcony any time you want and check on your loved ones. Sometimes when you call me, it may take a moment for me to come through. Yes, we already know when you will be contacting us because we know everything that you do. So we can be here and there very quickly in your time. As I told you before, it is not quite the same in our world because time has a different meaning here. I think it would be great if you could write down a description of how it somewhat works over here. It may help explain it to those who want to know.

I was very excited that Linda was talking about Heaven. The information was coming very quickly, and I hurried to write it down. I did not want to leave anything out. I had heard about the light that greets people when they pass over, and I asked Linda about the light.

Yes, of course, there is the light that greets you when you cross over, but there is so much more. The light makes the separation or distinction, if you like, of the passing from physical body to spirit world or world of spirit. Then, as you know, you are met by many people who you have known in your life, not just loved ones, but even people like Mrs. Prichard, of all people, because as you will learn, she was part of your life to learn a lesson. (Mrs. Pritchard was the neighbor mother cried over after she passed away whom I wrote about in chapter one.)

It is amazing when you get here. We all have such a laugh over everything, and it is nice to see familiar faces; some of whom you did not know had passed over when it was your time to pass. But we are all here now still laughing about everything—even the times when we had little arguments and disagreements. Yes, we laugh about them all. You will be amazed what it is like. It is like a little city, or a "city in the sky," made up of a mixture of people who were there on earth. But here, everyone automatically knows everyone. It may be for the first time, but there is no need for introductions.

Linda asked me if I understood what she was explaining to me and how it worked over there because she said it would help me to explain it to those people who wanted to know. Linda switched suddenly from talking about Heaven to mentioning the sermon that I received.

Yes, Angie, you will receive sermons from our world. The sermons are lessons that I want you to learn and teach others before you come over so you all will have less work to do over here. I wished I had listened more when I was there. Now it is like going back to school and learning all that Sunday school stuff all over again! Sermons are communications to help you to help others. This is what the communications are all about: to help others. Once people understand that they are on earth to help others, once they get that, then their work on earth is really done.

Linda changed course and talked about Mum. She had a lot to say. It reminded me of when you catch up with a friend, and you tell each other a quick overview of things, then you go back over certain situations in more details.

Mum understood this meaning of life. She got it. That is why she doesn't have to go to as many classes as I do, which is good because she likes to rest! I don't mean just sleep like it is on earth. I mean a meditative rest, where she can be quiet by herself. She has lots of people that come to her for help. She helps them understand what it is they have to work on in their own spiritual development, but it takes a lot of her energy. She was always good at helping people. She had the knack while in her physical form, and it is even more amazing to see her work now. She truly has a wonderful gift, full of love that is never ending and overflowing with abundance.

It was true: Mum loved helping people. She was always attracted to people who needed help, or maybe it was they who gravitated towards her. She would spend hours on the phone counseling family and friends, and, afterwards, went for a lie down because she was exhausted! I was not surprised to hear that she continued this work in Heaven.

During the months that followed Linda's death, there were disagreements within the family. Linda was cremated, and her ashes were kept in an urn at the family home. Some family members wanted them buried, so there would be a memorial place to visit. I understood this; however, we wanted to keep them next to our mother's ashes were in the living room cabinet, and then, one day, bury them side by side. I was surprised when Linda changed the subject again and referenced this disagreement.

> *I know you want to talk about the family, but I can't interfere too much because what you don't learn down there you have to learn up here, so I wouldn't really be helping you. But I can tell you that everyone is okay and I watch over them every minute of the day. I know what you all think and feel. I know you all miss me terribly, but my death had to be.*

Linda began to give me sisterly advice on how to live my life without her—advice she would certainly have given me if she was still alive on earth.

> *You have to learn to live a life without me. I was only one piece of it. I don't want to say small piece because that undermines the love I have for you all and the love you have for me, but it was necessary for me to go. You need to understand that. It would have been easy for you if I had stayed, but we all would have continued on the way we were, just plodding along, catching and enjoying happy moments when we could. I know this is going to be hard to understand, but you need to learn how to be happy all the time. I don't mean fun and excitement 24/7. I mean how to be happy being contented with your lives, with the people in it, and with the love that is around you now. Love is around you at all times. You need to open your eyes and mind, then see and hear it, and let it in.*

I sensed a sermon appearing, and I was right!

Explore Your World

> *A death of a loved one makes you analyze and reevaluate your life, and see where you are in your journey of life. If pain and sadness is what it takes to do this and the death of me and any*

other person, a loved one, is what gives you the jolt, then you must understand this.

I see you all having your own separate paths now. (Referring to Louise, Scott and I) *Explore your lives and see where the path takes you. We were all entwined, which was good but not for spiritual growth. Loved ones are only there as peripheral on the outskirts of the center of your life. Your life has a center, a soul, and this is what needs to develop. Having loved ones so close is like a crutch; you never need to go outside of the peripheral of your circle. You are now forced to go outside and explore your world. Remember to do this with the right intentions. That is the key that will make your life's purpose fulfilled.*

We will all be together one day and, yes, you will thank me and Mum for doing this to you. By leaving your physical world we were able to let you grow. Mum and I would never have left you if we thought you were not ready. Don't waste this opportunity. You will get what you need, not what you think you need. Just believe in what I say, and believe in your path. Don't get bogged down with all the human needs, desires, and thoughts. Think only spiritually: what do I need? Focus and practice on that. There is no greater joy than this.

Linda's voice faded out and, to my surprise, the sound of Mum's voice appeared!

Mum: Hang in there, love. This is your Mum speaking. I wanted to come and say hello. Can you hear me? My voice sounds younger to you, doesn't it? Like I was in my 30s! You can hear my laughter. I am wearing my lovely dresses and shoes with a heel, as they don't hurt my feet anymore. I am young again. I am telling you this because I don't want you to worry. I want you to know that I am all right. Linda is like she was in America, happy and contented with the cat, Harvey, so don't be sad for us. We are all right. One day you will know. Yes love, it is really me.

At this point, I began to cry. I could hear my mother's voice as loud and clear as though she was sitting next to me on the settee. I wanted to put my arms around her again and hug her like I used to do. Her love was all around me, and I knew that her soul was still alive and that she was with me.

Don't get upset. I am here, my lovely daughter. I want you to be happy; that is all. If you continue your work your spiritual work, you will have the best life you could ever have hoped for. Louise is okay. She is slowly getting on track, so no need to worry. Scott is doing okay. His new dog is helping him. They are two of a kind! ha! ha!

Bye Angie, will come back next time. I love you.

With words of comfort, followed by laughter, Mum said goodbye. I had been in my mother's presence for only a short period of time. This was a short communication. Was this how it was going to be: Linda communicating most of the time, then Mum coming in at the end with a few words of comfort? Although I loved communicating with Linda, I also wanted to have more communication with my Mum. It had been three years since her death, and I missed her dearly.

Chapter 9: Meaning of Life

I had been meditating for a few months and I really enjoyed my daily sessions. I had stopped wondering how it all worked, and appreciated any, and all, communication I received. I had connected and communicated with Mum several times. I hoped that she would communicate with me more often, and for longer periods of time. My wish was granted when, one day, after meditating for just a few minutes, I could see a picture of Mum in my mind. The sound of her voice came into my ear, loud and clear. I was so excited.

Mum: I want you to write down what I am going to say. Yes, it is Mum here. You will hear me loud and clear soon. It takes practice, and you will know when your handwriting changes whether you are in full form or full trance. You are just learning now so practice all you can. In a moment you will feel heat in your ear, and you will hear my voice. It takes a little longer to get all your senses to work, finely tuned, but practice makes perfect. You will be automatically able to hear me straight away if you are connected to my energy, and you will notice your writing will begin to change.

The Meaning Of Life

We can talk about life today. Life as you know it on the earth. Once you understand that, you will have a better understanding of its purpose and, eventually, life on this side. Life is a precious gift that should be cherished. Not just life for humans, but all life. I am talking about the birds and the bees, the animals, the fish, the insects, everything. All life comes together and coexists as one life. It is the joy of life that each animal, creature, etc. brings that must be cherished. For when you see the beauty of life in other things is when you will see the beauty of your life. All this will lead you to happiness.

It is not happiness that is gained through a career, a job, a new car, house, etc.; it is the type of happiness that is within. Not everyone understands this and, yet, it is so simple to understand. The meaning of life is happiness, which is obtained from seeing the beauty in all things. I am saying see the beauty in all things for seeing the beauty in things is also seeing the goodness in things.

Seeing the goodness in people is seeing the good in life. It is a basic thing, but people do not see the good. They see what they want to see: good if they want to see good and bad if they want to see bad. Take a look at all the creatures that you don't like, snakes for example come to mind. Yet, because they may not look nice, it does not mean they are not good. They have a role to play in the universe just like you do, so see their goodness and change the way you look at them.

Some people may look bad to you, and your initial reaction is to look away. But I say to you, look again and see them for the goodness that they are. Don't be fooled by misconceptions of how people look just because they may look different to you. Look at the whole person. Look at their eyes. What do they tell you? Are they sad or lonely? Happy or kind? How about their smile: do they have one? Are they reaching out to you through their smiles or through the lack of their smiles?

I have always taught you to see the good in people and do the best you can, and I want you to listen to that and take it seriously, to heart. There is no better purpose in life than to serve mankind through love and kindness.

Yes, you can feel your ears burning now, and your writing is getting faster and out of your control because I have so much to say, and I want you to write it all down as I say this to you so you don't forget. Get the word out: that is what I want from you. Always do your best, and you can't go wrong. How many times did I used to say that to you? You used to think that Mum went on too much all the time, but I wanted it to sink in, so now when I am not there in the physical form to tell you, the lessons are there in your head.

Fundamental Lessons Of Life

You have lots of memories of lessons that I taught you as a child, just basic lessons of love and kindness and all the stories of my childhood and my life. They aren't to be wasted. They are full of life's lessons, which is why I chose to have them in my life, as painful as they were; I needed them to grow spiritually.

If you take each one of my stories that I told you again and again, you can learn from them. Look back and remember them. Understand the message and share it with others. This will help people. People need to know life's lessons and, if my stories can teach them, then I want you to share them with the world. They are sad and full of pain, but pain and suffering are the fundamental keys to spiritual growth.

You have to look at history. Look at our spiritual leaders and see the pain and suffering of the great ones. Jesus, of course, is the most obvious one and, although his pain and suffering was the ultimate sacrifice to the world, each individual one of us has our own pain and suffering on a smaller scale. Our pain and suffering is only unique to ourselves and not the world. Yet, we can learn from each other's pain and suffering to help our own growth. You don't have to have your own pain and suffering if you are able to understand someone else's pain and to feel compassion for that person.

Life today is harder than the simple way it was years ago. I am not talking about technology because you can say it has made the world easier and a more convenient place. I am talking about all this advancement and technology today that has taken away the fundamentals of life—a simple life of helping one another and not everyone for themselves.

Look at the rural villages in South America for example; you will see people living well into their 100s because they do not have all this so called technology. They live off the land and live and eat simply, fetching their own water, cooking in the village for the whole community, living together as one family, and helping each other. It is such a simple life, yet people choose the life of luxury instead. I don't mean luxury such as a big house, fancy car; that is not always true. Luxury is the average person with a house and car compared to the people in the village I just talked about.

Although I was listening to mother's speech, my mind wondered to the sound of the noises coming from outside the window. As I became aware of the noise, Mum addressed the noise directly:

Yes, you can hear the noise of the cars outside and the lawn mower, weed cutters, etc. All these things create noise and pollution in the air. It upsets the energy and creates stress in what should be a peaceful world. I know modern day living does call for some technology, but is it always better? This may sound extreme but what about a push mower? They are quieter, give people exercise, but, of course, they are more tiresome to use. Therefore, people want the easier and quicker way all the time. There is nothing better than pushing a manual mower and feeling your connection with the grass.

That is enough about technology, but you understand the point here. Sometimes modern improvements do not always improve life. It is good to experience the city life with all the energy and excitement that it can bring, but this must only be one part of life because you will never learn the beauty of life that exists unless you spend time with nature. Once people are together with nature, they will be happy. They will learn to see the true beauty of life: being thankful for all God's creation and sharing this beauty with their fellow man. So, you see, there are lots of things you can do to help others in this world if only you open your eyes and look around. Seek out things you can do because only through helping others will you truly help yourself to live your life to the fullest.

Alright love, I think that will be enough of a sermon today as you like to call it. It is a teaching from me. Think of it as a gift from your Mum. What better way than to give you the meaning of life. I will help you as best as I can. Bye love, I am going now.

I felt Mum's energy drifting away as I came back to my active thoughts and my surroundings. However, just before the communication was completely finished, I heard Mum add the following:

Mum again: Start writing this up before it gets too much and all these notes stack up. You will have a hard time reading this writing if you don't. I have to go now. Things to do here. I've enjoyed spending this time with you. Remember, I am never far away. You are always in my thoughts. I am going to stop now. I love you. Mum.

I started to laugh to myself as she said these last few words, since mothers know their children only too well. She was right; I had written all these words down in a notebook and was having difficulty reading my hurried and scribbled handwriting. After each meditation, I decided to type them onto my blog immediately.

After I finished this meditation, I looked over the number of pages I had written. I had been meditating for well over an hour. For some reason, I still sensed that I had not completely finished. I decided to close my eyes again to see if there was another message from Mum. As soon as I did this, thoughts of Linda came through, along with a strong urge to write again. As it did before, my hand began writing words quickly on the paper, as quickly as Linda sent the words through into my mind. On earth, Linda was a fast writer, and as a secretary, she used to take dictation and write in shorthand easily.

Happy In Heaven

Linda: Yes, been waiting for Mum to finish. She goes on a bit, doesn't she! Just like she did when she was down there! She goes on and on, and doesn't stop! Everything is okay here, Angie. I love it! I never knew I could be this happy. It is hard to explain, but I feel joy all the time. It is like doing all the things you want to do without having to worry about eating, drinking, paying bills, etc.

There is so much space here that you can move around very easily and freely. It is like a social club! There is this meeting, that meeting, this event, that event. It is a great social life. You have your friends and family that you had on earth, but then you have more friends up here. It is like we are all connected. We are all family together. Love is what keeps us all connected. There is so much of it here that it lifts you up. I don't mean literally. It lifts your spirits, so to speak. That was my little joke! I always had a sense of humor, and I do now.

Everything is more light-hearted, not so serious here. We have a little laugh when we look down at you, but we also understand your pain when you experience bad things. We see your sadness and understand you. We don't feel the pain ourselves because we only feel love and joy. It is so wonderful here! You will never want to go back. But sometimes our souls need to grow, and earth is the best school for that, to learn life's lessons quickly. You can learn them here, too, but it takes a lot more work, dedication, and practice. Therefore, some souls choose never to come to earth because they would rather learn here. We all have choices just like you do down there. You have a great support network up here.

You can tell that when I'm talking to you nothing changes, does it? Funny really! When I say nothing changes, it really doesn't: just no physical body, no pain, and none of the bad things in life, such as silly arguments or disagreements. We don't get upset. Here, everything has meaning and is tied to the bigger picture of love and happiness. That is what people want for each other. We want that for you too, and my love for you and the family is just as strong as it was there. I want to protect and nurture you so I watch you all every day, all the time. I just want you to make the most of your time while you are down there. I can't tell you what to do, although as your big sister I want to! Not as a bossy sister, just that I want the best for you.

Have Meaning In Your Life

I can keep communicating with you this way as I know you miss me, and this helps you to work through your grief. Louise and Scott cry a lot, and that is how they deal with it, but I want them to live—live their lives going forward and know I am proud of them. Every time they think of me, I will hear them and know their thoughts. I want them to enjoy life with all its good and bad. "Life goes on" is an old cliché, but it is true. It is just different for you all now. You have to live your lives with the tools that are around you. In other words, make the best of what you have, your surroundings, the people in your life, and the things you do every day.

Have meaning in your life, and your life will become meaningful. Don't let the loss of Mum and me stop you from living your life. Life is a blessing, so don't throw it or waste it away. Take a look at what you have now, gather it all up, and use it as your foundation to grow. Don't think about what you have lost in your life, or you will be stuck in that place. Life is too precious! Reach out to others. Help others and your life will have meaning. I know this sounds a lot like mother told you, but this is today's lesson for you. Love one another.

There. You never thought you would hear me talk like this, but I have grown in the sense that I am already much wiser now than I ever was. I don't regret my time on earth or what I did or didn't do down there, but I am catching up on all the things I should or could have done down there! I am leaning to be a good person and to love everyone. I know I loved people down there, and people used to say I was a good person; however, there were parts of the me that were good, but then as you know, there were a lot of people who got on my nerves, but here no one gets on my nerves because, here, it is just too happy a place for that! Everyone is so nice that no one can possibly get on your nerves! Maybe that is why we have a physical body at one time because this is an example of how different it is here. You only learn the lesson of tolerance while on earth.

With that thought, my communication with Linda ended. She was gone. I came out of this communication feeling like I had had one of the marathon two-hour conversations we used to have each week. The communication was so clear that the sound of her voice resonated in my mind. I felt no different than the times we used to talk on the phone when Linda would give me some lecture on my life. She was my big sister, and her slight bossiness was just part of her role. I could see that this role had not changed, and it pleased me. She sounded just like she did while in her physical body: same sense of humor and witty comments. It was a great feeling to be able to communicate with her so frankly!

Chapter 10: Truth and Love

Linda's birthday was approaching, so I decided to go to England to be with Louise and Scott. While I was there, I went to the local Spiritualist church and attended the Monday night open circle. Open circles are weekly group meetings that are open to the public where people meet to meditate and build a closer relationship with God and the Spirit World. The churches have closed circles, which are not open to the public and are for the experienced church members who are mediums. The churches welcome you, even if you have no experience; everyone shares in the experience. Jonathan, the circle leader, opened the circle with a warm welcome and with a prayer, followed by a meditation. Jonathan told us to imagine we were outside the church and led us through the process of reentering the church and taking the same seats that we had at that moment.

Guided Meditation

I reached the front of the church and sat in my seat to the left, the original seat that Jonathan told each of us to take. I noticed a big, medieval style wooden table in front of me. A monk came and sat down next to me and placed a scroll on the table.

He seemed familiar to me, and instantly I recognized him as the monk from the meditation session from a just a few weeks ago: "Love One Another."

It was one of those old fashioned scrolls, which opened from left to right. He put candles on each corner to keep the scroll open and to stop it from rolling up. "'Look," he said and pointed to the scroll. There was a picture of a forest. The tops of the trees were dark green and bushy, reminding me of broccoli, with thick green stems with space in between. The monk began to speak:

Metaphor For Life

To realize what you really are. What are you really here for? First of all, you have that old saying, "You can't see the forest for the trees. I am an old monk who carries a white candle, just like you picture me now. I am showing you the forest, and I am clearing the forest just like the loggers do down on earth when they are clearing the way for a new road or a new housing development. You have been seeing only the forest for all of your life, and now it is time for you to see what real life is all about. I will show you so you can help others. As the forest is cleared you begin to see more and more of the land. This is obviously a metaphor for life. The treetops are so green and wonderful, all close together, touching each other like a blanket. This represents all the muddled and confused beings in the world, all vying for a piece of sunshine, a piece of happiness, not knowing what it really is they are seeking, so the view at the top is not clear, it is muddled. Underneath, there is much space at the bottom of the trees.

If they stop following everyone else they will see the huge, beautiful spaces at the bottom of the trees where the light is brighter than that at the top. It is clear, untouched, waiting for drops of leaves to fall to the ground in order for them to be reborn again into earth's natural place. People are so afraid of not getting to the top that they do not look below them and see what is in their reach. See the beauty that is there in front of them instead of struggling to look or to seek something that is unreachable, caused by the confusion that they themselves have created. Life can be so simple and enjoyable if people only realized the simple things in life are all around them now for them to enjoy. Of course, loving one another is the best and easiest foremost thing to do, but appreciating what has been created on the earth, this great universe is the best reward man can hope for. Everything you need is here. Stop searching for it in things that are not important.

At this point of the meditation I could hear Jonathan, the circle leader, telling us to finish the meditation and come back to the room. He instructed us to go back up the aisle out of the door of the church and gently become aware of our surroundings once more. After everyone in the circle came back into the active mind state, people were invited to share experiences.

Some of the people in the group were experienced mediums and did platform work, which meant they did public demonstrations of mediumship at local churches. There was a trained medium sitting on my left side who told me that he had seen my mother's spirit around me, and she had told him that it is her that comes and channels me and will help with my spiritual development.

These words spoken to me by a stranger validated that it was indeed my mother and, hence, my sister communicating with me. I felt inspired and ready to continue on my journey. I was slowly discovering the truth, the truth of life. I arrived home, full of excitement, joy, and inspiration. I had to meditate again; the night was still young. I closed my eyes and waited, willing the monk to appear. I wanted to see more of the scroll.

The Essence Of Man

This time I saw the monk holding honey in his hands, stretching it out in front of my eyes from one hand to the other, and then he said:

> See the beauty in nature. Not only do I want you to see it, I want you to taste it. Understand the true marvel of nature. It is incredible! No more beauty is there than that which is in nature and it is free, given to you with lots of love and endearment from the creator. Look around you at the beauty in all things. If you look you will find it. You see goo on my hands because you see, by touching the beauty of the honey, I have messed up the structure of the honey. But you must look beyond the goo to see that it is the same beautiful honey as it was before I twisted it and changed it from its original form. The beauty is there, so look beyond and see the essence of the honey, not the way it looks.

Then, the monk held a blue bowl in his hands. It was half full with water, which moved gently around the bowl. He continued:

> Giving a drink of water to anyone can be the most important gift you give. I am giving you one now out of the bowl. (I could taste the water.) You may think it is just water, but see how wonderful it tastes when someone else gives you the water? All of a sudden you want the water, and you taste it for the first time in a different light because it is given to you full of love and, again, this is free.
>
> Water is a gift from nature, yet you take it for granted, but you change the importance of water when you see it in a different

light, whether it is someone with a kind hand pouring the water into your mouth or watching it trickle down a stream or from a waterfall. So, when you see the water in a tap or a glass that is given to you, see beyond the limited thoughts you have and expand your mind. Look at nature's beauty in all things.

Appreciating this beautiful world is the best way to receive God's love, for he created the world with all its beauty, the seas, the mountains, the animals, and mankind. Enjoy it! That is what he wants for all his children. Just like a parent would give a child a new toy and see the excitement in the child's face, that is what God has done with the earth, given as a gift for mankind to enjoy! See them live happy lives with all his gifts that are right here in front of them.

I gave you this lesson of the honey and water, yet there are many more examples. However, the message is the same: see the beauty in all things, for you will truly see the beauty in life and in yourselves. This is important. See the beauty in yourself because you are magnificent creations of God, just like the honey. And when humans allow themselves to be distorted like I showed you with the honey, they forget how beautiful they really are. There are those who have lost their original form of God's creation. Their purity has changed or been lost. Find it again by looking at the beauty in life that is in nature and in all of God creation.

These are just basic things, yet they are the whole thing, everything. Life is full of analogies. They are life's lessons for you to learn. People have gotten away from basic love of nature and things.

Next, the monk showed me the bottom part of a dark leaf cabbage:

Take a look at the cabbage, at each leaf, and marvel at the intricate veins that run through it and at the rich deep color. Then, take a gigantic leap of faith and see the minerals, vitamins, and goodness in the cabbage. Food that is good for your soul. You may look at celery, carrots and see them as more useful vegetables and all the uses in cooking you can make with them, so you place importance on them when choosing them at the store. But look again at the simple cabbage, and see what value it can also bring to your table.

The key to this lesson is to look beyond what you can see, for when you do this you will expand and see the beauty in all things. Everything is God's creation so remember that as it includes snakes and insects! Take a closer look at them and marvel at their beauty. My teachings are simple and basic. All I say to you is to see the goodness in God's creation, and your lesson of love and happiness will be learned. Thank you for sitting with me today. I will go now. God bless.

The example with the cabbage resonated with me. I must admit, while growing up, that dark green cabbage was one of my least favorite vegetables. It was there on every Sunday dinner plate during the winter months my whole life. Dark green cabbage was mother's staple vegetable because it was good for you! To see the structure of the veins in the cabbage had certainly given me a new appreciation for this vegetable and the wonder of nature.

The Moment Of Truth

My final meditation that evening convinced me the most that life continues after death. You may think that all the evidence received so far had convinced me; however, this one profound experience changed everything:

I could see blue and green lilies floating in a pond, which reminded me of Monet's "Water Lilies." I could see and hear the water trickling down; it was peaceful. I looked up and could see a radiant blue sky. It was a beautiful sight. I could feel my body floating up to the sky through a white cloud. The cloud was moving, taking me away. I could see a ring of fire that the cloud was taking me through; I hesitated because I did not want to get burned. As I passed through, some flames landed on me, but they easily brushed away. They did not hurt! I felt no heat or pain. As I landed on the other side, I saw a bright, white light. I felt myself being pulled up through a tunnel of light. I easily passed through.

When I arrived on the other side of the light, I looked up and I saw Jesus on the cross. I was standing at the bottom of the cross looking up at him. The cross was very big. I could feel my head automatically move to the right. There, to the right of the cross, I saw Jesus again. He was looking at me with his arms wide open, hands facing upwards, towards me, with his head titled slightly to the side. He was dressed in a blue robe or gown, just like he is depicted in Renaissance paintings. He had a halo above his head, which lighted up his face.

Jesus spoke: "I have come to prove to you the continuity of life."

Instinctively, everything became clear to me. That is why I could see his dead physical body on the cross, and then I could see his spiritual body alive again. This is why he returned to the earth to show people that life existed after death. His soul is alive again in the spirit world, a world that is called Heaven. It is a place where all souls go after they have left their physical body.

Jesus continued: "The teachings in the Bible are of love and truth; that is all. They have been changed over time, but the real message is of love and truth. Help people to know the truth that life continues after death, and Heaven is where the souls are now. Follow my teachings of love and truth, and you will evolve as a soul."

When I came out of this meditation I felt the utmost serenity and inner peace I had ever known.

Mum And Linda Visit Me.

That night, I went to bed filled with joy, happiness, and excitement. As I slept, I felt an overwhelming sensation that someone was staring down at me. The sensation was so strong that I woke up. Startled, I sat upright in bed. The curtains were slightly open, and the light from the lamppost across the street shone into the room. To my surprise, directly in front of me, I saw a black and white image of Mum and Linda. The image looked like a charcoal etching that someone had drawn, except that a smile came upon Linda's face as she realized I could see her. At this point, I knew it was not a charcoal etching; it was them! As Linda smiled, she turned her head and looked towards Mum. Mum continued to look at me, lovingly. In my tiredness, I said, "I am sleeping right now. Can you come back later?" Instantly, I fell back to sleep.

In the morning I opened my eyes and looked around the room for Mum and Linda. They were gone! How could I have been so tired to tell them to come back later? Why did I say that? I had an opportunity to see them, talk to them, ask them how they were, and tell them I missed them, so many things! Yet, I blew it. I couldn't believe I had missed my golden opportunity. I know there are many people who may think that it was only a dream; however, I can honestly say that I have had many dreams of Mum and Linda, and I was fully aware that I was dreaming. This time I knew very well: it was not a dream; I was awake.

Chapter 11: Education for the Soul

I returned from England with an even greater enthusiasm for meditating. The open circles gave me more practice and experience with linking with spirit. The energy in the church increases your own energy level, which is why, I believe, Mum and Linda were able to visit me that night. Since I lived many miles away from the Spiritualist churches, Lily Dale, and Arthur Findlay College, I decided the best way to continue on my journey was through my own meditation sessions and inspirational writings. I was happy and contented doing this. Also, I had no idea how long this was going to last; I hoped forever. I was eager to learn more about the afterlife, and I asked for more information. My Mum did not disappoint me and came through with wonderful information on this subject.

The Other Side

Mum: People want to know more about the other side, as you call it. But it is "this side" to us. It is you who are really on the other side! Our side is normal to us; we think of it as normal just as you think of your side as normal. I want you to know as much as possible about our world because it will help you explain to others what it is like. That is the real interest of people on your earth. They want to know what it is like. I will help you by telling you what it is like.

Firstly, when you cross over, you are met by many people: family first, of course, and then many friends and even people you do not know. It doesn't matter that you didn't know them on earth because you have a sense that you have known them forever because you have, in many other lifetimes. You know many, many, people on this side when you come here, too many to count because, again, you knew them in other lifetimes. Just imagine your own life. Look at all the people you know today: passing acquaintances, people in the street, at the bank, "the store" as you say or "the shops" as I say. Then think back to your first school, all the children you knew there, all the children in your secondary school, your church, colleges, and so on, so forth, your first job, etc., etc. Just see how many people in your physical life today you have been in contact with, then multiply that by hundreds of lifetimes that you have lived, and you will have some idea how many are here on this side to greet you; not all standing in the front row of course, but like a big crowd at a pop concert or sporting event. The difference here is that you have the ability to know and remember each one of them.

The White Light

It is amazing beyond words. When you pass over, you see the light and you walk over a ceremonial bridge: a small bridge, into a beautiful garden with a white picket fence. A gate opens, and you step into this new world. Once inside the garden you can see for miles because the garden has no limit in size. Within the garden you walk around and are greeted by people that you know. Of course, the ones at the very front are your immediate loved ones, such as parents, grandparents, etc. Then you slowly make your way around to meet a few friends, more relatives, and some acquaintances, of course.

There are plenty of opportunities to catch up with everyone. It is very organized without any effort at all. There are meetings, events, and functions to go to, just like you do on earth. Where do you think humans get the ideas from in the first place? It is not that the spirit world made our world as a replica of your world. It is the other way around. You naturally want to meet with souls on earth, and you do up here also, so that is consistently the same on both sides. Call it human nature, if you like. Your soul, your consciousness, or whatever you want to call it, because we all belong together as one, whether on earth or up here.

Let me go back to how it goes up here once you pass over. I have already told you about the bridge, the garden, and the people meeting you, and then you look at the board and you are given your assigned room, space, area, a place where you go. It is determined by your immediate loved ones who are there to initially help you settle in and get reacquainted with the other side or this side once you are here. Then you catch up, just like you do there. You talk about how good it is to see one another. We review our lives on earth that we had together. All the places we went and the things we did. Even talk about things we wished we had done differently if only we had known because everything becomes much clearer to you on this side. All your mistakes, all your accomplishments, you can see them as part of the big picture, the picture of life.

We then talk about our loved ones who we left behind, how much you miss us, and that makes us feel sad for you, but not sad like you are on earth, but sad, in just a knowing way, as we can see you grieving. Grief may seem like a long time to you, but time is a split moment for us. We stay with you and give you strength to get through the human emotion of grief, but you have to know that your grief is real and necessary for you as a soul to grow. You will understand fully when you get here that your loved ones, when they pass over, do not grieve on this side. All they feel is joy and immense gratitude for being reunited with everyone on this side. They have come home for want of a better word. There is no better word; it is home for your soul and a big party and a reunion takes place.

On earth you have music and singers, and when singers pass over they sing on this side too, except they don't need all those instruments. Here, they can sing harmoniously without. We can go and listen to them sing. There are many, and you can choose which artists to go and see. There is so much to do up here, places to go: socially, for work and meetings, etc. Let me go through each one with you. Of course, the social one is easiest, so I will talk about that first.

A Big Reunion

It is one big reunion, as I began to describe to you what it is like when you pass over. When you are met by everyone, you go to your assigned place and then you initially are surrounded by your immediate loved ones so you can review your life and passing with them. They will tell you that they were with you the day, the week, up until your passing. They gather around you to comfort you. In fact, before you pass you actually see an image of your loved ones. They come to reassure you that you are not alone and that they will be waiting for you on the other side to take you by the hand and lead you through.

This is a very important thing to do because it helps the soul readjust more easily, as loved ones bring love, and it is their love *that helps and feeds the soul. Once you are here, we show you the ropes if you like. Actually, it is really just a quick refresher to get you readjusted and to help you to let go of your physical form, which you no longer need.*

The first few weeks, as you say on earth (days and weeks mean nothing here), you spend time just catching up with the news of loved ones, and you keep looking back to earth to see your loved ones and watch them and help them get through their grief. Then, you are given a review. This is done by a committee made up of a mixture of loved ones who you know, highly evolved souls such as guardian angels, and spirit guides. They assess your soul's evolvement and see where you need more development. It is not all done at once, but it is an on-going review first, like you have at work in your world. Again, remember, all the things you do on earth regarding the activities of the human soul are exactly how it is here. You have meetings and reviews. Can you see how the two worlds are inter-related?

Work And Meetings

The committee then assigns you work. Now, there are many different work types. Obviously, some involve helping other souls who have a need. For example, when small children and babies cross over they need help growing up and being looked after because a child and a baby grow up in spirit world and become an adult. Just because they don't have their physical form, they still have a soul, a spirit, or consciousness, whichever word people like to use. They grow into young adults. They just miss out on the physical aspects of their eternal life, such as eating, drinking, and human desires, pleasures, and experiences of life, whether good or bad. They skip that piece and develop a soul and learn to love one another, to be kind and help others, which is really what our souls are all about—loving one another, wanting the best for others in their development.

They still go to classes, just like you do on earth, but they learn only lessons of love and forgiveness, love and caring, love and helping, love and giving. They look down to earth and see lessons through glimpses of human life. In fact, all souls of all ages do this. Earth is a learning school. Think of it as a theatre and all the human forms are on the stage and we, the spirit world, are one big audience. So, we actually learn both ways. We come to earth as humans on the stage because we can't all learn life's lessons in the spirit world because earth holds the temptations of mankind. Think about Jesus in his temptation; that will help you understand. In fact, we all grow up to Jesus's age, and we all grow younger to Jesus's age, so there are no old or young people here for long. We all grow to be a healthy age and size. This helps us in this life because we don't need a babysitter, child minder, or caregiver. We are all fit and healthy in order to take care of ourselves.

As I was saying earlier, we have work to be done. This leads into this segment because when you pass over and you are not 33 years old, your work is to help the younger children and babies and the elderly re-adjust to their spirit age, so this is the work that you do. You help them change back to their normal age or selves, if you like. Obviously, some souls do not have a normal passing or death of human form, if you like. They may have been in an accident and were traumatized in the physical body. Of course, when they pass they do not feel any pain, but they have a sense of confusion. In other words, they did not have time to prepare for human death, so we, on this side, do our work and help them re-adjust.

Most people, when they die, have some idea of their upcoming death. Usually it is peaceful in the human form, and sometimes it is quick, such as a heart attack, but the soul knows when the attack occurs that it is going, so this is different than a car accident in the example I used. Obviously, when the human soul has a long illness, the soul prepares for death. The work we do on this side is to visit them in their human world to let them know that we are here and that we will help them. We comfort them; just like I did for Linda. I was with her, but I could not stop the process of her passing because it was her time. We cannot interfere or stop the process, although you and many loved ones ask and pray for this all the time. We cannot change destiny. It has to be this way.

So you can see some of the types of work we have to do over on this side, and don't forget all the times we come and visit you, our loved ones, in your sleep, in your home, and any time you want us to come, we come. You just can't see us. Some human souls can see us, and that is an ability that they have, but most cannot. You call them mediums in your world, and they help us communicate to loved ones.

Learning Schools

The other things we do over here include life learning of the soul, such as school for the soul. Yes, we have to go to school and learn about laws of nature and how to feed the soul, how to love, how to give, how to care. There are different levels of school. Again, it is like you have on earth. There are the first level classes, such as a classroom setup where you sit in rows. There are higher evolved souls, teachers, who come to teach the class. The classes are big, much larger than they are on earth; however, they don't need a microphone for the teacher because all spirits can communicate telepathically, so all thoughts do not need to be spoken. Some spirits do communicate with words, but it is not necessary. It is only a choice.

Once you have developed your soul on a level that has grown spiritually, you move up to higher levels of learning. These levels are smaller in group size and more detailed and challenging. They have assignments, homework to do. Sometimes it is helping souls on this side; other times it may be helping souls on earth. We hear your prayers and thoughts and do help you when we can without interfering with the long-term aim of your soul's growth on earth. The more lessons you learn on earth, the less you need to learn here. So, we don't want to interfere with your development. The higher classes are like boardroom meetings as you get higher up the class list. The very top is something like the Romans style where you lounge around, discussing issues and philosophy as Linda mentioned before.

Social Aspect

The other area I wanted to cover was the social aspect. This overlaps with the learning aspect, because apart from the classroom, there are conferences and meetings and seminars to go to. Again, just like you have on earth. It is very social over here, and you do have to select some to go to. You just can't say "I am going to do nothing." You have to choose a program for your soul's development. That is why we have committee meetings to review your soul's progress in the spirit world.

There is plenty of time to go to concerts and hear your favorite music. There is plenty of time to sit and talk with all your family and friends. You can even go and visit souls from your past lives and visit souls who will be in your future lives. You see, you make a pact before you go to earth with souls in the spirit world. You agree and plan some earth's life's lessons ahead of time, even to small details where a soul may be in your life for brief moment, or a month, or a year, etc. Whatever the agreement that was made before you entered the earth's plane. Take for example a person, a stranger that for no reason does a nice thing for you, which helped you immensely at a moment in your time of need or a time in your life where you had a bad period and a friend or loved one helped you through it. People say, "I don't know what I would have done without him or her." You feel you were in the right place at the right time or the wrong place at the wrong time. The people who were there to help you were part of the plan before you entered your human form. I don't want to say that your life is mapped out and planned for you before you enter the earth's form, but I am saying that certain events are preplanned, but as a human form you can change things, as long as your life's lessons are still learned.

I hope this makes some sense to you. I have tried to give you an overview of what it is like here, enough to get you going. I don't want you to get too confused with all this information I give you, but I want you to explain to others about the spirit world so people understand it and are educated about it. I am not asking you to go and change the world or to transform people's beliefs: I just want you to have a better understanding so you can explain to others who may want to know. Obviously there are different versions of the spirit world out there, I know that, but I want you to learn it from me, your Mum. Remember I am always with you my darling daughter, we are soul mates in "that world," "this world," it doesn't matter: our souls are part of one. Go now, and write out what I have told you so you will understand it, and we will speak again soon. Bye love, bye love. God bless, lots of love - Mum.

When I looked at the clock, over three hours had passed. It did not feel to me that I had meditated all that time, and I was anxious to read my notes. I couldn't believe the amount of information that mother had given to me. It all made sense: one big reunion, one big gathering, everyone learning and helping one another. So this is what Mum and Linda are doing! They are socializing, learning, and having fun. It is we who miss their physical form.

I took a few days break from meditating and typed all my meditation notes, which had begun to pile up, onto my blog. Even though I tried to stay ahead and type them up every few days, I often had weeks' worth of notes at one time. A few days later, I sat ready for my next marathon session and was pleased when Linda and Mum came through. I had missed them.

Purpose Of Life

Linda: Yes, I am here. I am always here. It is nice to be with you again. Just have faith that I am here. Mum spoke to you for a long while, so now it is my turn.

Start with life and the purpose of life: to be happy and to love. It is a lesson that you must all learn how to be happy and love one another. It is easy to do that here because there are no restrictions or limitations, but on earth there are many distractions and that is what makes the lessons so valuable. How many times have you asked, how can I be happy? What must I do to be happy?

There are many books written about how to be happy, yet no one really is. I don't mean no one literally because people can be happy, but often it is only for a short time. Something they do, see, read or hear makes them happy for that moment, but then once that moment has gone they resort back to how they were before. So the key to true happiness is to find what makes you, the individual, happy not just a moment of happiness.

For example, you may have a hobby that you love and spend all your time doing that when you can, but obviously you can't do it all the time because you have work you must do and all the other things you humans have to do. What I am saying is have an interest in your life that gives you enjoyment that you can look forward to. Once you have things in your life that you look forward to and that give you enjoyment, you will create your own happiness. It is the same as people who have a job that they love; it becomes a passion, just like a hobby or an interest because it is something that they do that makes them happy. Also, it can be an activity you enjoy such as taking a dog for a walk and seeing the dog explore new territory along the way. Sometimes it is just going to the park with someone you love—a child, a loved one, a parent, a dog, a friend. Spending time with people, family, and friends is a good way to bring happiness into your life.

Create your own happy environment on a day-by-day basis, and you will create your world around you that is full of love and giving. Giving is the best form of happiness because giving is true love. When you give yourself to another, there is no better example of true love. I am not just talking about the romantic love but love that you give to your child, friend, pets, or even a stranger.

When you open your heart to other people you are understanding the key to what happiness really is. It becomes a magnificent obsession. Once you start it you can't stop. Look around you at all the people you know. When you are with them, what is it that makes you happy? You will notice that it is the way you feel about them, and this feeling is created by the love you give to them and the love they give to you.

Humans are emotional beings, and they can only exist when they give love and feel loved. Just look at the lonely people on this earth and you will see that they are sad because they do not feel loved and they don't have anybody who they can love. Remember, it is a two-way street, so giving and receiving must happen. Of course, you cannot make other people love you or give you love, but you can give love to them and feel happy that you did that, regardless of if they give love in return. But you will find that the more love you give, it will come back tenfold. Build your love and happiness around you and you will be protected from the negative feelings of others. Love is a protector, love is happiness, and love is everything.

Please help others the best you can, at all times, not just when you remember or when you think you can. Help others all the time. Picture them as Mum or me if that helps, but always help them.

Linda finished her communication and, instantly, Mum's words came through:

The Power Of Love

Mum speaking now, love. I am forever yours. Our love, our bond with each other, is together for eternity in your world and mind. We are bound by our love, which can never be broken by a physical death, not by anything. A bond so strong, that our love can never be broken. My love is just as strong for you as the day I died.

Love is so powerful and it is that which the universe is made up of. It is the strength that holds life together on this side and on earth. There would not be an earth or life on earth, no humans, and no animals, nothing at all without love. Love is the bond, the glue, which keeps the world together. It is the reason for our whole existence, so strong, so much that it can't be stretched so much that it breaks because it is unbreakable. Once you figure it out, the power of love, you figure out the power of life, the power of universe, the reason for existing, the reason for creation, and the reason for our being.

Your heart is breaking now because the love you have for me, your Mum, was so great that you feel the pain of the stretch of the bond between us. When I was with you on the earth, the love we had was like an elastic band when it is relaxed. It was there but not always pulled or tested. It took the loss of a loved one, the loss of me, to stretch that elastic band and feel the pain, the human emotion of pain as the band is stretched.

You will see the band is not broken, never broken, just stretched. It comes back to the relaxed position once you stop thinking about me, but when you become sad you start stretching out the band, the elastic band again. That is the best way I can describe it to you. Does it help you understand how love never dies? How the physical body is only that: a physical bond. The love we had was part of our souls and, as you know, our souls never die; they just lose physical form.

I think you are getting the picture now, aren't you love? I think that is enough for you today. I see you are upset and emotionally exhausted from this session. Write up your notes now. I will be back again soon. I love you, my darling daughter. Love Mum.

I understood completely what Mum was saying. I knew our love never died just because she had passed away. I could feel her love. Love never dies; it lives forever.

Chapter 12: Heaven on Earth

Writing, while in a meditative-state, was a tool that helped me to easily communicate with spirit. It kept my concentration and focus in one place, eliminating any distractions. As I wrote, inspired thoughts from spirit came into my mind and spilled onto the page, like champagne flowing from a bottle after the cork has been popped. I did not always know which spirit would communicate with me, whether it would be my mother, Linda or at times, the monk; neither did I know whether I would receive philosophy, details about Heaven (which was always very exciting), or personal messages and advice.

Throughout the meditations, my eyes were closed. Occasionally, I squinted my eyes while turning the page; however, this would at times, distract me. When my pen moved easily and quickly across the paper, I knew the words were inspired by spirit. When I became aware of what I was writing and tried to guess the next word, the pen stopped moving. Sometimes, I physically tried to write the word I thought came next, but the pen would not move. It had a force of energy that kept it still. Once I cleared my mind of any thoughts, then, and only then, did the pen move again.

The depth of the blending was different each time. I could not control it. Sometimes the energy between my mother and I blended so closely that I felt her presence and an overwhelming sensation to cry. I even felt a shortness of breath, a symptom of mother's illness before she passed. These sensations did not last, and were there to establish and confirm our connection. When I communicated with Linda, I saw an image of her first with my psychic third eye. She always had a smiling face. I would acknowledge that I could see her, and then I would ask her to talk to me. Sometimes, the communication was a sense of knowing: I sensed the words that they were saying. Other times, I heard their voices. Usually, I heard my mother's voice more than Linda's. On this day, I sensed my mother's energy.

The Bonds Of Love

Mum: Yes, love, it is me. I want to tell you in your words so you can easily explain to others. People will understand more if they can find out from you how it works. It is like spoon-feeding you the information. There is no point in me giving you all the philosophy to help others if you are not able to string it all together in some form of order that makes sense.

I want to tell you about love and how people need more love in their lives. The stories of my life, some that you witnessed firsthand, created a bond, a deep bond, with me and my children that remains today. Just because Linda and I are not in the physical form, we are still with you all, every day. You cannot break these bonds. Our love is the same now as it was then. I am a mother who loved her family so much that the bond created can never be broken, not in your world or this world. The bond is as strong and as real as in the physical form.

How was our bond created? It was created because you saw and felt the love I had for you, my children. You were all that were important to me, and I would have done anything for you. I was always looking out for you. You all knew that, and that is what made our love grow strong. I taught you all how to love one another, to think of the other person, to share your thoughts, your dreams, and your day with one another.

We were all connected in our daily lives and our thoughts. So you can see that did not change when I passed over to this side. Your thoughts of me, and then Linda, did not stop. We are all inter-twined in our minds, our thoughts, and it is these thoughts that never go away. My thoughts are with you and I know your thoughts are with me. We were unique as a family because I raised you that way based on my loveless childhood. My greatest joy was you four children.

All that joy came from the bottom of my heart and rose to the top. It overflowed into your lives and other people's lives we touched as a family. Just look around you, and see all the people who have been in our lives and shared in the entire family's love. Your friends became each other's friends in a way; they were extensions of you. So, the love came back into the family. I know it is hard now with us gone, but you must go on with your lives and finish your time on earth so one day we will be reunited again. In

*the meantime, just concentrate on helping one another and look
after people the best you can.*
  Love Mum xx

Mum's life story would take another book: she had an unfortunate
childhood and was unloved. Mother poured all her love into her children,
filling our lives with so much love. As mother's energy left, I saw Linda;
she was wearing a blue and white flowery dress that she once wore to a
wedding. She appeared very slender as she did in her teenage years,
before she gained much weight, which she battled with for the rest of her
life. On this day she looked lovely.

<u>Discover Your Journey</u>

*Linda: It isn't how you remember me, is it Angie? Well,
I'm not that big anymore. I have slimmed down to when I was a
size 12. I have come to say hello. We are here to help you Angie.
Keep meditating and you will get better, more confident at this.
We are here to help you the best we can.*

*I want you to write with some humor. As you know, I had a
good sense of humor. I remember saying to you that you had a
pudgy nose and asked "Are we being recorded?" instead of giving
you a straight answer to your questions. Even though I was dying,
I was trying to make you feel better during that awful time for
you. You see, I knew it was bad for you, but on this side I don't feel
any bad emotions or sadness because we only feel joy and
happiness, but I do have my memories. I remember how I felt
looking at you, Louise, Scott, and all my family and friends who
came to see me. I saw the love and the pain that you all had, but
there was nothing I could do. I felt pain and sorrow for you
knowing that I was leaving you feeling that way. There was
nothing I could do, but now I am on this side my pain has gone. My
suffering those last few weeks has gone, but for you I know you
relive it and think of it often. All I can say is that it is a learning
experience for you as a human being and that it makes you a
stronger more compassionate person.*

*When we cross over to this side that is the person you want to
be: caring and compassionate. It is sad for those people who pass
over who never experienced sorrow or a loss that caused the pain
and suffering that you experienced. It is the pain and suffering
that evolves the soul. The soul can only grow when it knows*

sorrow and the pain that goes along with the sorrow. So please, don't dwell on my loss or dwell in the sorrow and pain that you felt. That is not the point of your soul's purpose. You feel it, experience it, but then you must continue on with the rest of your life's learning experience: loving and helping one another, forming bonds and relationships with people, helping people.

One day it will make sense to people, usually before they die and certainly when they pass over. The goal is to help people when they are younger and have time to enjoy the true value of their human form by making them aware of the purpose of their life in everyday terms. To discover your journey in life is the best gift you can give to humanity. I am not talking about a get rich scheme; I am talking about how to have a good life within the one that you have because when people are always wanting and wishing they are not enjoying life. They think they have to chase after this or chase after that to be happy or rich, when in fact all they have to do it to love one another, help one another, care for one another, and they will be rich—rich beyond their imagination. For true happiness lies in love and caring and forgiving one another.

Linda is waving goodbye to me now. Mum is saying "Bye, love." as she waves to me.

Linda had referred to the time, just a few weeks before her death, when I had asked her whether she thought I was taking good care of her. I looked down into her eyes, waiting for reassurance that she was comfortable. Instead of responding "Yes," as I had anticipated, Linda exclaimed "You have a pudgy nose," followed by "Are we being recorded?" I laughed but felt a sadness knowing how brave Linda was, all the while keeping her sense of humor. Often, I relived Linda's time in the hospital in my mind; it didn't get any easier. Each time when I thought of her lying there, waiting to die, all my emotions came flooding back to me as if it were yesterday. Yes, the meditations did make it easier to ease my grief, but the grief always returned. I felt sadness when Mum and Linda waved goodbye.

The Truth Of Life

Sometimes I meditated using the techniques I learned at Arthur Findlay College and Lily Dale. One of my favorite ones was to imagine that I am flying through the sky on a magic carpet and that I land on a beautiful island. This time, I could see a campfire, and I landed my carpet in front of it crackling. Then, I waited to see who came and sat next to me.

I was very excited to see the monk sit beside me with his scrolls. It felt like a long lost friend who stopped by for a chat. He rolled out his scrolls.

Monk: Come to give you a wise lesson. There is so much to talk about. You need to make the most of your time on earth. Simply listen to what I am going to tell you. I want to talk about "the truth of life." It is a hard title to understand, but once you read the content, you will understand the title.

Life was created by our creator, God. One single God who today has many meanings for many people, but there is only one God, the Creator, and it is his will that the earth was created in the first place. God is a ball of energy that evolved with a huge magnetic force and that is what gave power to the creator. It gave the creator great intelligence, intelligence to use, that created the universe, the earth, and the planets. Once the creator set up the universe, and all its planets, then came the next logical form of creation: life on earth as we know it today.

God created the water, the oxygen, and the chemicals that sustain us. God created animals, plants, and sea life so the earth could grow and develop a life that was interdependent. This was an important lesson in itself because the earth cannot survive without the eco system that has been created. It was created this way on purpose so mankind could learn lessons by looking at nature to see how God's creatures survive. We are not talking about how animals kill one another, but rather, the reason for their survival depends on interactions with other species. Humans can learn from animals, which is why the animals were created first. You have to learn to get along with other things in life, learn from the experiences, and know that survival of a species is the only reason why we should kill another.

That is a lesson that humans should learn. They should not kill one another in war or just for the sake of killing; it should only be for the protection of the species. This is a big lesson because throughout human history man has killed for no reason at all, yet find justice for the killing. Mankind cannot survive unless they understand the consequences of their actions. All this destruction of one another will in turn lead to the destruction of the earth, the earth that God, our creator, founded out of his love for the universe. He used his energy and intelligence known to him to create. He looks down at what mankind has done and is doing to his creation, and he sees sorrow for the lack of human love.

Once he sent his son to the earth to teach those who did evil in his world, but this did not create peace or harmony. Instead, it created more pain and suffering in the world. We look at the earth today, and we see the same kind of greed and power that we saw then. God loves all his children, yet they forget that one God exists, and they create their own God. Mankind cannot survive in a world where there is hate, fighting, and war. Mankind does not know the truth. Also, there are some that think they know the truth, but they joined others and show hatred: how can they say they know the truth when their actions speak louder than words?

The truth of life and the universe is that God created the universe to bring his love and intelligence to all of mankind. That is what the dream was for the universe. Make man in his likeness so they can experience the love and great knowledge of the world they live in; otherwise, he may as well have stopped after the animals. But intelligence was missing. He needed to develop a race, a species that had intelligence. The animals have love; you can see that in most animals when they take care of their young. You can see the intelligence starting to form with certain types of animals such as cats and dogs, horses, lions, tigers, which are hunters because they need some intelligence in order to survive.

Then you go one step further and you have humans. They are born with a unique brain that can process their intelligence and know right from wrong. I am not talking about intelligence of the technical type, although as humans you use technology in your society today in the name of progress. I am talking about simple intelligence of knowing what is right and wrong, the ability to make a decision based on the knowing of right and wrong. It is so simple, yet people do not make decisions based on what it right or wrong moral decisions. Instead, they use intelligence for themselves. They consider other things far more important to themselves such as how to make more money or how to do something better than someone else. Always for a selfish, competitive reason. Even people who try to live a good moral life still toy with choices of temptation, for the desire of a better life.

The truth to life is the intelligence that humans are born with, and once that truth is realized you can use your intelligence to help the rest of mankind. Find ways to prevent war, find ways to live in peace. You may ask, "What difference can I make? I am just a small person in this whole world." But take a look around you, and you will see what it is you are doing in your lives that do in fact contribute to the bad misdoings in the world.

I will give you an easy example. You buy clothes and other goods made at the expense of less fortunate people than yourself. If you stop buying these things, then obviously you will not contribute to their torture and inhumane lives: the poor living conditions, the intolerable working conditions, and the measly amount of food they are given. When you stop contributing to this, then you can truly say, "I am an intelligent person, and I choose to do the right thing." That is what God wants of all his children: to do the right thing, love one another.

Let me give you another example of what you can do in your life when you think there is nothing you can do. Start listening and open yourself up to what is going on in the world. You can't say that you don't know; therefore, it is not your problem. You have the intelligence to look around you and see the poor treatment of mankind against the species. Energy needs to focus on all that God created. Do not focus your energy on what is just for you because what is good for you is what is good for mankind.

Heaven On Earth

God wants to create on earth what he has created in Heaven. I am not going to use another word because Heaven does describe the world we live in here in the spirit world, and it is God's plan to recreate Heaven on earth. In order for him to do that, in order for that to happen, he has to change the thoughts of mankind by getting them to use their intelligence that God gave to them.

Yes, there is intelligence in the spirit world because that is what the soul I; since the physical body is gone, the soul has the intelligence which lives on. The challenge on earth is having the physical body, which has so many needs compared to the soul in spirit, and it is the way mankind replenishes their human needs in the way that this created pain and suffering on earth.

The truth of life is to find a way to nourish the soul and feed the physical body without creating the destruction of mankind. Mankind has the intelligence to discover this truth, and yet it chooses to use its intelligence against the very essence that it was created for. By writing this down, people can read it, and it will help them put their lives back into perspective. God is saddened that people have lost the way. He is saddened that they find materialistic things that they believe they need in life, rather than say that what they need is the truth, the intelligence of knowing the truth.

You cannot stop world wars, but you can make a difference by not adding to the pain and suffering of people exploited for the benefit of others. Start by making a list of all the things around you in your life, and ask yourself if the basis of that is love, or is it exploitation of others to satisfy your own needs? You have the intelligence to ask and figure this out. All these are tests in your life. All humans are on this earth to be tested. It is like an intelligence game. A true test of intelligence played out on mankind.

You are not controlled by anybody or anything. Not by God, he only sends his love, his kindness; he only wants the best for each soul. When you choose to come down to earth, in your human form, to learn this true gift of intelligence that is a choice the soul makes and chooses to participate in in the game of life. The goal is to return to Heaven with a higher level of intelligence, an understanding of love, caring, because it takes intelligence to figure that all out. You cannot say "I didn't know" when you return here because you had the intelligence as a human to figure it out yourself, if only you wanted to.

God gives you the freedom of choice to do whatever you want to do on earth. So, if you want to be rich and you ask God to be rich then by the simple laws of nature, the power of attraction, you can be rich. But if you want to live and grow intellectually through the love of God, then also by the laws of attraction, you can do this.

I hope you take note of today's lesson. Look around you and see what you can do to help mankind. If you need help, just ask for it,; use the law of attraction. That is it for today's lesson. I am so glad you took the time today. I will be back again soon.

Chapter 13: The Soul's Purpose

I found with each day my ability to meditate became easier. I closed my eyes and waited for something to happen. It was fascinating to me that it actually happened and that all this information was so readily available, if only you allowed yourself to tune into it. It had become somewhat of an obsession to me. On this day, Mum talked to me about Linda's death, it was very moving. I felt her love, as her energy blended with mine.

Mum: I want to talk about Linda and how she could not accept my death, the pain she suffered not being with me when I died, and the guilt she lived with that made her ill. Yes, love, it was the pain and guilt that caused Linda's illness. She could not live with the pain anymore. It took control of her life so much that she could not live anymore; she could not take it anymore. She is happy now, so be happy for her. I want you to be happy for Linda and for me. Living with pain is bad for you, and it hurts me to see my family grieve so much. I want you to remember the love I gave you and how I taught you to do good things in the world. That will make Linda and me proud of you all. Start doing good things and good things will come to you. Bad times are only there for you to appreciate the good times. I will go now. Bye, love.

This was such a short message but very important to me. Linda had been consumed with guilt regarding Mum's death because she had not been there to take care of Mum the week before she died. When Mum passed away, Linda felt her decision to go on vacation was selfish and she hated herself for that.

Using A Keyboard During Meditation

It has been a little over three months since I began meditating. The meditation sessions were averaging two to three hours long, then another two hours to type my notes onto my blog. I decided to experiment with actual typing my notes while meditating. At first, typing was a little uncomfortable since I am not an accurate typist. I had to keep my eyes open slightly to look at the keyboard. I wondered whether spirit could actually use a keyboard through me. I sent thoughts out in a form of a question asking Spirit if we could try and use the keyboard. When I began to meditate, I saw a beautiful colored rainbow, and I felt as if I was floating in the air up through the clouds. I sensed the energy of the monk.

Monk: We can move your fingers to the appropriate letters, so just let us come through. We have a lot to say to you, so let's start with getting this typing right so we will make fewer mistakes. Notice your breathing is getting a little rapid. I just want you to be aware of it. It will be a signal to you that you are in the trance-state. The aim is to put down what we are saying. Keep focusing on the keyboard and it will come to you. First, we want to communicate with you as much as possible. I will go slowly so you can get down what we want to say to you. Later, it will come quickly and you can go faster.

Love Never Dies

Love does not die when your loved ones lose their physical body and pass to the other side. They only lose their physical self. The love you felt was a strong force of energy that you and your loved ones felt, just like the energy that lingers in a room after a person has left. This energy can be a good energy or a bad energy, so when that person leaves the room you can still feel it in the air; you can sense it. Everyone can relate to that, and it can even change your mood. You can feel the bad energy for several moments when a person leaves the room who has said something bad or was angry. The opposite happens when someone has left the room who makes you feel happy! This feeling of happiness, this positive energy that was created when the person had this happiness, still remains when the person has left the room.

This is the same as when you feel the love of someone. That feeling you get of love when someone leaves the room remains with you, and you want to snuggle up with that love and keep it forever. This is the same when your loved one has passed over; they have this love that is so strong that it remains behind in the room with you except that the room is not just a temporary space; the room is the space that is the energy of your whole life. This energy is saved in the special room or space of your life for eternity. You can access it at any time when you look at a picture of your loved one or when your loved one comes into your mind.

If you have a memory of your loved one, or you see something that reminds you of them, automatically you think: how your loved one would have liked this, or your loved one should be here to see this. At that time your loved ones are really with you because the same energy, the same love is with you in the room or the space with you. That is the best way to describe it. They are with you. The memory lingers with you at that time just like the memory or the energy in the room that is left when a physical person leaves the room. That is the best way to describe how your loved ones visit you. It is an easy analogy so people can relate to that and understand how the process works

Your loved ones are always there with you. Sometimes they are in the distance and looking in. They wait for you to contact them and their energy draws closer. It is when their energy draws closer that you can feel them. Sometimes, when you start to cry for no reason, their energy is so close in the air in the room, in the space around you, and you instantly think of them. Sometimes the energy is stronger; usually it is when you cry. This is when the energy is strongest because love is there. Love is the emotion that makes you cry, and the deeper the love the more you cry. It only lasts for a short time because they do not like to see you in that state of emotion.

They like to see you happy, so they back away with their energy and the crying stops and you feel better. You feel better because they have left you with love. When you think of them they are around you but not so close. It is only when you think of them in a time or moment of your life such as a past memory is when they get closer, and they visit with you.

I found this part of the meditation very interesting: *So this is how it works*, I thought. When I think about Mum and Linda, it is because their spirits are around me. This was a comforting thought. It also helped me to understand how the two worlds co-exist.

Obviously, they are not with you all the time; they cannot be. They have lives of their own in the spirit world, and they have work to be done. However, when they see their loved ones in distress about anything that is happening in their lives, they come closer and give love and support and strength through their energy. Always call on them. Most people do this through daily prayers or just a prayer in times of need. They hear your prayers; even those people who do not pray, thoughts are heard and prayers are answered this way. Please don't think that because your loved ones have gone that they are no longer with you because the love you had for them cannot be broken just like the love that is in the air, which is energy.

Energy cannot be broken. What I am saying is energy is not tangible; it cannot be broken; it is the law of physics. It is not made of a matter or raw material; it is a component of energy that just exists. It is up to you, the human race, to decide what you will do with the energy of the earth. Energy is created through the mind, through the thought process. So you see, if you think of your loved ones, you are thinking of the love created by the energy in your mind and in your thoughts and in your being. It cannot go away once it is created. It is always there, and it can be summoned closer to you at any time. It has just moved to another dimension other than the physical world. The spirit world is in the physical world without the earthly elements needed for a physical body. The spirit world is all around you but functions without all the elements essential to the survival of life on planet earth.

Yes, we can get used to the computer, but it may take a while. In the long run it will be better for you—maybe? I am smiling at you now, as I know it will be better for you but maybe not better for us. Let's keep going for a while. This is like a new toy; once we get to know how to use it, the better we will be. We have spoken about love and how this energy of love does not go away and cannot be destroyed through what you call death of the physical body.

Why Does The Soul Exist?

Now I want to talk to you about life. Life is the fundamental gift from God our creator to all things. Life is precious and should not be wasted, yet so many people waste their lives on frivolous things that they learn nothing during their span of time on earth. They learn only the physical needs of the body and forget that they have a spiritual body, which is the reason for their whole being and existence on planet earth. Earth was created by our creator for the spiritual soul to learn love and compassion. That is it. Learn the truth of life. That is what every man's purpose is: to learn the truth of why God created the earth. Once this has been learned, then your soul can grow and evolve.

It can evolve quicker on the earth plane with all the temptations of mankind. Yet, people do not understand this. They live in ignorance of this and believe they are living a good life just because they attend church or give to a charity, but often people are only doing this because they think that is what they should do. Would they do this without recognition? Yes, of course, there are souls that do this but they are few. We want all souls to live helping others, but many do not understand the nature of the existence of their soul in the first place.

This is not taught in schools or churches yet it should be the main lesson, the main class of life. Why does the soul exist, should be the question that every soul asks. Yet this is not asked, and souls do not know their purpose on earth. They can go a lifetime without this knowledge, so when the soul returns to the spirit world it has to go to earth again until it does understand life's lessons, or, if the soul chooses, it can stay in the spirit world and learn life's lesson on this side. It does not matter which side the soul learns its lesson, only that the lesson is learned.

If people start questioning why they are on the earth and seeking out answers and the truth, they will have a much more fulfilling lives. Usually it takes the death of a loved one, or the death of many loved ones, for the soul to figure this out. Losing a love one creates compassion in a person, or more compassion for those who have it. Once people understand the meaning and purpose of life, they will accept their loved one's death and know they are with them at all times. Haven't you noticed how people in the Spiritualist movement have been able to accept the passing of loved ones more easily and continue on with their lives? I am not saying that they did not feel the physical pain and emotions that the human body has; I am saying that they have a sense of peace, a sense of knowing where their loved ones are, and that they are still around without the physical body. Mind to mind communication is as real as the energy left in the room as I described earlier today.

Seek The Truth

The purpose of life is the number one lesson for people to learn, yet people do not know why they are here. The analogy of love as energy in a room should help a lot of people understand you. Write this in your book as a lesson that was taught to you through your meditations and your understanding of the spirit world, which came about through the love of your mother. Your love for your mother was so strong that you refused to accept that she was gone after she passed and it was this searching for answers, searching for the purpose of life without your mother's love, which caused you to seek the truth.

Find the truth in life that we do exist out of our physical bodies and that love is the proof of this. The fact that you can feel your mother's love with you as you do is proof that life continues after death. Love is an emotion caused by energy created between souls that can never be broken. Time does not take away or weaken the energy.

It is the human form that stops thinking about the loved one who has passed to spirit world, who weakens energy and connection to that person. So when they pass over, over time, they communicate less with each other because the human form has lowered that energy by not thinking about the loved one. The loved one in the spirit world also lowers their energy and stays busy with their life too. However, the minute the loved one on earth thinks about them they return to earth to visit them, and the energy is built up. Again, this can go in cycles

You can go months, days, years, etc. without thinking about your loved one, but the minute you do, the loved on is there. Then, the human emotions are triggered, crying, joy, comfort, happiness, a feeling of contentment after the thoughts have gone. If mankind knew how it all worked, they would enjoy life more to the fullest. Understanding the purpose and meaning of life is to learn and understand love. The huge energy feeling of love is there so that all humans can tap into and feel at any time. The love energy is there for all mankind. That is why it feels so good when you help a stranger and people in need. You are turned into the love energy of the universe and then, only then, you are fulfilling your life's purpose. Thank you for sitting with me today. I will be back again soon.

I received a lot of information on a range of topics from the monk. I am amazed how easily the topics intertwine giving a deeper insight into each. On a lighter note, I found that typing my notes whilst meditating was not beneficial to me; there were too many spelling mistakes! Some words made no sense at all and were impossible to decipher. Afterwards, I spent just as much time figuring out the actual words, and then retyping parts of the meditation notes as I did with my handwritten notes. I decided to stay with my notepad and pen!

Chapter 14: A Real World

I was often told through the spirit communication I received to put the information into a book. When I communicated with Mum and Linda they spoke to me in the same tone in which they did while on earth: sometimes lovingly and sometimes sternly. This time, Mum came through in a motherly way to put me back on track. I doubted my ability to write a book. Although I kept copious notes of all the communication sessions, I could not visualize a book. This meditation cleared my vision.

Mum: I want you to start writing the book now before you lose your focus and aim. Look at all your notes you have so far, and put them together in some sort of order. Once you start doing this it will come to you regarding the storyline and what you should write. Start with the story of a young girl who loses her Mum when she thought she would have her forever or until her mother grew naturally old as you hope all loved ones will do. When her mother died she felt like she had been robbed of her love that had always been there and was suddenly taken from her unexpectedly, beyond her wildest dreams. Her nightmare was a reality; her mother with all her love had been taken away and you, as her loving daughter, could not accept this, could not accept that the love had gone. The love, which was so deep, so strong a bond, between mother and daughter, as any bond could ever be, that you were determined not to let it go. You were determined to seek the truth of life and refused to believe that life did not continue because a love so strong could not have died.

You sought to find the meaning of life, and through this, you found that your mother's love did not die with her physical death, that it lived on beyond the physical world. Through this you discovered a whole other world, a world where the spirit lives on, where the love is just as strong as it was in the physical body. It did not die, and now you want to share with the world what you have discovered.

The Physical World Versus The Spiritual World

The spirit world is a real world that exists along with the world in which you live on earth. The spirit world is a real world full of life that exits without the physical form. That is all. That is the only difference between the spirit world and the human world. There is no physical form. Once people understand this difference, they will see the truth of life.

The purpose of their lives can only be discovered once they understand that their soul continues after their physical death. It is not a strange phenomenon that the soul exists beyond the physical death. You only have to look in the Bible to see references of spirits returning to give proof that life continues after death. Yet, people seem to disregard this and only look at the parts of the Bible they want to believe. I say to you that life does exist after death, and once a soul in the human form understands this he or she will know the meaning of life. Sometimes it takes a death of a loved one to know this or a near death experience or some profound event in your life but not all human souls experience a profound event, so they go through life without awareness of the spirit world.

Go now and write. If you do not write it now, then other things will distract you. Just start writing and it will come to you. Start with your mother's death, how it affected you and your family. Then, the big loss of your sister, which is what really threw you into this. How you could not accept not knowing why she had to go. Why did God take your sister so soon after your dear Mum? It was too much for you to bear. Then, move onto how it evolved into your knowledge of seeking the truth. Your journey to Arthur Findlay College and Lily Dale "just getting your feet wet a little," as you say. You had to have the answers, so you set out on a mission to get the answers, and the one place you knew where to get the answers from was the very place where your Mum and sister went.

This meditation helped me to visualize the book. I left this meditation in the book so you, the reader, can follow the steps I took in creating the book. I hope you find this information interesting and relevant to the story. The following day, my mother gave words of encouragement about the book and about life.

Freedom Of Choice

We are here love. We are so pleased that you are writing. We feel your sadness about everything. Let us help you. All you need to do is let us help you and we will. Start living for today and tomorrow will come. I know that is a philosophical statement but it is true. You must live your life for today. Stop waiting and hoping for things to happen. If you want things in your life, in the future, then plan them today. That is all. Ask yourself what it is that you want, and then figure out a way to get there. When you don't know what you want, it is the same as saying I don't want anything because, if you want something, then you must know what it is that you want. Once you have figured out what it is you want, the next step is easy. Make a plan to make it happen. It is not just the spirit world telling you what you want because that is taking away your freedom of choice, and that is what God gave his children: the freedom to live their lives.

When there is no light at the end of the tunnel, you have to make your own and turn it on. Figure out what you want, and turn it on. Figure out what is important to you most, and then figure out a way to go. Focus on your goals, and they will become a reality

One step at a time. That is the message for today. Don't try and do all things at one time because you will find that no things get done. You can't take the time back, so it is important you don't waste your days and plan them each day. It is okay if you don't want to plan any activity for the day, but then you have to say to yourself each morning or the night before: "I plan not to do anything all day." Then, you will not feel guilty that you didn't do anything all day because you decided to do nothing all day, and then it is all part of the big picture. Each and every second of the day you think that time does not mean anything, but it does; so spend it wisely just as you do money because time and money run out, so don't waste it—plan it. We will go on to the next thing now: life.

The Value Of Life

Life is as good as you make it to be. You can sit at home and say I am unhappy about my life or you can decide that you want to do something with your life. It is how you spend your life that will determine how much value your life has to you. Value, like anything that you have, the value you put on yourself and your life, will determine the meaningfulness of your life.

If you value life, you value all things. If you value all things, then you value the true meaning of life. I know it sounds like we are going around in circles, but life and the importance you put on life will determine the meaning and purpose of your own lives. Stop and think about people who go through their lives and are so busy they don't stop to figure out what they are doing to themselves or to other people or to the planet with everyone in it. Don't you think they would be surprised by their actions if they knew what the consequences are? I don't mean in a malicious way, but in an "I didn't know" or "I didn't realize" way. Everything that you do has consequences whether good or bad, so think about what you do each day. This is important because people do not think about what they are doing to other people.

Just as I thought I had finished my meditation for that day, I sensed the energy from the monk. I sat and continued to write.

The Lesson Of Life

Monk: I want you to start looking at all the ways to help people in your life. Look around at all the many organizations that help people and help them to help people. I am talking about organizations that want to help people who are hungry. Feed them food to nourish them, and pray for them to live a happy life not wondering where their next meals are coming from. If you look hard enough, you can easily find them. I cannot tell you which organizations to join, but open your mind and your heart and the right one will come. You cannot live a life merely based on your own needs. Your life can only be measured and be meaningful based on the number of people you help in this world. Put all your talents and experiences together, and go out and make a difference. Educate people on the work that needs to be done. Educate them by drawing awareness to the poverty of the world. I am not saying to work like TV shows that ask you to send money to them; I am saying by doing things yourself in the community.

Go and seek out the poor who cannot feed themselves or the poor who cannot keep warm. All you need to do is open your heart to them; the rest will come. Find a need, then figure out a way to fill it. What I am saying to you is to share what you have. If you give money or you give a helping hand, you must learn to give. There are many ways to help other people. Once you decide to do it, you will see which direction you have to go.

The rewards you get from helping the poor are on-going, long-term, and require more of a commitment from your soul. The real rewards come from a long-term commitment to helping mankind. The more that you commit your time, energy, and love to a long-term cause, the greater the reward will be. Once you recognize that you will find your true life's work. What I am saying is that no human should go hungry. To eat food is the basic survival of mankind: food and water. How can we support mankind without it? The illnesses come later and form some cancers and other diseases, but hunger can start at any age and can kill just as much as disease. You are all on the earth to learn how to help one another. This is what we call love, and love is the only lesson of life. Love one another; that is all you have to do. How do you show love? How do you love someone? By loving, helping, caring, and giving of yourself to another person.

Go and feed the hungry, and you will have served your life's purpose well.

Your friend, yes, your monk.

The monk signed off, as Your friend." Over the last few months, yes, we had indeed become friends. It filled me with emotion. I cried. A few days later I felt the presence of a new energy. As I began my meditation, I saw an image of a Native American Indian who had a very stern face in sharp contrast to the gentle monk. He was sitting in a circle in front of a wigwam smoking a pipe. He stopped to say hello and smiled at me.

Native American Indian: Man is the destruction of his own race. We have lived in a world where man caused, and continues to cause, the destruction of entire nations and cultures. Man's arrogance is what caused this. Arrogance comes when man stops believing in the true meaning of life and concentrates on his own emotions and needs. Man's desire to look after his own interest first has caused the suffering of many. Man's own desire for strength and greed at the expense of mankind has brought much pain and suffering to the world.

Education about the truth of life and man's purpose on this earth is as critical now as ever. Man must learn about tolerance and forgiveness before they destroy one another and the earth. You can help by giving love to your fellow man. All man can help by showing compassion to fellow men. This is not a new concept, yet man does not follow this basic concept. Men should live together as one and show love to their fellow man. A simple life is the Godliest form of life. It makes man closer to God by denouncing all personal things he or she acquires and thinks are needed.

Will go now, as this is a start. More to come.

And with those words his energy disappeared. I did not know what to make of this experience: did he come in replacement of the monk?

Chapter 15: Happy Again

It had been five months and three weeks since Linda passed away. I was still tormented by her death and sought answers to my questions. Why did she have to die? Did she do something or ingest something that made her sick? Was her death predetermined before she came to earth? Did she choose the way she died? Did she choose a brain tumor? Why not a quick heart attack like mother? Did she have a choice at all? Was it her choice or God's?

I thought of Linda every day. Many things reminded me of her. I took down photographs of her when I was sad and put them up again when I felt better. I relived the last few weeks of her life. Slowly, I thought about the happy times. She had a great sense of humor, and one day I stood there, looking at a photograph of Linda taken on a trip to New Orleans. While walking down Bourbon Street, we came across a man standing in a doorway with his eyes closed who appeared to be sleeping and apparently intoxicated. Linda immediately stood in the doorway next to him and pretended that she, too, was asleep and intoxicated. As I recall the moment, and remember Linda's sense of humor, I felt happy again. When I had those strong feelings of happiness or sadness regarding Linda, it usually meant that she would visit me during my meditation. I liked it when she visited me. It reminded me of our two hour Saturday morning conversations. She spoke to me as frankly as she did on those Saturday morning marathon calls! This day was no different.

Linda On Her Passing: Time To Go

Linda: Angie, can you hear me? Been busy here. Lots to do, but can help you write today. Want to talk to you about me and Mum. We are here, helping you get through these difficult months; they are always the hardest. Don't worry about the family; we are taking care of them. We watch over them every day. They are just going through life's learning experiences so we can't interfere too much. As long as they are safe, they will be alright.

My death was determined before I was born Angie. You know that, so stop going over the last few weeks and months of my death. I was supposed to go that way, it brought out the most compassion in you and everyone else that you could ever have known. It is up to you to use that compassion the best you can, to the best of your ability; otherwise, you will waste it. Don't waste it. It is a gift, a gift of compassion. Not many people have this gift. Don't be misled and believe that I had to die so you will have this gift. That is not true. I had to die so I could be with Mum. She needed me on the earth, and she needs me now. I love being with Mum; that is all I wanted to do. After she died, I just wanted to be with her. I tried to say that to you all the time, and what you didn't realize is that was how I really felt. Yes, it got a little easier living without Mum, but the pain was still there. I just couldn't live my life without her.

I tried to make the best of it. Tried to look after you, Louise, Scott, and the kids, but all I thought of was how much Mum would have liked it. How Mum wasn't there to enjoy it, and I couldn't stand it any longer. Then, looking after Jimmy just added to it. Everything was too much. My brain was overloaded with grief. Even if I had survived, it would have been a lonely and sad life without Mum, then losing Jimmy.

I was happy with Jimmy. He understood me most of anyone I knew, and when he got his diagnosis, it was the straw that broke the camel's back. I couldn't take it anymore. I wanted to live with Jimmy, and I couldn't live knowing that he wouldn't be there. We loved each other, Angie. I was happy with him. It broke my heart again when he got the cancer. I didn't want to live without him. I didn't want to start over again. Even going back to Mum's house would have been too much. It would not have made me happy going there. It is best this way. Now I can be with Mum and Jimmy. I am with them every day. I wish you could realize that. I know you do, Angie, but I wish the others could see that. I know they miss me and you do too, but I was only a piece of your lives. There is so much to life that you all don't see. It is here for you to enjoy. I want you to enjoy life. I want you to live your lives and be happy. Just enjoy the fact that you are alive and on the earth.

When you think of me, I want you to think of the happy times. I want you to talk about me in your daily lives and say, "Linda would have liked this. Linda would have loved that, remember *when Linda did this?" When you remember me this way, I remain part of your lives today. When you start thinking about me, when you only think of the sad times, then you only remember those times that were so few in my life. Why remember a few weeks when you can remember a whole lifetime of memories? The last few weeks had to happen that way. It actually gave you time to accept my death, my passing, which we did not have with Mum's passing. Yes, it was uncomfortable for me at the end, but I wanted to have every last possible moment with you. My pain was not that great; uncomfortable was the word, but it made me happy to see you there showing your love and kindness. I wanted to go, Angie. I know that is hard to believe, but when the actual time came, it was hard to say goodbye to you, but I could see Mum waiting for me. I was torn between the two worlds. I was happy because I was going to be with Mum, but sad to be leaving you because I knew how much you were all going to miss me. I had done all I could for you—all I could. You can survive without me and will have more happy memories to come. I lived a full life. I loved you all.*

Slow down and take one day at a time; enjoy the world and all that God gave us. Yes, I wish I had been more or even slightly religious because now it all makes sense. You don't appreciate the world on that side until you get here, then you see all of God's creations, of mankind, life on earth, the planets, how it all comes together to create life that we know.

The families you are born into are there to teach you, as we are, life's lessons. You pick your families, and you pick your life's lessons. You could have picked a family where we all lived until we were 90 years old, had a peaceful, uneventful life, or you can pick a family like ours who overcame adversities and struggles, who enjoyed seeing the world through traveling, through our love for each other, yet only have a short life. You don't always get both. So, don't cry for me anymore because I served my purpose in all of your lives and now I am living the rest over here with Mum and everyone else. It is so wonderful here, full of joy and love. I couldn't possibly ever want to go back to earth. I can love you and watch over you from here. I know as humans you miss me; it is only natural. It shows the love that we had for one another, but don't keep grieving for me. You must remember the happy times and embrace my life and my death.

I know you think I went too soon, but how soon is too soon? What if I had lived a few more years? Would the pain be any less? Was it less at Mum's death at sixty-seven years? No, not at all, so don't look at my age as only fifty years because sixty years would have been just as hard, but know you have ten more years to learn how to live with grief. This is the lesson that I want you to share with others, so you are actually starting now. I don't think it ever sunk in with you with Mum's death—I mean the grieving part and helping others, but it will now with my death. If that wasn't a wake-up call for you, what is?

I know I am speaking quite frankly with you, but I need you to start living your life and to stop spending time mourning me any longer. I am very happy, and I want you to be happy on that earth. Illnesses and deaths are part of life, and you have to learn how to deal with them. Go and do fun activities with nature, bike rides in the country, running in the fields. Join organizations that help people, churches, clubs, and young groups. Life is fun; it is what you make of it, Angie. Set your goals: three and six months. Remember, they really do work. I used to put a big damper on things, ideas you had, but on this side, I can help. When it is for mankind, we can help; that is how it goes. So, please don't be sad for me anymore.

I will go now. I know you can see my smiling face, and I want you to smile. I am giving you a little squeeze now; everything is going to be all right, Angie. Trust your big sister. You know that I am always here for you, always have been, and that has not changed. Send my love to everyone. Tell them I am always around and can hear everything they say ha! ha!

TTFN. Love, Linda xxx

I felt Linda squeeze me in a close embrace. I did not want her to go. She had answered my questions. I understood more about her death and felt a release of emotion. When I meditated the following day, Linda was so light-hearted and uplifting that I felt happy again!

Busy Bees Up Here!

Linda: Mum and I are two busy bees up here. Mum sits on committees and has a lot of meetings she goes to and I keep her on track so she doesn't get all confused which one to go to. I am good at that, organizing people, just as I was down there.

Honestly Angie, it is lovely up here. You will love it when it is your turn, but you have a long while to go. You have been given work to do down there! Don't think you just have to wait until you get here to do kind work, kind deeds. You are lucky you get to do them down there; it will only do you and mankind good. Life will be better for you when you do this. It will bring balance to your life. Once you get started there are many on this side who will flock to help you. There is nothing greater for us on this side than to watch the soul in the human form help other souls on earth. This is the hardest thing to do so we all rally round and help. I know what you are thinking that it should be the easiest thing to do help one another, yet people don't always do it, so in reality it becomes the hardest thing to do.

Everything is fine Angie, going the way we planned it. I know you keep thinking about my death, but you wouldn't be living this life if I was still there, and I wouldn't be able to help you from this side. So, you see, it had to be this way. I can help you, Angie. I want to. That is what I have done all my life on earth, and it hasn't changed. I want to help you live a happy life, not to dwell on our deaths any longer. We are fine Angie, so happy here. We watch over you all every day.

We see all the good and bad things that happen around you, but we don't change anything or interfere because it is not necessary to do anything. They are all silly things, part of life's lessons, and if we interfere you lose out on the lesson. I know it sounds like a cop-out to you but really, we only interfere if and when the time is called for and you or I, or Mum, do not get to choose that time. That is done by the higher committees closer to God. Yes, just like the movie, that black and white movie: A Wonderful Life. Yes, angels do come down. They only interfere when absolutely necessary. So those silly life experiences that seem like a struggle are not in vain. Heaven knows, I had my fair share of them. So stop thinking that your problems are really bad because they are not. Know that it is all part of life.

Mum sends her love. She has been so busy here. I thought I was the social butterfly on earth, but up here it is the other way around. Mum is busy all the time, but not too busy to watch over her children and grandchildren. She loves us all very much. We were so lucky to have her; you will see when you come over this side. She is on committees that monitor and review the soul's progress on earth, then meets with souls on this side before they make endeavors to incarnate or reincarnate on the earth again. She looks at your progress and helps people understand where they need help.

Jimmy and I are together; it is lovely. We are pals and hang out together. We have such a laugh over you all down there. He says "Howdy!" in his best American accent.

Although Jimmy was British, he loved the American accent and often used to mimic it, especially after watching cowboy movies. Suddenly, I hear Jimmy's voice.

Jimmy: A life of love, love and kindness, is the best way to go, Angie—the best way to go. Remember that and you will do well. Always a pleasure to speak with you! We're off to see the new souls who have passed today. It is a celebration here when new souls come here. Actually, I mean old souls returning home. We all meet them and it is a fun time, a happy time for all. I can hear all the chatter going on now, so we must go. I know Linda talks to you regularly so will keep in touch another time. Take care of yourself, Angie. I will go now. Bye, Angie.

I see Linda running with Jimmy.

Hearing Jimmy's voice again and knowing that he was with Linda reminded me of old times. It felt as though they were alive and well living in England, not Heaven. They described their daily activities just the way I could picture them as if they were on this earth. At that moment in time it felt like they were their old selves again and up to their old antics!

Chapter 16: Creation of Mankind

It was a few days before Christmas, and I had not meditated in several weeks. I had taken a break as my family told me that I was becoming obsessed with all this spiritual stuff. I traveled to England to spend Christmas with Louise and Scott at Scott's home in the South of England. It was our first Christmas without Linda. Naturally, I thought back to the previous Christmas, to the time when I saw the bird, the omen of death. I remembered my conversation with Linda, her reassurance that it was an omen for Jimmy's death, yet still having an unsettled feeling. The day before I left for my Christmas holiday, I decided to meditate. I was getting withdrawal symptoms, and the urge to meditate was overwhelming. Instantly, the monk, my friend, came through followed by Mum and Linda. The monk showed me an open book with pages that had holes cut out in the middle.

Why Did God Create Mankind?

Monk: I want to talk to you today about your book. There is much work to be done. Now, get started on it straight away; time is ticking by. You have the outline, so now we have to fill in the middle part. I want to talk about mankind and how mankind came to be. Why was mankind created? This should be the question that people ask. Why did God create mankind on his earth? There is much discussion about this but it comes down to one basic meaning: God created mankind to show his love for the world. He loves the entire world and all the things he created in the world. Mankind was just the next process, the next step in his evolution of the world. Mankind is a complicated animal compared to all living things in the planet, but God wanted to create mankind to experience all the things, all the pleasures that God had created on this earth: the sea, the ocean, the mountains, the trees, the birds, the animals, etc. This creation, this earth, was so beautiful, that he wanted to share this with mankind, so he created mankind in his image. This is true, so they could share in the joys of the planet and the universe. But God looks down and watches his creation and he sees what mankind is doing to his creation.

Man is taking more liberties with the planet than God had hoped. Part of being human is to learn respect for all things and you do this through love. Love as a verb, doing loving things, loving one another and loving the planet and all that it has. But, mankind has lost its way and has forgotten the most fundamental part of life, which is to love others: "Love one another as you love yourself." Yet, this simple concept is so hard for most people to grasp. They forget that love makes them happy. They forget that love brings joy to the world. Do you not know what the true meaning of love is? Love is the essence of human life. Without love there can be no mankind, for without love you will have violence and war, and mankind will self-destruct.

The Act Of Love

So you must never underestimate the importance of love in your life because it is so powerful that it can work both ways for mankind, and it is up to you to understand it and the path you want to take. What people don't realize is that choosing love is the easiest, that it is the simplest and the happiest thing that they can do. It takes less resistance to love someone than to hate them, yet people do not understand this simple concept. All they have to do is look around the world and see the kind of destruction I am talking about, brought on by mankind and hatred for one another.

Start to look around you and see ways you can love people. I am talking about simple gestures of kindness, given with love. Once you start to do these acts of kindness, you will bring love, peace, and joy to all on earth. Acts of kindness should be on the top of your mind all day from the minute you open your eyes until you go to sleep. You will find that once you start these acts of kindness you cannot stop and others will notice and say to you "You are always kind to people and people love you," and they will copy you and start being kind themselves. Once people start being kind to one another, they will fill their lives with love and joy. They will appreciate God, creator of the earth, and the world and all that is in it. They will love the earth and take care of it because it is a gift from God to mankind and should be appreciated through their love. This is all I am saying about love.

Giving of yourself to others by caring about them and reaching out will bring more love back to you than you can imagine. I say to you, go and show love to someone today and see how it makes that person feel. Once you have touched someone's heart you have shown true love and God will be pleased. Many times people get caught up with all the complications of life and find themselves falling down a black hole and find no way to climb out. Everything becomes over-whelming and others are blamed: "If only they had not done this or said that." Yet, what people do not realize is that it is they themselves who create the negativity in other people around them.

I know this sounds confusing so let me explain. You blame someone because he or she said this or they said that, but ask yourself, why would a person say that? Then look deeper and see the pain that they are suffering. By your words, by your actions you say something that triggered or recalled anguish, unknowingly to you, and so that person lashes out at you for discovering that pain. You then feel like the person is being mean to you, but take the "you" out and look back at the person and see the pain. To truly see someone else's pain is to love them, to love them and make them feel loved, because when people feel loved, when people know they are loved, is when the pain goes away.

That is all I have to say about the pain, but I want you to always remember to do your best every day to make someone else's day brighter and better than when you saw them. If you do this, you will find the world to be a better place to live for you and all mankind. Love and loving one another, loving the universe and all its glory is the true meaning of life and is the finest joy of life. Look around you at your friends; see which ones are joyous and love life. Then ask yourself, how can I be that way? Why do they have so many friends? Why are people drawn to them? Take these traits and copy them. You learn something from everyone whether good or bad, so keep the good traits, and when you see the bad traits, ask yourself what is the cause of these? When you understand this important concept, you will have the key to understanding mankind.

Mankind is not so complicated because we are all mankind so those bad traits you see in other people, you have in yourselves to some degree, and that is why you can easily recognize them. Mankind is not so different from each other. You look at the fighting in the world, and you can see that men are fighting for what they think is their just cause, their right, what they believe is right. So take that on a small individual basis. Do you not fight for what you believe is right? Do you not fight for what you believe is justice? What your own belief of justice is? So don't judge people who fight wars if you yourself fight wars within your life. There is no difference, no difference at all. You cannot stop the war of nations, but you can stop the war in yourself.

There are many life lessons to learn, and we can talk about them in more detail, but that is your lesson for today. I will leave you now and will say this: "Don't wait so long next time to meditate, as we have much to say, much to do."

Until next time. Your friend, John, the monk.

Merry Christmas To All

Mum is here, Angie. Linda and I have been around the family watching you all, and that makes us happy to see you all together. We know you miss us, but there is nothing we can do about that because it is that way, and you are learning to live your lives now. It will get better. I know it was a shock losing Linda so quickly and suddenly after me, but there wouldn't have been a better time for everyone. You are all there together and can support one another. You must all work through this together. The timing is right now for you all to be together because soon you will be leading different lives and won't be able to be together as often. This was another reason for Linda to pass over when she did. You were all able to be there together and support her on that side before she passed, and now you are all there supporting each other.

Linda is here and she wants to know if you sent out all your Christmas cards this year and not to forget anyone. Did you write a list? Linda asks! She knows you didn't, but you should write your list and remember everyone on it and don't cross them off if they don't send you a card back to you like she did, because that is not the way to show love to people. Linda is laughing.

Love Mankind

Linda: You will see, Angie, that on this side you love everyone because all of mankind is all of mankind; we are one. I know you find this hard to believe coming from me, but that is how it is here. We love everyone and everything. If all this love was on earth, wouldn't it be a wonderful place? That is how it is up here: a wonderful place because here is so much love; people love one another so much. We love our lives, each other, we love to learn, we love to visit one another, we love being around each other. The energy is so high, full of love that you get swept up in it, like a wonderful whirlwind. That is what life should be like on earth, but unfortunately, it is not because humans get in the way with their fears, mistrusts, doubts, etc. and they forget hope. All the things they need to make them happy they forget or just don't realize what they should do to be happy.

Over here is great, Angie! I know I go on a bit about how happy I am here, but I really am. No worries up here! I do my best to be around the family and send my love to you all so you will be happy, but I can't physically be there for you and, for that, I am sorry. I am sorry that you don't get to see me in my physical form, but you have enough memories of me in my coats with fur around the hood to keep you laughing for a long time. I want you to laugh when you think of me. Toward the end it was a bit stressful and overwhelming; however, that's all better now, so don't worry about me.

I want you all to have a Happy Christmas and to enjoy what life has to offer you. Life can be so good if you make it meaningful. That was what I learned when I passed over and maybe a little bit toward the end, but life can be meaningful if you make it that way. Loving and understanding others is the key, as you have already been told.

Say hello and give my love to everyone. We will be with you all at Christmas and want to see you enjoying yourselves because when you pass over here we will have plenty of time to talk about all this. I am even looking forward to that day, so make the most of your lives down there. You had me in your life, and now I have gone, so just accept that and enjoy people around you now. Surround yourself with people and fill any holes in your life with love.

Will go now, Angie. I want you to enjoy yourself. Love, Linda

Mum: Bye, Love. We're off now. Merry Christmas to all!

It was a wonderful meditation. Christmas was getting better already. On Christmas Day, Louise and I drove to Scott's house. We stopped at the rest area on the way and bought two cups of coffee. As we sat there drinking our warm beverages, I looked around the large room at other customers and the employees, wondering if they had lost a loved one recently. I heard one young man in his early twenties order a cake, and his mother scolded him saying, "Grandma will have dinner ready soon." After some protest, he bought the cake, something to do with a "big appetite." I listened with both joy and sadness knowing my Mum was not here to scold any of her children. After feeling sorry for myself, I looked at the employees who probably did not want to work on Christmas day, and I hoped their shifts finished soon so they could be with their family. I felt fortunate that I was spending Christmas Day with my sister and brother.

Chapter 17: Planet Heaven

As far as I remember, Mum loved to go to fortunetellers as she called them. I don't remember exactly the first time she went to one; I believe it started with a gypsy who knocked on the front door. There is a superstition that if you turn a gypsy away at your door the gypsy will cast a spell on you and your home. My mother certainly believed in this, along with many other old wives tales. When the fair came to town in the springtime, you could guarantee gypsies would knock at your door trying to sell you trinkets or a palm reading. Mother used to buy both.

One day, I remember my sister Linda coming home from work. She was very excited. She told us that she had heard of a great fortuneteller who was not a gypsy but an elderly lady who lived in the center of town. Instantly, Mum made an appointment with Mrs. Davis who described herself as a psychic, and that was the beginning of many psychic readings throughout her lifetime. Mrs. Davis was so accurate with her information, with her predictions, that my mother became instantly hooked on psychics. Mrs. Davis was held as the standard by which all other psychics were judged, and Mum and I saw many of them over the next thirty years in which to compare

It was always an exciting time when we got news of a new psychic. Whenever we traveled on holiday, vacation, anywhere all over the world, we would always, somehow, gravitate to the psychic reader at the market, fair, boardwalk, etc. We paid anything from a few dollars/pounds up to a hundred or more. If we were allowed to tape record the sessions, we did; otherwise, we took a note pad and wrote down the information as fast as we could.

Although this past time brought us a lot of joy, it also became a crutch in our lives. We began living our lives by referring to what a psychic had told us. For example, if one told you that you were going to get a promotion at work or a new job and you did, then we would say "See, the psychic was right." Unfortunately, Mum was told she was going to move house, and refused to spend any money on new furnishings for her home.

Instead, she would say, "I will buy a dining room set when I get my new house." Thirty years later, she still had the same old dining room set.

I share this story with you because I continued to visit psychics in hopes of receiving good news for the future. I needed something to look forward to. One day, when I meditated, Mum came through with a motherly message.

Mum: Don't waste your life waiting for things to happen like I did. Stop asking others for help. You know what you want so you don't need to ask others all the time. Start focusing on what you want and make it happen. You have all the knowledge to do this, so why do you ask others? Have faith in spirit, and you will do right by spirit. We want what is best for you and the universe, so you will be guided by spirit to help the universe and, in turn, you will help yourself.

As soon as mother had given me this advice she switched gears and to my surprise she talked about Heaven.

Planet Heaven

Mum: Life in Heaven. I want to educate the world about life on this side. You already have some information from Linda about life on this side. I can tell you more. We all live together on this planet, called Planet Heaven. We all live together in communities just like there are on earth. There are towns and cities but not very many villages and small towns. People tend to congregate in the towns and cities because there is much learning going on. There is more activity, just like in the cities on earth, which in turn builds up energy and it is the energy that keeps the spirit-energy flowing: energy creates energy.

Spirit is just a ball of energy, a ball of consciousness. It can create many shapes and forms so when it loses its physical body it creates a form in spirit Heaven. We can take on many shapes depending on the level of vibration. Of course, when we are closer to earth, when we visit earth, we take on the shape of our human form that we once had. This is so our loved ones, when we want to communicate with those on earth, can recognize us as we once were. So it brings the spirit back to life in human form if you like. But once on this side, in our levels of energy field, we don't need to appear that way. We only need to appear like a human when dealing and communicating with humans.

In the spirit world we all have different forms that we take on depending on who we are communicating with, what level of evolvement the spirit is in, and then we take on the form, which serves that purpose. This may sound confusing to you, but let me explain a little more. A form does not need arms and legs for example. It does not need legs to move about or to walk because we can move as spirit in a blink of an eye, so to speak. For example, we do not need arms or hands to write with, or eat with, or to get dressed because they only benefit earthly needs that we do not use over here. We do not need forks to eat with or use a pen to write. We don't wear your physical clothes, so we don't need to get dressed. We don't need arms or hands for any of these purposes. So, yes, we have no arms and no legs because we do not need the use of limbs.

What we do need is our intelligence, our consciousness. We do not need eyes to see, as you can see, hear, and sense things without any of the human senses that you need on earth. We can choose if this thought goes to one person or to many people. Of course, you can use your thoughts to imagine anything you want, anything you like. If you want to go to a pop concert your thoughts go out this way, and you are attending a pop concert. Just like when you have a dream at night and you dream that you are attending a pop concert, or are on holiday lying on the beach. Just as you dream of these things and imagine yourself there that is what it is like in the spirit world. What you dream or imagine is a reality to you in the spirit world. So you see, you can do anything you want, go anywhere you want, and say anything you want, just through your thought process.

Wouldn't that be a wonderful thing for the soul or spirit when it is on the earth? Just close your eyes, and send your spirit to watch a pop concert, and then when you open your eyes your spirit comes back to you. That is what it is like here. You can visit anyone you like! Set up your thoughts to visit a relative or friend or loved one and then you are there. This is how Linda and I work. We think of being together and our thoughts combine and we are together, but with any kind of energy, energy comes and goes and must be recharged.

Feed Your Soul

We recharge ourselves by feeding off each other's energy and by feeding off the energy that is all around. We have good and bad energy just like you do on earth, so we have to process the bad energy, recognize it, and understand what it is doing. Bad energy zaps energy just like it happens on earth. Then you recharge yourself. Haven't you spent time with someone who has taken all of your energy and left you feeling exhausted? When you meet someone, someone who is kind and happy, or you watch a comedy show, etc., and you feel all energized again. Well, the same concept happens over here.

You can meet new spirits who pass over who are confused about where they are and what happened to them. You use your energy to show them the way. If you do this often, your energy is taken so you need to re-energize. We get this at the wonderful reunions of people where there is lots of energy around. We are taught this valuable lesson from the very beginning because having a high energy level allows you to recharge your soul. Once you have your energy level stable and don't go below the line, you can achieve so much more. You have the energy to learn more about the universe and God, our creator. You will learn, I mean understand, why God created the earth, humans, and the need to have all these spirits. Why are there so many spirits in the afterlife, in God's Heaven? What does God want with them all?

If you look at the big picture, you will see that spirits are energy that makes up the universe. God is energy; energy exists and God wants it to be positive. Yes, you can say we need negative energy to balance the positive. That is what we achieve on earth, the balancing of negative and positive, but in order to achieve that balance on earth you need help from the spirits which have passed over.

Spirits are like helpers and guides. They are there to help the spirits in their physical form achieve this balance. Believe me, the human form of spirit is out of balance, created by human man-made thoughts instead of God-like thoughts. The balance is to bring God-like thoughts into the man-made thoughts of the physical body. Once this balance is achieved, God's work is done but human souls are so out of balance it has taken many spirits, many guides to come down and intervene.

You may wonder if spirits have always been around. Yes, since the creation of time. Spirits have made themselves aware to mankind more and more as the human spirit has become so out of balance. Now, there is a much bigger effort to make contact with the human form so we can help level the balance. Again, I refer to the positive balance of the energy that supports life and spirit as we know it.

Does all this make sense? Because God wants all his children in the spirit world and in human form to have balance that brings energy to the soul. Feed the soul, feed the spirit is how God looks after his children. Don't concentrate on your physical from, just concentrate on feeding your soul, your spirit, with positive energy. Now, there are many ways to feed your spirit energy. Energy creates energy, so when you do something good to help others, your energy level rises, and then you have the energy to repeat this and help others. It is a simple concept, yet people on earth do not always do this. Feeding the soul, the spirit, is the way to God's heart, God's purpose, God's creation, the universe and all that it holds. Start thinking of ways to feed your spirit, to raise your energy levels, and you will be closer to God on earth than you can imagine. For the idea, the concept of helping another soul does not end when you lose the physical form. You must start now and you will have more energy than you can imagine, and more energy will lift your spirits.

To understand more about our work here is to understand how we can help other souls in this world. Philosophy is the best, the teaching of helping others by doing the right thing in your life. Yes, the monk has given you great teachings of life that you can interpret and follow on earth. That is why he has given them to you. They are for all humans to follow if they open their minds to the bigger world out there and not just the earth form.

Life On Other Planets

Other planets do have life, but not in the human or earthly form that you know. They are highly evolved planets without the need or use of earthly elements, gases and life forms. We can visit any of the planets with our minds, our thoughts, as I described earlier, but at this level of our communication. It is easier for us to communicate with earthly souls and souls who have recently passed over. Communication with other planets is reserved for those souls who have a special need to communicate with energy fields on those particular planets.

Do not get confused and think there is life on other planets because life as the human form understands it is not on other planets. But, there is energy on other planets, different levels of energy that feed different needs of souls, spirits in Heaven. It has all to do with intelligence and the level of energy needed to feed that intelligence. It is a concept that a human mind cannot grasp because there is no earthly equivalent.

Try to stretch your imagination and imagine spirit forms that are closer to God in likeness. Their spirits have evolved for many, many, years and have long lost any earthly experiences or memories, so they are now in a higher vibration plane. They still need energy to feed their energy and are beyond the realm of the form of energy level after earth. They are drawn to other planets that God created and feed off the energy that is there. This provides them with the strength and energy level that is necessary for their development.

Planets were created for a reason. Everything God created is for a reason, and everything he creates now is for a reason, even down to life on earth: the life and death cycle of our human life on earth, including the grass that grows. So don't underestimate God's power, his energy to create a universe, because energy has its place in the world, the universe, even spirits--no, especially the spirits that are forever evolving on this side

Earth form is only a small step in the life of the spirit. It is an early development and the energy fields on earth are all that are needed to sustain that life form. Don't worry about Linda and me visiting you on the earth vibration level. It is easier for us to do this since we have not long passed from that energy field to this energy field. We can visit any time and are around you all the time, just as we were on earth.

We want you to make the most of your life on earth so we help you. Other people on earth are helped by loved ones too, but they don't realize that they are. If you look at coincidences, for example, there is no such thing as coincidences; they are spirit guided to help you stay on track in your life. So, don't ignore their meaning. Even when you meet someone in a chance meeting do not think that it is indeed by chance because again; it is your spirit guides who are helping you, your helpers.

Sometimes you see something and it reminds you of something else, a person or an event. When this happens, spirit is telling you that you are on the right track and are confirming this for you. However, when you are off track, you feel a frustration in your body, a tingling, or sickness in your stomach, they are all signs from spirit to say "Pay attention." Again, it is your energy level that is receiving the message from the energy field in spirit. It is a form of communication, so don't think you have to see a ghost or hear a tapping on the wall etc.. We can send our thoughts to you, into your head, your consciousness, or to your stomach. The sickness feeling is when something is wrong. At the opposite end, we also send you feelings of absolute joy. Your emotions are all triggered by energy fields around you, and by being in tune with this energy you can recognize it and proceed in your life accordingly. It is amazing the power of energy, and once you can recognize it and tap into it, you will live a more fulfilled and complete life. Energy is the source of life, the source of the universe.

Chapter 18: Power of Love

It has been eight months since Linda passed away. I do not want to say death because that implies the end of her life. I do not believe that her physical death was the end of her life. She has passed over into her new life, and her soul continues to live on in Heaven. I have found out many things about the continuation of the soul after the physical death. It is this belief, this truth, that life is continuous that has brought great comfort to me. I am no longer afraid of death, and I do not believe that I have lost my mother and sister. They are around me every day as your loved ones are around you every day.

A friend once told me of a time, shortly after her mother's death when she was in her garden pulling out the weeds. It was a task she did not particularly liked to do, however, one that had to be done. She knelt down to the flowerbed and started to pull out the weeds from in-between the flowers. As she remembered her mother, an avid gardener, she felt her love and guidance around her. Her hands moved easily and effortlessly. She was amazed how quickly the time had passed, and before she realized it, she found that she had pulled out all the weeds.

Often, when I talk to people who have lost their loved ones, they all have similar stories about not remembering exactly how or what happened, but knowing they felt different while performing some ordinary task, while thinking about their loved ones. The power of love does live beyond the grave, and below are several meditations about love and the power of love.

Fulfill Your Life's Contract

Monk: Now let us begin. (He sounds like a school teacher today!) *You should educate people about our world so they will learn what they need to know before they cross over. You should teach others that their life on the physical earth must not be wasted. The more they understand this the more they will fulfill their life's purpose. Mankind must learn to love one another and help one another all they can. These are the basic elements of human life. They must love one another, so I say to you, we must teach people this basic truth, why we are on this earth. We are on this earth to learn how to love, with all the restrictions, obstacles, and complications of the earth form. Man must learn that he is not in control of his destiny but is required to fulfill his life's purpose, the contract made before he came to the earth. Yet people go through their lives and ignore this contract that they made with the Creator before they came to earth, into their earth body.*

So, how do we teach it? Firstly, we need to educate them that the spirit world does exist, that life does continue after death. Once they are aware of that they must ask themselves "Why am I here on this earth?" Once they ask that question then they are ready to except the teachings of spirit.

The teachings of spirit provide all the tools necessary to fulfill your life's purpose on earth. If you complete those teachings you will have less work to do on this side when you cross over. (This echoes Linda's meditation earlier: if you learn life's lessons on earth, you have less to learn when you cross over)

The Power Within

I want to talk about love and how people should bring love into their lives on a daily basis. It is simple yet people don't listen. Love is the creator of all things, all desires. Without love you cannot have a world. It is so powerful that people do not even know how it works in their lives or in this world. Love is energy, just like we all are energy. Love is an extension of that energy. When you use it you create more energy and more energy comes back to you in abundance. Love truly makes the world go around. Love is what makes life and what makes life worth living. Without love there would be no life, no need for existence. Love is the magic ingredient that creates a life that is worth living because without love there is no life.

Find ways in your daily life to create love all day, every day. It can start with the small things such as appreciating every minute that you are alive on earth. Every minute that you are alive is an opportunity to love and be loved. Love your neighbors, love the man on the street, love the car that you drive, love the food that you eat, love the job that you do. Change the way you think about the world and you will find love. It is the power that is within you, within all of us, yet we choose not to use this power. We choose to search for something other than love. Things that are not love and expect them to make us happy, but how can they make us happy when they are not based on love but based on expectations and hopes of the human soul.

Your Spiritual Soul

The human soul is far away from the spiritual soul from which it came, from which it remains part of still. Yes, part of still. You still have a piece of your spiritual soul in Heaven that stays here. It is this spiritual part of you that gives you that gut feeling that you have and your consciousness that lets you know you are doing right or wrong. Have you heard that expression "a guilty mind"? Yes, that is your consciousness, your spirit from this side talking to you to let you know you are off track from what you should be doing, your life's purpose. So, listen to it when it comes.

It is a simple thing but people are not aware of its importance to their life's purpose, their life's work. People believe that they are in control of their lives. Yes, they are to a certain degree but when it comes down to choices, decisions of right and wrong, then their higher self, their consciousness steps in. You may ask yourself about the evil people in the world and wonder why they are not answering to their higher selves.

I say to you: they have undermined their higher selves by refusing to pay attention or listen to it. Again, part of human nature is to make a decision, a conscious decision on what is right and wrong. Evil people consciously try to ignore their higher self, and the more they ignore it the less influence the spirit plays in their lives. You, in the human form do have control over the amount of spirit you let into your life, just like when you meditate and allow spirit to work with you. Evil people choose not to allow spirit to work with them and block out their spiritual side completely. When they eventually cross over to the spirit world they will pay for their redemption. They will have to go through many sessions of reviewing life in the human form and will not be able to advance or progress out of the hell that they created for many, many years—more than a lifetime in human years and an eternity in our world.

God loves all his children, even the ones who commit such terrible crimes. They do pay in this world but the end goal is that

God brings all his children home once they have learned their life's lessons whether on earth or whether they are learned on this side. God is forever loving, forever caring. God is love. Love is the most important word in the world. Love is the world. Love should be the word that everyone talks about all day: ways to love, how to love, be loved, etc. Everything you do should have its basis in love.

That is what the lesson is for today: A simple one, but most important.

Thank you for sitting with me today. Your friend.

This lesson, on the importance of love, summarized to me the importance of life and the reason for our whole being. It is what makes the planet work. It was not surprising that following this lesson from the monk, Mum continued with the same theme of love. I imagine them all hovering around me while I am sitting in my living room saying, "It's my turn next" because immediately, as the monk finished his last words, I sensed my mother's presence!

Love Makes The World Go Around:

Mum here. I want to add some words to the monk's message today. I have been waiting for you—not in a bad way, just looking forward to visiting with you today. You are doing fine so let me just say how happy I am that you are enjoying these meditations as you call them. Linda is here too and sends her love. Yes, that is the theme for today also: love is the center of the universe. Love is what makes the world go around, not money like the song says! Just a little joke, Angie!

Love is the key to life. Love is the key to the world, to the existence of mankind. Once people figure that out the earth will be a better place. I know you feel and give out love more than you ever did in your life because life experiences have brought you to where you are now. Love is there when you need it; love is there when you need to give love to someone else. Love is there to make the world go around. It may sound simple, but often the simplest things are the truest and the dearest. They do not have to be complicated. It is the little things that create happiness.

I am always here, Angie, so get on with your day today!

Bye, Love. Love, Mum.

The teachings today are very clear. Love is the center of the universe, the center of life. Love is the purpose of life. The following day the monk continued with his teachings about love and peace.

Make Every Day Count

Monk here today: Today's lesson is about God, our creator. Gods wants the world to be at peace with itself. He wants the people in the world to get along and help one another. It takes a disaster to bring out the love in the world, which God would like us all to have—all this love, all the time, people helping one another. Yet people choose only to help when there is a crisis and not when the need is there as it is all year around. People do love one another, but they have forgotten how to show this.

You may think that it is a tough lesson to learn when you see the destruction. It is not done deliberately or out of malice. It is done by the force of nature that the earth has created through its use of energy and use of supplies. Natural disasters, as you call them, are man made by the human race, except they don't see it like that. They think all disasters are an act of God, but God loves his children and does not cause these disasters. It is human actions that cause these disasters, yet humans do not like to take the responsibility for their actions.

Out of disaster does come good. It is the law of nature, the yin and the yang. Out of bad does come good and God wants only good for his children. So you see, good will rise and people will learn a valuable lesson: to love one another through their help and support during a crisis. God certainly does work in mysterious ways, and it is this inner feeling of wanting to help mankind when humans step up and help one another.

I want to talk about the world and how God loves the world he created. Yet, man is destroying this world through greed and temptation. God wants man to love the universe and help his fellow man. God created the earth to share the beauty with mankind. He created a universe, a stage, a school, for mankind to learn and grow which they have done, but lately they have taken so much from this universe that it is causing disasters in the world. Yes, God won't interfere for he made mankind in his likeness to learn their spiritual path on the planet he called earth.

Yet all this learning is causing havoc on the earth and humans are out of control. They need to remember why they are there in the first place. They need to know that God loves them and wants the best for them. Mankind has moved away from God in so many ways, but God wants to remind them of the purpose of their lives. The purpose of their lives is to love themselves, their neighbors and love the world. It is a simple task to ask, but many do not do this. They love themselves but forget to love others. It takes a natural, or should I say man-made disaster, to bring out the love in the human soul. Don't think that all these sermons are negative or that God is not pleased with the human race: that is not true. For God loves all his children and wants what is best for them, so when he sees they are not living their life's purposes, he wants to remind them of this so they will get back on track once again. He wants them to live meaningful lives on earth but feels they can only do this once they realize life's purpose.

Go now and write down what I tell you so you can help others understand this simple concept. A simple concept, yet many people don't live their lives to fulfill their life's purpose. Make every day count, make everyday a blessing, and God will be well pleased.

I sensed the monk's energy drifting away and I prepared myself to come out of the meditation. My mind did not completely clear, and I felt inspired to write again. The monk's energy continued to blend with mine and he added:

Your mother is a special soul who has progressed so rapidly because of her love for mankind. She had such a lot of love in her heart while on earth that her soul has advanced quickly when she passed. I know she visits you, and for that you are truly blessed. Learn from your mother's life on earth and follow her simple gestures of love that she used to do. Speak nice words to people, showing love and thanks to all. Yes, she may have had moments of crying at times when she was upset but they were human emotions, a protective mechanism for her, one that all humans use. The key is to have the love, the elements that you show to help others. That is the piece that people forget to do. The act of kindness to people is the piece that most humans are missing. So when you see the destruction in the world and the devastation of the human soul, remember that acts of kindness are all it takes to help one another.

Stay focused on your goals of helping mankind, and you will success in living a purposeful life. Write down how you will help the world, and remember to do this and not just write down the words to forget it. I am here to help and guide you, give you words of wisdom and a little of life's philosophy, but in the end it is up to you which path you follow. As humans you get to make that choice. Go, plan out your path and live a good life. That is all I am saying to you today. There will be many times to speak more of philosophy. Start your journey now. That is what I say to you today. Go now and I will be back to sit with you again.

Thank you my friend. God Bless.

What a wonderful thing to say about my mother. I knew she was a special soul who loved her family, friends, and strangers. When she watched the events of 9/11 in 2001, as innocent people fell to their death, she cried. She felt their desperation and their fear, as she knew hope was gone.

Chapter 19: Yellow Brick Road

When you lose a loved one, there are those days when you feel better than other days and there are those days when you feel sad and lonely without them. One day, I was feeling sad and had difficulty focusing; I missed my Mum and my sister. It was taking me a while to settle into a meditative state, so I used a visualization technique. I visualized a flight of stairs and began to walk up them. When I reached the top, I saw a chair at the end of the hall. I walked up to the chair and naturally sat down in it. Immediately, Linda came and sat next to me.

Joy And Happiness

Linda: Hello, Angie, I am here. Mum is here, also. We want to help you today. Yes, you are smiling now. That is what I bring to you: joy and happiness. You cannot help but smile because I am close to your face and radiating my energy onto your face, onto your body, filling you with joy and happiness so much that you cannot help but smile. I want so much for you to be happy and not to worry about silly things. When will you ever learn that those things just don't matter? What matters are love, joy, and happiness and that is up to you to create. Now don't you feel better, Angie? Now that is all it took, a little visit from me to bring a smile to your face.

The book you are writing is mainly about me and how you found out the truth of life through my communications with you. You see how happy I am, so you know what a wonderful world I live in. It is a world that you and all humans will live in when you pass over. I was not this happy when I was on earth. People only think they are happy on earth because they measure it by the standard of happiness on the earth, which you know to be happy. But when you cross over, you see this wonderful place so full of love and happiness that it is incomprehensible to the human mind, the human mind which is part of the soul, the spirit. But when that spirit gets reunited with its full body, its full spirit on this side, it becomes whole again and the picture is complete. That is how I feel complete, and once you are complete the happiness just grows and flourishes.

Don't mourn for me because I am so happy beyond words to describe. I know you miss my physical form, but see beyond that human limitation. Open your mind to all there is. When you open your mind you will see the truth of life, the truth of the soul, and then you too will be happy in your earthly form. Now talking with me, doesn't that make you feel happy and contented? Yes, of course, it does, just like you felt when I was in the physical form. The feeling is still there.

You can think of me at any time and this nice happy feeling will come over you each time because I am still around, and when you send your thoughts out to me it gives me permission to move closer to you and say "Hello." It is up to you how close you want me to visit. Like today, you knew I was around in the kitchen, you could sense me, and yes I was waiting for our meditation session to start, and now I am really close to you so you can feel my presence as though I was there talking to you in person, which I am, just not in the physical form.

It is a shame that souls in their earthly form do not tap into this experience, this energy because it is so easy for mankind to do. Once they put their minds to it they too can just relax and wait for their loved one's energy to come close. Unfortunately, Hollywood in its wisdom has painted a dark cloud over this process and many people stay away from it. Yet they are missing out on a wonderful opportunity to be with loved ones every day. This is what we want: we want to be with our loved ones on the earth because we are around them, just on a different vibration field. We are so close in our energy fields that we can communicate quite easily, yet the human body with its earthly influences does not allow this process to happen. The churches and institutions have made this natural connection a taboo in your world and in such has eliminated this natural process in the name of Jesus Christ, which is ironic because Jesus loves all his souls, all his children on this side and that side, and wants us to help one another on both sides.

One World

Sometimes his teachings were changed to fit man's concept of what was normal and acceptable to them, the human form, yet by doing this they eliminated man's potential of grasping both worlds as one. They are indeed one world and not two, yet the human form does not allow this to happen. I want to help you close this gap between the two worlds and make it one. Make it one for those who want to be part of it. Once they understand how the two worlds are really one world, they will live a happier, fuller, richer life. What more can I say about that? It is that simple, yet it is such a hard concept for the human mind. Just look at me Angie; I have not gone. I have not gone anywhere. Just because I lost my physical form does not mean I feel any different about you or about my love for you. My love is still there even stronger if that is possible for you to understand because everything on this side is fuller and richer than anything that it was on earth.

Colors are richer and deeper here. The sea is a beautiful blue green, and the sky is an amazing blue with dazzling sunshine. All the things you imagine are brighter, clearer, and more beautiful. At night when the stars are in the sky, they shine so bright that it is never dark here. There is never night as you have on earth. Everything is perfect just like when God created the earth. The picture you have of Adam and Eve in the Garden of Eden is how God created the earth in the first place; that is how it is here. You see, he created earth and man in his likeness. He created his kingdom on earth as it is in Heaven, his kingdom in Heaven. Then as humans evolved in his kingdom on earth, they changed God's creation so much that the earth became how it is today.

Humans have forgotten God's creation, and that it was created for the good of mankind. Instead, they use the earth for the good of themselves. I am not saying that all humans are bad or disregard the earth because they do not. We are saying that most souls, in the human form, do abuse the earth. They abuse through their use of the elements in the earth and through their thoughts because bad thoughts will lead to bad things.

On this side, all those human qualities leave and only the goodness of the soul is left and goes forth, back into God's kingdom of Heaven. It is so beautiful here that you can't wait to come back. I mean, souls who leave the Heavenly kingdom to come down to earth to learn their lessons can't wait until they return here. We all discuss this when we decide to come down. We

141

discuss how beautiful it is up here, what we are giving up to come down to earth. Yes, we all pick when we will come back to Heaven. We pick when we will come and leave the earth.

Choose Your Life's Lessons

It has to be that way because it can't be forever so to speak. You have to decide what your life's lesson on earth will be, then pick the human soul you want to be, and then plan your time accordingly. I am not saying your life is all completely mapped out because you do have freedom of choice. I am saying you choose who, where, and what type of human soul you want to be. It is kind of fun really. People meet here to discuss their soul's progress, which family to be born into and map out a schedule, if you like.

There is such a lot that goes on here: plans for this, plans for that, many committees, many meeting rooms, seminars to go to, etc. We have such a good time here. I love it and, of course, I get to be around Mum whenever I want to, except she is busy with her schedule. But all in all, we are together as much as we want.

Life is so meaningful that you want to learn. It is amazing how the soul works, how it lives off energy but has this intelligence to it: intelligence or consciousness or thoughts that are ever evolving and learning. It is all about the intelligence that is the best way to describe it. I am not talking about being book smart intelligence, because that is a human form, which is so limiting. You learn what is given to you, and so you do not really learn anything. You only learn by testing your mind, your ability to learn what is not being given to you, to learn about life forms in the world by learning about the energy that create life forms.

What is energy? How does it work? You learn on earth by studying books or being told about it, but when you are on this side you are energy, so you live and experience it so much more because you do not have your physical form to weigh you down, to limit your conscious thoughts. You trust your intelligence.

In the human form you ask: "How can that be?" In the spirit form your intelligence understands how it is. You have a better understanding of the earth, this Planet Heaven because you are part of it all. When you are in the earthly human form you limit your imagination, your mind to what can be understood in earthly forms. I want you to go beyond that and understand what the world is made of, what it is about. It comes back to one word:

energy. God is energy, everything is energy, and when you understand that you will understand the world and how it works.

Now that is a lot of information I have given you today, Angie. I hope it all makes sense. I have given it to you the best I can so you can explain it to others and, in turn, it will help them understand life's meaning and help them to enjoy their lives more while on that side. I want you to be happy with your life while you live in that body, and by giving you all this information it will make you understand life's meaning and the purpose of life to you. You will live a more complete and fulfilled life while you are there.

This is a blessing, Angie, a blessing that we can communicate as freely as we do. So I don't want you to waste these communications. Go forth and share this, and it will fall into the hands of those it is intended for. So don't worry about that; you will be helping more people than you know. Like everything, those people will be drawn to it, just as you were drawn to it. Some people will just be curious and want a quick read. It doesn't matter. All that matters is that it will help those who it is intended to help.

The Yellow Brick Road

Linda showed me a picture of a book with edging around the outer pages. She began to describe a layout for the book. *Angie, I want you to write inside the box on each page, for when it is words from spirit it needs to be distinguished from regular text. It makes it more appealing to the eye and less confusing for the reader. This can be done with a red rose for Mum, a daffodil for me, and a sunflower for the monk. This will distinguish your notes in the book and make it less confusing and appealing.*

As the reader can see, I took Linda's advice and used artwork to differentiate between spirit communications, although I decided to use the image of a monk instead of the sunflower.

A book's appeal is the cover of the book. Although they say "don't judge a book by its cover," you must have some appeal to draw in the reader. Your book will get lost if it is all written with the same format. You need to differentiate the segments so the reader can understand what is being said and look for what appeals most to them. It is just a little advice to help you with your layout. This way you can incorporate many things without it becoming messy and confusing to people.

Best to start with my death and how you accidentally came across the automatic writing when you least expected it. It came so naturally that you began to build upon it and learn as much as you could. Your journey has developed into a world of love and beauty where you have discovered you have not lost me. You have discovered that I am still around more than you realize I think, Angie. Yes, I am around you all the time just whenever I want to without jeopardizing my work and my commitments on this side. You see, I am around you now as you write this, Angie. I just want to give you some more ideas for your book. I know you have a lot already, and now we need to look at the layout of it. As we said, you can start with my death, how I came to you in California at Kate's house, and from there you went on a mission to discover the truth and confirm that it was really me. You even went to mediums to confirm this, took your work to Lily Dale so they could confirm this. You even tested me a little by asking for information only you would know, but as you can see by my writing that it is me who inspires your words, not you, Angie!

You can see my sense of humor coming through, which I am afraid you never did have one as funny or as silly as me. You were, and still are, so very serious. Just look at the writings and you can see my personality coming though. Anyway, enough about that!

You can see we still keep our personalities on this side. We don't lose very much when we cross over apart from the physical body and those human elements and problems. It is truly like paradise here. Remember the movie the Wizard of Oz *and the yellow brick road with all the beautiful colors? Again, that is what it is like here: a beautiful pathway or journey on the yellow brick road to follow the discovery of yourself and who you are. It is a joyous and happy journey full of love and excitement as we walk our paths. Can you feel the excitement that I bring to you? Imagine your life on earth is in black and white, and when you cross over it is in multiple colors, and your whole soul comes alive with so much pleasure you can't wait to move along the path.*

I am describing it as easy as I can for you, Angie, because I want you to be completely clear on how it is here. Can you see and hear how happy I am? I will wait for you to come, and we will be together again just like we were before in our little house in Virginia. I am even happier than that. I have everything I want here: love, friends, and family—all that is needed on earth. So you see you can create your own Heaven on earth just like God wants to create his Heaven on earth. It is bringing God's love to all on earth and living your daily life with that love for yourself and all mankind. Except on earth there are so many earthly factors and issues that get in the way.

Love: The Secret Ingredient

If you learn to live your life without the issues and concerns of life and live with God's love every day, you will find happiness on earth. You don't have to wait until you get here to find happiness. All it takes is to accept God's love and live your life accordingly. God's love is all you need. It can create a wonderful life for all, and yet people choose to live without it.

You don't need to go to a church to bring love and harmony to your life. It is all around you: listening to the birds chirping is God's love, listening to babies crying is God's love. There are so many ways to hear, see, and feel God's love that you don't have to be in a church to feel his love. It is all around you if you open your heart and your mind. Once you do this, it will grow and you will be full of love. You will feel the love and know that you are closer to God. That is what God wants for his children, to feel his love, and this will bring you closer to God.

What a simple concept that is all God asks. Unfortunately, it took my physical death for me to understand this. I tried when I was on earth. I loved my cat, Harvey, so much that it gave me all the joy and happiness I had ever known. However, I just did not see the big picture that it was love that made me happy.

The secret ingredient to life is love. Imagine if I had loved all parts of life as much as I loved Harvey; just imagine how rich my life would have been. That is what I am saying to you now, Angie. Love everybody and everything in your life the best you can, and you will see your life transform beyond your wildest dreams. This is what I say to you. Start loving yourself and your life and you will be amazed at what comes into your life when you do this. Eliminate any stress and anxiety by removing yourself from the situation. Live within your means, and you will live a contented life. Be happy with what you have, and you will never want for anything else. So simple really!

Help others to see this and fulfill their own paths this way. Don't forget who you are, where you came from, and thank God for all he gives you every day. These rules are so simple, yet people don't receive education on this only if they belong to a church or have family who believe in this philosophy. Please help those who do not see this and help them. Show them the way. I will give you all the love and happiness that I can send your way. That is what it is all about, Angie. Focus on love and do things in the name of God and you can't go wrong.

That is it for today, Angie. I hope this has been helpful to you.

Your loving big sister, Linda.

Chapter 20: Manual for Living

It was the month of January and winter was in full force. The North East region of the United States suffered through many snowstorms and blizzards. Like most people, I decided to stay indoors; I used this opportunity to meditate even more. The meditation sessions were lasting longer and longer. I found that I could easily enter a meditative state within minutes. On this occasion, my mother visited me for a short while, and then a long communication came from Linda. I felt a warm glow inside of me as I felt their love draw near.

Mum is here. It is so peaceful here in our world. We are very relaxed and happy. The feeling is like no other: feeling only happiness. We are both here helping you. We are very pleased to talk to you about life. There are more segments today about life on the spirit plane. Linda is here to tell you more.

When Souls Cross Over

Linda: You see all the volume of energy. Some ghosts get stuck in between the plane fields because they can't accept they have gone. They feel their lives were taken from them before they were ready to go. I am talking about those who die without warning from a heart attack or an accident. It is up to them when they cross, when they want to acknowledge that death happened, and they are here in the spirit world, or they refuse to accept their deaths and remain in the astral field so close to earth that they can appear as ghosts to the human eye. We try and help them as best we can from this side and most usually accept help immediately, but there are always those few who try to get back in their bodies and remain confused. Eventually, they all complete a passing. The ones who take their time, the ghosts if you like, choose to linger like this until they are ready. It is not a bad thing in any way, just one of those things that happens sometimes on earth. Then people in the human body help them from that side, and we help them from this side. They are not left in the in between zone for very long because, ultimately, they reunite with their natural form. There is always one in every group. But again, I must say this is not a bad experience for the soul, just a minor delay of their choosing. Sometimes they linger to say goodbye to people and places on earth that they love. It is not a bad thing; it just takes some people longer than others, and after all, all souls are different with their personalities.

That is part of the work we do here, to help souls cross over. It is an important part because they have long forgotten all their memories on this side, so we surround them with all our love, which reminds them in an instant. For ghosts, that memory takes a little longer to recover as they are still attached to their memories on earth. At no time are souls or spirits in distress. It is all how it is meant to be. Souls are very resilient, and their energy rebuilds itself and adjusts naturally on this side. People should never think their loved ones are stuck anywhere because they are not. They are in the adjustment space when they cross which can be in an instant or slightly longer. We all help each other here so no one is left behind.

You may wonder whether it is only bad souls that need the adjustment. I say no. All souls go through the adjustment process. When bad souls cross over they adjust in an instant, as easily as good souls. The difference is for bad souls they go to a different place to learn from their mistakes. Yes, learn I say, because only if they can truly learn that what they did was wrong can they move forward and be redeemed and be brought back into the plane with all other souls. Evil souls, such as Hitler, remain in that place to give repentance for all their evil deeds. This is a long process and so can take much time before they are released and put on the path to redemption and the path of light to see God and the truth of life.

It is important to understand that your lives on earth have an impact on your soul's progression over here, so it is important to do the right thing and live life the best you can by helping one another. When you pass over you will find how well you lived your life's lesson on earth, and you will be well pleased if you have followed the path of truth. Please understand I am not saying all humans should be a priest or a nun all their lives; I am saying just live a noble life, full of love and kindness for your fellow man, and you will have lived a good life.

Well, Angie, that is your lesson for today so I will go now.

Love, Linda. Bye, Angie.

The following day Linda had much more to say about life in the spirit world. I particularly enjoyed this communication with its reference to life's purpose and life's learning lessons. It was another one of Linda's marathon sessions lasting over three hours. I saw Linda on my left side; she was smiling very brightly with her big, beautiful eyes. She looked very happy.

A Manual For Living

Yes, Angie, I can speak to you now. You have been very busy, haven't you, with all my things. (Referring to her old letters and paperwork which I had been sorting through.) *Sorry it is such a lot of work, but it is only things, Angie. Let's get started on today's work. Talk about my life here, Angie, so you will have more information for your book.*

Today we have been studying philosophy, the teachings of the great leaders, and prophets who were on the earth, including our creator, God, and Jesus Christ. Remember foremost that God loves his children, and the great prophets were there to teach his message with his son Jesus Christ who sacrificed his life on earth to be the ultimate teacher. Yet, mankind did not listen to the message; instead they turned one philosopher-prophet against the other, done in the name of God and caused strife in the world. You see this more clearly on this side, and it makes so much sense to me now. Philosophers and their teachings are such a big part of your life's lesson up here. No, you don't have to write papers or take exams. Ha! Ha! Just a little joke! But you do have to learn and understand the meaning of life. This is the theory part and, of course, we get to do the practical part just like some classes on earth.

Your life here and on earth is made of a practical and theoretical learning in the classroom and in the world. We are assessed on our progression and the understanding of the truth. It is so much easier to understand it on this side, and I really enjoy it all. It is a time when we all come together and learn as one. Everything you do here through learning is done through a

149

guidance of some sort, whether it is your classroom tutor or your personal committees or committee members, you are never just left to figure things out for yourself. You are taken by the hand and shown the way.

There is so much love here that it makes learning a wonderful experience, and everyone exceeds and does well. I am learning so much up here: learning about relationships with people. They are the most important things to have. It is through relationships that you actually learn about yourself. For example, you bring out the best in someone or the worst in someone depending on your interaction with them. Imagine that, Angie, such a simple concept to get, yet many go through life on earth and do not understand this simple concept. Of course, on this side, it is so easy to understand everything but, again, I say to you, or I point out to you, that this is what makes your experience of learning about life while on earth so challenging. It is a game if you like.

You are sent on earth to figure out the meaning of life and your purpose of life. Unfortunately, not everybody figures this out. It is your life's purpose to love one another and the simplest and easiest way to love one another is to bring out the good in someone by showing your love for them. Again, it is so easy on this side to see and understand this, yet it is so hard sometimes on earth to see this and understand this. There are people on earth who do understand this but find it difficult to practice it in their daily lives.

Creating a manual for living your life's purpose on earth is the whole purpose of me bringing this information to you, so people can figure out what they are supposed to do with their lives on earth and practice this daily. Practice is the keyword here, and then they will have won the game of life and will have fulfilled their life's purpose on earth while in human form. This is such a powerful statement and realization of life on earth and yet it is so simple for people to follow if they choose to listen to this wise old spirit on this side! Yes, Angie, I am giving myself a little credit here - trying to make you laugh or in hopes of making you laugh! I don't want you to take all this so seriously. Think of it as having a sneak peek at the test on earth for all humans, a sneak peek that does not give the test of life away because without understanding what it is and how it works will do no good to you or any human soul unless it is understood and practiced.

The Final Test

The final test, the final grade, is when you pass your life's lesson by actually completing it. So don't think it is something that is given lightly—a sneak preview. It should be considered the greatest sneak preview of a test you could ever really want because this information is so valuable, and you will fulfill your life's purpose beyond your wildest dreams.

Once you cross over to this side you will be so happy that you lived your life and followed your path. Again, it is a simple thing so go and tell the rest of mankind so they can learn too and you will do me proud, Angie—just joking! I mean, make me proud. I like having a little fun with you, Angie, trying to get you to lighten up a bit more. Earth is a wonderful experience. All people need to do is to figure out how they can enjoy their lives the best possible way. Many people believe that it is through fancy cars and houses and designer things, but as you know, Angie, you can't take those things with you when you cross over to the "pearly gates," as you say down there. You only get to keep your good personality and sense of humor, like me!

The point I am trying to make is that your soul keeps only thoughts, memories, and personality, none of the material things. So the soul should make its memories and thoughts as happy and as loving as they can be, so they can bring these over here and have less classroom time here and more time for fun activities. I have already told you some of the fun activities we do such as meeting the newly crossed over souls. That is really fun, one big social party and get together. Then, of course, it is the life's reviews I mentioned before. Then you get to choose if you want to view a pop concert or sporting event. You can go anywhere you want to go. Just send a thought and you are there.

There are wonderful singers who sing beautiful songs all day here. The music is uplifting and makes you feel like you are floating on air, which you are so to speak! It naturally draws you in. All the sounds, all the notes here are beyond what you can imagine on earth: Heavenly sound would be the closest thing I could describe it as. Musical notes are everywhere because they uplift the soul.

Everything is uplifting here. We like to listen to other souls who make visits to their loved ones, just like you listen to people's stories on earth because listening to stories, telling stories is another interaction of the soul and each time the soul interacts, the higher the energy of the soul and the more love that is created.

Love is the key to everything. Love is what creates the energy and unites the soul both in Heaven and on earth. Unfortunately, earthly human souls have not figured this out. Yet, you have seen TV programs of the perfect family life, where everyone is happy Pleasantville, for example, comes to mind: a picture perfect town. Well, that is how it is here, very pleasant and picture perfect in every aspect of life, all the time!

I don't know how to describe it to you any differently than that. Life here is so pleasant and everything is so easy to understand and do. If you want to eat, you just think about what you want and there it is. No calories or fat to worry about because you don't have a human body to eat it with! So remember what I said before: it is all in your thoughts. Everything you do is in your thoughts on this side.

Thoughts Are Energy

Let's review this again. You can do, see, and hear anything you want on this side because it is all done through your thoughts. You can create anything in your mind, just like the law of attraction that became such a big phenomenon on earth. You create what your thoughts are, what you think. Obviously the process takes a little long to happen, and it is harder to understand, but once you understand the process and you get it, it does work. On this side it is easier because you don't have those negative thoughts to counter balance your good thoughts. In the earth form all these thoughts get mixed up together so the universe doesn't really know what it is you are asking so you feel, you find, you don't get what you want. You get what you don't want because the thoughts are there and are mixed up between what you want and don't want.

On this side, everything is so clear that your thoughts don't get mixed up so you can choose what you want. Let's talk about an example. Imagine I want to eat an orange on this side. All I do is think about the orange, imagine it, picture it, see it, peel it, taste it. You can do this process in your mind as a human. Just close your eyes; imagine an orange, picture it inside your head, with your thoughts, peal it, then imagine the juice squirting out of the orange. You can smell the fresh orange juice as it squirts out. As you break the orange apart, you feel the texture in your mind as you suck out the juices. Once you go through this process you can actually taste the orange taste in your mouth and smell the orange flavor as you peel the orange. Your mind is so powerful that you can do this exercise with many things.

You see, your mind is your soul, is your spirit, and is your energy of life, which you can control on this side and that side of its life. I was going to say natural life here, but you may get confused as what is natural. I say to you that the life of the soul is as natural as it gets. It is the human body that limits the soul's natural ability to do many things. Most of the limitation is man made from rules of society, rules passed down through many centuries. I will not say since the history of man because man never had all these rules and limitations when man was created. It has only been since man became what we say earthly educated that rules were laid down by other humans to limit and control the minds of others. They were not made out of malice but initially as a mechanism for human survival since the time of the cavemen. People started learning, believing in what they thought was right from wrong, with themselves being the judge of these matters, but in reality they passed down their own limitations and beliefs of right and wrong onto other humans and, thus, limited man's mind and thoughts.

Know The Truth Of Life

What we want to see happen now is full circle. We want the minds and thoughts of humans to open up to the possibilities, the truth of life—knowing this truth of their lives and why they are on the earth. This has been shut out for many centuries because the church rules have squashed human development of the mind and soul. The mind and soul, the creation of God, should be free to learn and expand its knowledge and capability, but it is so restricted on earth. All those rules and regulations create all this havoc and animosity between cultures and nations in the name of God. I am sorry to go on about this so much but it is important that people understand they are in control of their own minds not anyone else. They must use their minds for the good of mankind; that is all God asks of his children.

Now on this side, that is what we do. Our thoughts and our energies go out to all souls on this side and that side for the good of mankind. It is easy to do here because we don't have that physical body that restricts us like it does on earth so we are able to follow God's purpose on this side. The whole point of communicating with you and other humans on earth is to educate you about the soul and the purpose of your life on earth so you don't need to wait until you cross over to start fulfilling your life's purpose, the very reason you are there.

Again, it is like looking at the test paper, a sneaky look, which benefits everyone, every soul. The more good you do while in your body, the physical body, the greater you will please God and advance your soul's development. Again, go back to the thoughts you have in your head each day and ask yourself: what are my thoughts? Why am I having these thoughts? You may think about a friend or a loved one and the phone may ring. Your thoughts come into your head from the energy of the person who was about to call you. You see, all thoughts are energy, but if you understand this then you can tune into the energy on earth.

It is this process that makes it possible for you to connect with me now, Angie, but I think you understand it more and more so it makes my work with you less to do. I won't be doing this forever with you, Angie, because you need to evolve your soul, develop your soul even more, and, in fact, eventually, I will be hindering your development. I am here doing this now to educate and teach you, to put you on the right track so to speak, but you understand this very well, so my work is nearly done and you will move on to the next step.

Don't worry, Angie, it won't be yet, and when it does happen I will still be around but will not give you all these lessons anymore because you won't need me. I will be around watching, checking on you from time to time. But I need you to get going on this and start writing. Just do it, Angie, and I will be pleased.

I love you; remember that I will always be here for you. Go and write up my notes. I will come again; I will go now.

I felt sad knowing that Linda would not be communicating with me forever, although I knew deep in my heart that at some point she would have to move on with her life. I felt anxious not knowing when that time would come. I felt I had much more to learn and I was not ready to lose her again. I hoped and prayed that it would be a long time away. As Linda's energy left, I realized she did not come by herself. As soon as Linda was finished the monk came through with words of wisdom continuing on from Linda's message. It had been several weeks since the monk last communicated with me and I was pleased to feel his kind, sweet, energy again.

Monk: Make Every Day Count

Very pleased to come through this strongly today. Very much want to talk about life on your planet. It has become so much more complicated than it was ever before. Your technology changed all that. Not so sure to say in a good way but in a practical way to live in a world with so many souls. I want to talk about human life today. We need to get back to basics so to speak. Basic teachings of life: make every day count. Every day, do some good deed for the day, and you will find you have fulfilled an obligation to yourself, to God, and to his universe. It is a simple but important concept for all to follow. I want you to start today to do this and write down each day your special deed of that day. You need to do this or else you will forget what your life's purpose is about. Look at the big picture, and imagine that if everybody did a good deed for the day how many great deeds would there be in the world. Have you done your deed today? It can be a small deed as a smile to a stranger or a big deed as serving food to the people, no matter, whatever you decide to do today, ask yourself: which good deed did I do to change the world? That is all I say to you today. Go and start your good deed of the day.

Although I did not write anything down, I began to practice this simple advice. I made a point of doing a good deed every day by saying nice things to people, whether it was asking how they were doing that day, or just simply wishing them a good day. I would like to think that I did these things naturally before; however, since I became aware of it, I felt differently than before. I felt happier after the interaction, and I hoped that they did too. After I had finished my meditations I decided to go outside and shovel the snow off the pathway. Thoughts of Mum and Linda lingered in my mind. I wondered about the last time that they had shoveled snow: were they watching me now?

Chapter 21: The Group

It had been very difficult for the family since we lost Mum and Linda. We were faced with dilemmas about certain situations, such as what to do with the family home? The house had become like a museum with Mum and Linda's furniture and personal items. One vote was to keep the house in this condition for another year, and another vote was to sell or rent the house. There had been several heated discussions about the house between myself, my siblings, and the family. I was very pleased when Louise and Scott asked if I could meditate on the situation. It showed support and belief in my communication with spirit! Linda came through and immediately said:

Love Is The Answer

Firstly, I must say that love has been taken away from the equation here. Love equals what? is the formula, and it is missing from the equation. I want to say how nice it is to be here again. It has been a long time since we spoke. I want to talk about the family. Yes, Angie, it is me, Linda. I don't know why you always seemed so surprised. You seemed to be in a bit of a mess, so to speak. I do not mean to poke fun at anyone, but again it is the human factor that is so funny to us, but we know it is so important to you so we do not make light of it in a bad or disrespectful way.

My advice today is to let those who have difficulty with the decision come to the right decision on their own. If we interfere with any decisions or take sides then we will be put in a difficult situation and, again, we do not interfere with human decisions. We can only offer our guidance. Our guidance is always based on love and the best decision for humanity, so one must ask oneself: what is the best decision for mankind and not what is the best decision for you?

I have told you this before about decision-making and cannot say more. It is up to you how you use it for decisions in life. Again, is it for the best of mankind or for you? Some people do not always think about their actions, or long-term effects, so always make decisions that are good for mankind and you cannot go wrong.

Love is the key and foundation of all good decisions—that is all. So simple, yet so hard for humans to accept this. Don't play around with human emotions. They are fragile based upon your expectations of one's self. Controlling one's self, one's emotions are simple when based on love. Again, I sound repetitious and don't mean to belittle human emotions, but often they are given too much importance based on one person's need. Life is so simple when you love one another as God loves you. That is all.

I will talk about other things today. Today, I will talk about life on this side, on our side of the world. Yes, it is the same world that we both live in, but it is separated by the thoughts and emotions of the soul. Again, this is based on the physical body and the non-physical body. When you use the physical body, you use all these human emotions that weigh you down and become a burden to you. When this burden has been removed, you are free to live your life the way God intended you to.

I have lost my physical form as you know and do not have all those emotions; however, I remember them so well and can relate to your human problems today. We feel all your emotions when we are close to you. We feel sad for our loved ones when they are sad or troubled. However, this is your learning experience while on earth, while in the physical form.

Love is the key, the only answer you need. In my world, love is everywhere. Joy is everywhere. There are no physical or negative emotions only joy and happiness. It is so wonderful here that I want to share some of my happiness with you. I can do that by being around you and lifting the energy that surrounds all. I can certainly do that for you today and uplift your spirits to be like mine! That is a little joke because your spirit cannot be as uplifted as mine because it is weighted down by the physical body.

You can see I am smiling now and your mood has changed. You are uplifted, and I have enabled that to happen and can uplift Scott, Louise, and all the family. So, don't worry about them because my love is with them as we speak and always. Yet, I must say to you, I do not offer a solution or interfere with human decisions. It is against our wishes to do so. I must abide by these.

It has been so wonderful to be with you today, but I must go and let others take more of a role in your development. So I say goodbye for today, my lovely Angie.
Your sister forever, Linda xx

With those words of advice Linda was gone and instantaneously I had a new communicator, not Linda or Mum or the monk, but identified only as "The Group."

Group: Yes, from your group today. Names are not important at this time. Start writing as soon as possible the next chapter today. Write about Linda and her escapades over here. That will be interesting and will get you focused again. Just a start for today. We want to thank you for today and want a schedule for you to do this regularly.

I was surprised to get such a short introduction from the group and did not know what to make of it. I included this insert because I was soon to receive much more communication from the group.

Life Is Everything

It had been just three days since I was first introduced to the group. On this visit they talked about the experiences of the soul. Their energy felt as if it had an importance about it. This is in contrast to the monk who had a gentle energy. The Native American Indian's energy felt abrupt. Linda's energy was usually light hearted and made me smile. Mum's energy was always heavy and felt loving. As the group began to communicate with me, I saw both Mum and Linda smiling at me. I know they had come to watch over me and to let me know that they approved of the information I was about to receive from the group.

Group: Life is everything. Life is choosing. Choose a life that serves humanity. We want to talk about life and choosing a life that serves humanity. No other kind of life is more rewarding. It is the right path to take. Feel the love that surrounds this life. It surrounds you when you are in tune with the universe. Stop chasing after material things, and live your life as simply as possible.

Life is full of beautiful things that come to you with love from God, our creator. People do not see the beauty of the world because they are focused on looking at the wrong things. They are distracted. All it takes is the loss of a loved one to open your eyes to the beauty of the world, but that takes time since people blame God for taking loved ones. Yet, it is not God who takes them.

Man has freewill on this planet and it is man who chooses when to die, when that time comes to rejoin our world. Yes, it is determined by your spirit before you are created in the physical body, but when the time comes, the spirit with its earthly thoughts does not want to complete this predetermined passage for some are attached to earthly emotions connected with other spirit souls on earth: family and friends.

Once you leave the earthly form, your soul can really begin to live, grow, and develop. But it also needs the earthly form to enhance its development. Once the spirit passes over, it continues to grow and develop in a natural sphere of which it is part: returning home. It is the earth form that is alien to the spirit not the spirit form that is alien to the earthly form as you on earth seem to think.

We laugh when we hear of you thinking of us as extraterrestrials, people from outer space. I must admit, that your idea and concept are not far off, yet I repeat it is you, the earthly body are the aliens to us. We are superior intelligent beings who understand the world and life on all planets and the development and capability of the soul. Yes, I say capability of the soul because there is so much more to the soul than the physical limits put on the soul by its earthly form.

Soul Takes Many Forms

The soul takes many forms over its lifetime. I am not just talking about reincarnation on earth. That is just a small piece of your soul that returns each time—not your whole soul. You see, your soul is very adaptable and can do many things. It is not your whole soul that returns to earth each time but a small piece. Does that give you some idea of the endless limits of the soul? The limitations are endless. The soul is not just one whole soul that occupies your body while on earth. The soul is connected to a bigger part of the soul that remains in the spirit world, which is then connected to a bigger soul, and so on, and so forth.

The earthly form is at the bottom of the pyramid so to speak. It is under-developed and has to learn that; that is when it starts in the premature stage if you wish. The soul needs to evolve, so it can fulfill God's bigger dream of making the soul God-like in his image. You see, the image is a big energy field that is connected at the center of the universe. All spirits, all energies, feed naturally back to the core of the universe which is God.

Imagine the human form as a small dot in the outer edges of the universe. As it gets bigger and bigger, it gets closer, because it joins with other dots, energy fields, like a piece of snow that falls from the sky and forms a blanket on the ground. That is how the soul is in size, in relation to God. It is a piece of snow, a snowflake, a part of the massive particles of snow. You get the picture of this? The snow goes back to the universe in reverse. It is a simple concept to understand. I cannot describe it any better. So you see we are all part of the same blanket of snow: just tiny snowflakes.

The feelings you get as a snowflake are, therefore, only relevant to your life on earth at that time, and you love only other snowflakes that you touch, that you live with on earth, that makes up your small blanket. When you lose someone from your blanket, you feel the hole, you sense it, and you see it. But God sends another snowflake to fill the hole. Only humans do not always see the new snowflake that fell onto their blanket because they are standing in the hole and cannot see out, beyond the hole. It takes time to pick up this blanket and feel the love, warmth, and comfort it brings.

Many times it takes another loss to get you out of the hole, to see the bigger picture. That is what has happened to you. Your mother's death put you in the hole, and you could not see the truth. You were still trying to just fill this void but not understanding what it meant. It took the loss of your sister, so soon, to make you search for the truth. Knowing the truth will allow you to live your life in the physical body to its highest potential.

All humans have this potential, and it is often wasted because they do not realize it and they focus on earthly possessions and things. Earthly problems stem from this: possessions. All wars are fought over possessions; all disputes are possessions. Once you let go of these feelings of ownership and realize that God gave his universe to you freely, without any payment in return, then you can see your life's potential. Repair your blanket and see the big picture: the one blanket of the universe of God. Do not let grief keep you in the hole because your soul will never evolve.

God bless you. Thank you.

Chapter 22: Love is the Secret

The following week the group appeared again with guidance on healing the soul through love and kindness.

<u>Healing The Soul</u>

Group: Hello and welcome. It is nice to be here again. You have learned a lot about life and the universe. Amazing isn't it, how it all comes together? Feel you have learned a lot lately and spiritually you grow every day. We are pleased you are coming along nicely. Want to start now with more important things today, now that all those niceties are out of the way. Want to teach you about the universe how it is made up of energy.

Sometimes the energy gets blocked for one reason or another, and that is when illnesses on your planet occur. Do you see happy, contented people with illnesses? No! Look around you. People who are sad, who have a lower flow of energy attract certain diseases. Think of it as a flow in the energy field that surrounds them. The energy field can be seen as an aura. Some people on your earth can see auras, but it is deeper than that. If you connect with the spirit world first, then look at the person. You can see the energy field much more clearly.

You have been practicing a little with the spirit world allowing us to communicate with you, but you need to be able to use this gift wisely. There is no greater gift on earth than to heal people. Healing people is healing their soul, their energy field. Some just have a glitch in the soul, the energy field, a blockage, and you need to remove that glitch through your healing techniques. We decide what level of spirit involvement you will need. All we ask is that you dedicate your time. Set up specific times to heal people and I promise you we will come. It is not a practice type of thing. We heal the same on day one with you or day 100 with you. It is you that needs the practice; discipline is a better word. To provide consistency for us both to work is a partnership. Once you set up a time to practice and work you will notice that healing will take place. It can be done by having the person in front of you or absent, for 'spirit' knows where the healing should go.

The Healing Energy

Practice on your friends first, and then see what happens. You will become more confident and people will come. Think of Field of Dreams: *build it and they will come. You can help many people in this world through love and kindness. Healing is the mixture of both. Healing is the work of God: giving love to people. They will feel God's love when they have experienced a healing session because it is God's love that comes through and heals the bad, negative energy in their field. They will feel elated, lighter, happier, and calmer—all the signs of positive energy. They will receive positive energy through spirit. This is the healing energy. Have I explained it well? Good, you need to know how it works so you can explain it to others, the patients. Not too keen on that word patient, rather children of God who need his love. There are lots of people who need his love. Look around and you will see that you do not have to look very far.*

You will feel the love of God as you heal. It will pass through you to the person, and also you will be healed yourself at the same time. So you see this cooperation comes through you to the person being healed, and, in return, you will feel the love of God as it comes through. There is no better feeling in the world, so you see it is not really work in that you are doing. It is actually greater attunement into the love of God. You understand this? Good, let us move on today.

Love Is The Secret To A Healthy Life

Man is in need of love more than ever before. The world is changing, and man's love for fellow mankind will be the savior of the world. It is not up to God. He gives man freedom of choice; freedom to choose his path. What I say to you is man has the key to the universe if only they open their minds and allow love to come in.

Love, love, love is all it takes. You have the secret of life so don't waste this wisdom. Pass it along through your work, through your action. Love grows tenfold when you give love. You have found and discovered the knowledge of our world. You have opened your mind to our world, and now you have received the truth, the gift of love, gift of knowing the truth of life on earth—a wonderful gift that not many people understand. I am not asking you to change the whole world; I am asking you to change your world and serve God in the name of his love. Love is the secret of life. Go and show your love to mankind. Feel his love, and you will live a long and happy life free of man-made diseases. Yes, man-made, because people create their own stress and unhappiness and create negative thoughts, which are energy. Negative energy attacks the body in the same way good energy and laughter affects the body. You will feel God's love as you work. Accept it, treasure it, and know it comes with all the love that God can give to his children.

Seek And You Will Find

Life is not all what it seems. Life can be simple if you want it to be, or complicated if you seek outside the box, but it is much more rewarding when you seek. For when you seek you will find. Many people do not seek the truth and find they live a life of non-belief. A simple but non-eventful life of non-achievements or contributions to society, but there are those who seek, seek answers on the meaning life, which in turn makes their life worth living.

Seek the truth, and fill your life with meaning and purpose. Don't try to analyze everything. Accept what information is given to you, and you will receive all what you need to know and understand about your life's purpose. No one can tell you differently. You will discover for yourself what you need to know. You will not learn if it is handed to you on a silver platter, so never envy people who have a silver platter. Feel sorry for them, for they will not learn life's lessons this way. Life's lessons are the purpose of life, and they all resort back to lessons of love. Once you live your life with love, you will have served your life's purpose well. Learn to live life with love, even those you do not want to love, love them more.

Many more lessons to come. The great love of earth is the love for mankind, all mankind. Please be aware of this and love mankind by helping and caring for all. Make the most of your life. Have a circle of friends who make you feel good, and share your dreams and goals of seeking the truth. These friends will help you on your spiritual path. Make new friends who share your dreams and visions, not those who want personal and monetary gain only. You will find more happiness with friends of similar interest because they share same spirits.

Universal Love

Our world is different to yours, but in many ways it is the same. We seek love and truth, yet we learn it in different ways. Over here, we learn it through our contribution to the whole universe, not individual love. Everything here is universal, so everything you do is shared by all spirits, not by one. It affects all spirits, all the time. We hear and see at the same time, telepathy. We all grow and learn from all souls; that is the main difference between the physical form and non-physical form.

Imagine a world where you all benefit from just one soul. Not on earth. People only benefit themselves, and that is why the love is so hard to understand. Always involve others and see how they too can benefit from your actions. Don't benefit yourself only, for this is truly a loss to you and to all. Words of wisdom, but needed to show you now to grow spiritually with love. Love all you can. Even if you don't want to, love them all. You see you have come full circle today. That is the purpose today: to put you on track again. Be aware of your actions and remember to love all.

The Silver Chord

See the brightness of the sun. The white light is even brighter, yet it does not hurt your eyes. This bright light is the energy of God, his Holy Spirit, which is within us all. That is what draws you to the white light. You are already attached by a chord to it—the silver chord that is inside you—so when you connect with the spirit world, whether through death, near death, out of body experiences, or meditations, your internal silver chord is naturally drawn to the white light and draws you into the energy. Once you learn how to tap into this energy, you can mix with life in both worlds.

Life Is A Journey

Life is a journey, a pathway to the future journey of the human soul. As long as you work towards this pathway, your life will appear simpler, easier because you are going with the flow of life.

When things happen that seem to just fall into place, then you are on the right track; it is when you try to force things or go against nature, the natural universe, that you run into roadblocks. Always remember that you are where you are meant to be at all times in your life and that you are not there by accident.

We sensed you needed a little pep talk for today, so we will leave you with that. Again, it is nothing that you do not know already. Welcome to our world. Names are not important at this time, but we will speak again when it is necessary.

The following day, Mum continued on the theme of universal love and the purpose of life on earth.

The Work Of Spirit

Angie, I am here. This is Mum today. I want to talk more about your life. Life is best when you serve mankind and love mankind through your work. I am not talking about the corporate world but a world where you can help your fellow man. Life is best when you do the work of spirit. Make your life count while on this earth. Be aware of your daily hours. Don't let time slip away from you.

I want to talk about life in spirit world. Our life is much simpler and easier than life on earth. Our needs are less because we do not have the physical constraints to deal with. Of course, these constraints are learning challenges for us, but let's not take them so literally. The best way to live your life is to help others, as you know. Here in the spirit world, we help one another grow. Loving, sharing, and caring are what our souls do in the spirit world. We take the time to share our learning experiences with one another so we can all grow.

We grow as part of one big soul, one big spirit, which gives us strength and great energy, to create more energy, which, in turn, creates this greater force of the universe. This energy can be developed in all levels of the Planet Heaven, so the greater the love and cooperation between souls, the greater the compassion for all souls—the greater the energy levels, the greater the vibration field for all souls. We feed off this energy field to develop our own souls. You will note that on earth the energy field is so low that you do not help mankind. Loved ones help us on an individual level or on a level with a small group of friends and family in their circle, but the energy level does not develop. The greater the love, the greater the energy field; that is all.

Mankind will learn, sometime, the importance of bonding together so they can create an energy force so strong it will keep and sustain. Without this energy force, mankind will self-destroy, self-destruct, and the learning place we call school, earth, will cease. Mankind must learn to love fellow men. "Love one another as I love you" is the great quote from the master, the great teacher of mankind. Love one another is simple yet so hard. May we suggest you practice this in your daily life and watch how it grows?

Put others first before your needs. Everything else is desire that varies depending on one's frame of mind. Remember that they are only desires that you have which change with time. Your only need should be to have love, just more love. Your life will be fuller when you follow my words of wisdom and follow your heart. Your heart is God's voice talking to you; always remember that. It is your guide in life and circulates the blood around your body to all the necessary organs.

My lovely daughter, always remember that. Make decisions based on your heart and not your head, and you can never be wrong. You will be following your path, and your heart will keep you on track. When you get heartache that is just the depth of the learning experiences and the degree to which you have learned your lesson. The deeper your degree, the deeper the pain and the deeper the learning experience. It is not always the bed of roses you want it to be.

Those people who live a life that seems to be a bed of roses do not have the experiences needed for soul development, so don't think they are better off than you. They may benefit economically in human form but not spiritually, and their souls do not grow as they must. Instead, they choose to learn life's lessons in another lifetime. We, on the other hand, have chosen a level to lead our spirit down a path of enlightenment and enrichment and are on track. Just keep on track doing what you are doing; that is all you need to do.

Many people on earth do not realize that they are there to develop their souls, so they spend their days aimlessly, just getting by. Help them figure out the correct path so they too will be enlightened. Not an easy task, but they will be enlightened through your work. Expose them to the spirit world, which will open their eyes to the world that they live in, amongst, alongside the spirit world. They live in two worlds, which is one great universe, and they must share their earthly experiences with their soul counterparts in the spirit world. They do this through a recognition and acknowledgement of the existence of the two worlds and through understanding that the human form is only part of the big picture of life, the big world we truly live in.

Linda followed with a quick hello.

Linda: Yes, Angie, it is me. Just a quick hello before you go. Been busy, Angie! You won't believe how busy I have been, just the like the old times at work! Well, I am just as busy up here. Remember how people used to come to me with their problems? Well, they are still doing it up here. Things don't change, really, Angie. Just because I lost my physical body, underneath our spiritual body is exactly the same: my outgoing personality, my friendly personality, my sense of humor, it is all there! People from near and far come to talk to me. Word gets around!

Mum and I have such a good time. We are like social butterflies up here. We go here, we go there—always to do with someone's problems. We often go together to help people with their problems, usually those who have just had their life's review and are not too happy with what they saw, so they want to talk about it. We help them go over it again and again, just like when you used to call me with the same problems again and again, and when I gave you the same advice, which you never listened to! Ha! Ha! Really, it is just the same now. We give people advice; we like listening and helping them out. We are a pair of "nosey parkers" and enjoy a good soap opera.

When you get here, we can all do it together. Can't wait until that day, but it is not now, and you will never have a time limit. We want the best for you and will help you all we can. Mum said it is good that Louise is getting back on her feet; it will do her good. Susan is getting settled, and Scott is making peace with himself. Brian? What can we say other than that he never ceases to amaze us with his kind and lovely nature—he gets that from me!

I want to say that I have evolved such a lot. I have been up different levels of Heaven to take a look; although I am not on those levels, I can still go up and take a look. You know me, always liked to have a nose! Want to see what it is like once I get there but having so much fun on this level down here. I can move really fast—quickly, wherever I want to go. Whether it is here with you or across the pond, it is like I Dream of Jeanie: *Bing, I am here! Bing, I am there! Oh, I used to love that show! Remember I used to say how much fun it would be to do that? Well, I get to do it all the time.*

Take care of yourself. Much work to be done.

With those words Linda was gone. I smiled when she mentioned the TV show *I Dream of Jeanie* because, as a child, Linda, enjoyed watching it. She used to refer to that show throughout her lifetime. With all her travels between England, Australia, and America, she often said "wouldn't it be wonderful to just blink your eyes and be in a different place like *I Dream of Jeanie*"? It was nice to hear Linda talk about how she "used to love that show" because I felt as if she was here in the physical form. Her personality, her enthusiasm and sense of humor remained the same in the afterlife. I would like to say that this meditation from Linda came on the one year anniversary of her passing. There was not any mention of her physical death, just joy and happiness in Heaven!

Chapter 23: A Tour of Heaven

I was able to distinguish between the strengths of my communications. Sometimes the energy level between the spirit world and I was stronger than other times, resulting in a deeper blending of thoughts and consciousness. On this day, I sensed the strong energy of the group as an exhilarating sensation filled my body. I sat there, on the settee, with all the excitement and hopes of a young child on Christmas day. Then, the vision came—or should I say the movie came! This was a most exhilarating meditation. It was a marathon session, lasting close to three hours.

<u>A Tour Of Heaven</u>

I see a garden. It looks like the Garden of Eden. People are sitting in and around the base of a tree, talking. The tree is open like a child's play house. I hear people explain how they can travel up and down the tree, the Tree of Knowing, to different levels. They can slide down or around the tree, similar to a helter-skelter at a fun fair, sliding down onto the ground. I hear them say, "We do this for fun only, as we do not have to come down this way. We can shoot straight up or down the tree trunk—anytime! This is our environment. This is where we live every day and spend our days." It was so peaceful and quiet, and yet, a lot of activity was going on. I see the magnificent blue sky. The sun is not too bright, a warm 75 degrees with no wind. It is so peaceful, so serene. I want to stay here with this nice feeling. I see happy people and children are playing.

I am sucked up through a hole and come out through the top of a tree into a world that is golden yellow like the sun, but it is not hot. The feelings of high energy rush through my body, giving me strength, making my body feel lighter. I quickly go through a green layer of energy, which gives me a coating of stability. I go through a purple layer of energy, giving me spiritual wisdom. Then, finally, I shoot up further, out into the white light of God.

The group speaks to me: Feel his love as it surrounds you, falling down around your body, coating you in his love, his warmth, his energy, until you feel his warmth, his love. Your spirit will be drawn like a magnet up out of your head, through the top and pulled close to spirit world, a place where you can meet and communicate with your loved ones, your angels. See the angels. They have wings, not because they need them but to let you know that they are angels floating around. They are here to bring us love, appreciation for all things and to help us and guide us in times of need. Feel their love as they bring forth their love to you, circling around you many times with love and energy. Once you feel their love and energy, you are free to move onto the next level.

The level is purple in color, which is soothing to the soul. It gives you rich knowledge and wisdom. Take as much of this wisdom and knowledge as you can. You can feel and absorb it. You grow strong. You pass through the yellow place and this bakes and cooks you. So all the ingredients of the cake sink in, and you are ready to leave this yellow place and move directly into the light of God.

You reach the light of God and feel fulfilled, prepared. You have been waiting for this moment. There are many people here to greet you. Look around and see whom you recognize. Who was the first person to come and shake your hand? Is it a loved one? Perhaps your mother, or father, grandmother, grandfather, brother, sister, husband, wife, or is it someone you don't know or even your pet? Is it a man or a woman's hand? Feel the hand as it is put onto your shoulder as the two of you embrace. See the head; do they have short hair, long hair, no hair?

I see Mum, Linda, and I can see the monk. I also see a man who is a healer with reddish hair, blue eyes, and a slight goatee-style beard. (This man smiled as I described him.) The group told me that he was my Healing Guide and will keep me on track. He checks off progress each time. When you have seen who has embraced you, then see what it is they are showing you. Is it a picture, an object? When you have seen the picture, describe it. I see a picture: Many people walking through a street, following a lady, sitting on a donkey. She has a baby. It is set in Biblical times.

Then ask for an object. Ask them to give you an object that is meaningful. Hold it in your hand; feel what it is. I feel a key, an old fashioned type. I see a door and open it. Does it squeak? Or open easily? Or do you have to push it open? It squeaks but opens easily with a slight push. I go down a few steps into the kitchen with pots and pans hanging up. They are expecting me. They have made me a pie, a blueberry pie. I see it; I taste it. It is made with fresh ice cream, homemade ice cream. Pie is warm and looks inviting. A lady is standing, wearing an apron. She looks like my granny—my granny! She has made me a pie. She says, "You can have whatever you want over here, Angie. It is so easy to make. Don't think I spent hours making this. It was very quick and easy and looks delicious. Your father is okay and enjoys his life. Health not too bad, he gets his check-ups and copes with it. (Referring to my father's diabetes). I am always with you! I look over you, even with all those children and grandchildren I have! I look after all of them. I take care of them the best I can. You are the only one who comes to visits me. They don't know how to, but you do. You know how to do it; therefore, you will experience a greater joy because of it. Linda comes and visits me, similar to what she did while on earth. She comes as often as she can; always a good one, so kind and remembers her old granny very well. She loves me just like she did on earth. 'Our Niecee,' we call her. Aunt Dot and Aunt Nancy, they are all here. You will see everyone once you pass over, but not yet. There is much work to do down there first. Enjoy your pie, and then you will have to go. This is just a social visit today, but more will come later as you develop. Will go now, Angie! Continue on your path. Give my love to everyone, especially your father."

As I leave, I see Linda, and she holds her arms out open wide to greet me. We embrace. She takes me for a walk in the garden. I see a beautiful yellow flower on the left as we walk down a red brick path. The path is smooth and shiny, but it is not slippery. It is easy to walk on as though we are gliding. "Watch the flowers; see how they gently move into the wind. See all the beautiful colors. There are many colors, and I notice the tulips. Yes, Angie, spring is coming. You know what that means? New growth. New life. Remember all the scenes you saw today. Time to go, Angie!"

Linda disappeared, and then Mum suddenly appeared:

Mum here, my love. Always here! I am still the same. You got to see your granny and Linda today. Always nice to visit! Just wanted to let you know I am here, love. Always with you, watching you. I want to tell you, Angie, that life is not what it seems. There is so much more to life, yet people do not see it. You have begun to see it, but you must continue your development, a regular schedule and commitment with balance in your life. Don't let it overtake you. Don't forget. Just schedule weekly sessions, and you will see how quickly they will add up. That's all I am saying for now. Finish your book. Schedule time to write. Will go now, Angie. Just a quick visit today. Don't forget to schedule time, and we will come.

I felt the end of my morning meditation was near. The group finished by saying:

As you say goodbye to your loved ones, thank them for coming to see you today and know you can see them anytime you practice this exercise. See them as they wave goodbye, and feel the love between you now. It is the same feeling of love you had on earth, lighter in some ways, a glow, a happy reunion. I want you to walk back into the garden, into the white light, back to the golden glow, through the energy field of purple knowledge to the layer of green solid ground. See the soft brown soil on the ground. Put your feet on the ground, and feel your feet in the soft soil. See the grass growing; look at the blades of grass blowing in the gentle wind. You are back in the garden.

I could feel the sensation in my feet as my toes wiggled amongst the grass and the soft soil. It felt real to the touch. In an instant the vision was gone. I came out of my meditation with an amazing feeling of euphoria, as though I had just won the lottery. To my surprise, the following week, I was taken again to the garden with the big tree but not before a brief visit from Linda.

Linda: Just want to say hello, Angie. That's all today. Not much to tell you. Like old times isn't it? Talking on the telephone! You are figuring it all out about the continuation of life in our world. I knew you would, Angie, and I know you can feel it. What a joyous feeling it is; that is when you know that it is right. The truth is right; you feel euphoria. Always remember that feeling. Euphoria when things are right. No need for drugs or alcohol to feel this way. When you are close to the truth, then you feel this sensation and your thoughts are where they should be.

I will go now. Linda smiled. *I love you, Angie. I want you to be happy.* She smiles at me again.

I felt Linda's energy disappear, and I was transported back to the garden where I could see the big tree. The energy of the group surrounded me.

I see the tree of knowledge again with its branches. The branches are thick and bushy and look like broccoli. It is amazing up here. I can see everything. I see many planets. I can look down at all the planets! I feel like I am flying all around the orbit. I land on a silver color planet, chrome-like. The group speaks. This planet takes samples of earth to see what is working and what is not working. You see all the test tubes; they are for your benefit. Also, the people do not need to wear white cloaks or be in the human form as you see them, but you will be able to understand better this way if you can see them like this. I can see silver countertops like those seen in chef's kitchens, the stainless steel ones.

Monitoring The Earth

We would like better cooperation, better communication with the human forms on earth so we can work together and create a better life experience for all human forms while in the physical form. That is the purpose of human reincarnation or carnation to experience God's earthly planet with all its beauty, minerals, and pleasure. Yet people do not always recognize the earthly beauty and do not get the message or the best from their life experience while in the earthly form. They constantly keep us busy up here by monitoring the earth to decide and correct the damage that is done. The earth must be preserved for thousands of generations to come, and it is our work here to do that.

You ask what type of work we do over here, Angie. Well, that is one of many jobs that we do. You will find we have similar jobs to those on earth such as doctors, scientists, teachers, etc. because the earth is a replica of our world, only on a smaller degree. It is not the other way around, as you tend to think. Our world is bigger in size and cannot be measured. It is inconceivable to you on the earth in the human form. We do a lot of work on this side to keep you on earth, on that side, in the earth form that you exist in. Don't believe that it is all by chance because it is not. Nothing is by chance; you know that; nothing is by chance.

It will take many years to educate the world, just like Darwin's theory, and to be accepted, but one day it will and our worlds will live as one. You in the earthly form, with your mind, will be able to travel to this world as you are experiencing now and we, as you know, already come to your world. There are some human souls who are able to see us with their human eyes, but the number is few.

It would be a lot more if people opened their minds to this world and let us in. Small children can usually see us, but they are told that it is wrong to have an imaginary friend, so they forget and disregard us, so they forget their ability and live their lives with prejudices learned on earth. There is no prejudice amongst children. When they grow up, they are taught prejudice and they change the way they think and see the world. If all humans opened their minds and hearts they would see a much bigger world and would feel the love in the world, God's love, the purpose of his creation—love.

Department Of Love And Emotions

Going into a red field, looks like red rhubarb in a field. I walk through it. They move aside. This is the department of love and emotions. Yes, emotions of love—the human emotions, the scales of love. When the branch stems are blowing gently, the love is flowing gently around the universe. When the wind comes and the stems are blowing furiously it means there is some unsettlement on the earth. We can monitor how long this phase will be, can be days, weeks, or years.

We can also watch it change color, change energy fields, and review whether a good or bad period of human life is happening. A team watches and monitors this. We look at where the disruption is, whether it is caused by nature or is man-made. We do our investigation and sign up for this job, just like on earth. We, *like you, have investigations. Again, as I told you before, we have many jobs in our world, which are the same as earth jobs.*

Let us go into the green room. The green room is where we prepare the souls who are returning to earth. They come through here and take a look at earth today and plan where their souls will develop best: which families, what country to be born in that will help their soul to develop. But sometimes they come to help the soul development of other people. That is why you get death and physical ailments and all sorts. They are reviewed before you go down. Some choose just a simple, easy, carefree life and some choose a life with their kindred soul, which serves no purpose in their own development but for the development of others. You see it works both ways. You can help develop another soul by sacrificing your soul or not, whatever is needed.

The brown room is next. I want you to guess what is in this brown room. Brown should remind you of your old brown, school uniform, as it does your sister Linda—she is saying. Yes, the brown room is the school or education committee. No, we do not wear brown colors. Our clothes are just an image for you to make the point this is where the education committee is located. The workers come and assess you both on earth and on this side. It is very busy much more so than the red room. More discussions take place rather than watching the emotions in the red room, which can be mundane.

The blue room is the spiritual room where we look over the part of your soul's progress. Souls must progress when on earth. Eventually all souls on earth have to be monitored, guided, and put back on track when off track.

The yellow sunshine room is full of new life and growth. We like to see a lot of energy. Yellow indicates new growth. This is important. Need to have many new souls to grow and develop.

This meditation ended suddenly and without me being brought back to the image of the garden. It certainly wasn't a bad feeling but, rather, a waking up from a nice dream feeling and wishing you could go back to sleep for a few more minutes to finish. The energy had been taken away from me in an instant. I do not know why it ended so suddenly. I believe I was shown everything I needed to see at that moment in time.

Chapter 24: Two-way Communication

Each day when I began to meditate I had no idea what type of a meditation session I would experience, and more specifically, I did not know which spirit communication I would receive or the strength of it. Some days the energies blended so well as if they were sitting next to me. Other days, words came into my head as inspired thoughts. At all times, I was fully aware of my surroundings. Depending on the strength of the energies, and their blending, my meditations varied, making my experiences completely different.

<u>Live In Harmony</u>

Group: Hello, good morning to you today. You have chosen a regular time and place. It will be much easier this way. There is more writing to do. Education is important. People should learn as much as they can about the spirit world because it will help them with their lives on earth. People don't understand the benefit it will give them to live in awareness of spirit, which will enhance their lives.

Once you are in tune with the universe, and in tune with your surroundings, then you can truly be happy to live, to love, and to appreciate life. Live in harmony with your soul and your spiritual soul. They are one, you know. When people are out of kilter with their soul they experience problems in their lives, as you know and have experienced yourself. You see many around you who do not live in harmony, and they struggle with their lives. You must educate people so they, too, can live a life that is worthy and that they deserve.

You are very fortunate to be able to communicate with spirit, or should I say, you are fortunate that you exercise this gift because there are many who can communicate with spirit but do not know this and do not try. You are fortunate that you communicate as you do. We are pleased. Let us move on to today's work.

You need to love yourself and others first before you can love God, because you are all part of God. If you say that you love God and do not love one another, then you do not love God as you say you do. Try to love all people; that is a true test of love. Send out your love and prayers to those people in the world who are less fortunate than you. You should be sending out your healing thoughts on a regular basis, for example, when you schedule your meditation sessions. It is all energy, you know. Remember that. Everything is energy; the more you create, the more will go out into the world. Imagine if everyone sent out healing thoughts, healing energy, to the world, what a better energy field there would be for all to share. But people do not expand their own energies beyond the space in which they live. This is an important task that should be scheduled into your work. Let us move on to other things.

A Two-Way Communication

Your book must read as a story and not a manual or a preaching book. It must be a story so readers can relate to you, and you should speak to them, where the reader will forget that your loved ones are even dead because you will have brought them back to life again though your book. That will be the message of the book, bringing loved ones back to life, which is what they are: they are more alive than you know! Their spirits are alive and well and free from the physical constraints that hold the soul down. It is you, in the human form, who is a dead soul. Death from the human body frees the soul and allows it to live its eternal life in Heaven, in our spirit world. So, when your mother and sister come and work with you, they are real, they are really there and alive. It is you that has the limitation. So don't paint them as dead ghosts. Paint them as they truly are. They are free souls, free spirits, who visit and communicate with you just as they did on earth in physical form.

This is a two-way communication: one talks, and one listens. Although it is spirit that does the most talking, we are all communicating. There are times during telephone calls and conversations with friends when one is talking and one is listening, more than the other, just as it is when we communicate. Don't lose sight that it is a communication of you and spirit, of two souls communicating, not just a one way communication, and remember we have a sense of humor up here, so please include any humor you can.

Our world is happy and full of love, and with that comes humor. Laughter is, indeed, the best medicine, and remember when write your story to include laughter and humor. We do have souls that laugh over all of you down there. When you communicate with us, you can see and sense a happy soul with a smiling face. You can see that we are happy, we smile, and we laugh. We can also be sad. We are all these human emotions, but on a different level. We do not experience pain of the body because we do not have an earthly physical form. We do have emotions, however, that are deeper, such as extreme happiness, love, and laughter. These are good emotions. Remember, there are no negative emotions as you have on earth, only good ones.

I think I have given you enough information today to get you on track again. Remember, we are here to help you and will help you if you do spirit work for the good of mankind.

Will go now, Angie. That is it for today. From your guardian angels.

As the energy from the group slowly faded, I sensed a happy energy surround me. It was Linda bringing a smile to my face.

Linda: - Just a quick word from me. I have been watching you trying to learn as much as you can as always! Always the studious one! I want to talk about your book. It is coming along nicely. You should incorporate as much as our funny conversations as the philosophy. You don't want it to become monotonous or boring. Some humor from me will make it interesting. Just talk about you, how you have learned to communicate with me, and how you wrote down what I told you. That will be interesting to readers because it talks about more than just me in Heaven. People will find it hard to believe. Some will want to believe; however, some cannot relate. But they can relate to you, your story, your sorrow, and your pain. You can put all the meditations I gave you together. People will want to know about how they helped you and your life, how it took you out of your grief and gave you hope again. Have some fun with it! Make your book fun, and people will read it. If it is too sad and serious people will put it down. I want you to smile and laugh when you think of me, Angie.

Having so much fun here! I can't wait until you get here and see what it is like. Just a happy place with lots to do, and no squabbling over silly things like money issues and bills. They are all there on earth to help you learn life's lessons. The trick, or the key, is to learn how to manage without them, and once you do that, life is easy. It is only hard when people worry about money and bills. I know for some people this concept is harder than others, but if you learn to live within your means, value every penny you have and spend, then you will see how easy life becomes. Ask yourself, do I really need this? Do I really need to spend this money? Can I make it without it? Once you value and respect money, your lives will be so easy, so simple, more like our life here. Then you are free to enjoy your life, your friends, and your family. I know we enjoyed all our shopping sprees, and that is fine once in a while, but learn to live modestly, and life will begin to grow.

Take care of friends and family, and treasure them as if they were a million dollars. You will reap so much more reward from life. That is all I say to you today. Go now and practice your writing, now that you have had a little help today.

With those words of encouragement Linda's energy drifted away. Thoughts of the previous year returned. It had been one year since Linda's misdiagnosis. I remembered the pain in her head, her inability to guide a fork or a spoon into her mouth, and her reliance on a walking stick to keep her balance—all allegedly symptoms of depression. Now, one year later, she was alive and happy in the afterworld. What a difference a year makes. On the following day my Mum communicated with me and continued to describe life in Heaven.

Communicating With You

Mum: It is lovely having Linda here with me. We have a great time and do many things together. We go to all the reviews, events, meetings, etc., and other times we just hang out. We both loved America and are around you all the time, as well as being with Louise, Scott, and the kids in England. It is very easy to travel back and forth, to be around you all simultaneously. We watch you all the time. For us it doesn't feel busy. We have plenty of time to interact with you. We join in on the conversations, and lead you to say things as well. Yes, we can guide your thoughts, which in turn, comes and goes and can sway you one way or another. We don't interfere; just bring you to the punch line or the reality of the situation a bit quicker and most importantly a bit clearer.

We want to be part of your lives because we love you all and have not really gone. The quicker everyone understands this, the quicker we will start being including in conversations. It is like the TV show in the 1960s, Randolph and Hopkirk-deceased, *and how Hopkirk-deceased was always around dressed in a white suit, adding his two cents worth to help his partner solve crimes. That is how we are around you, how all spirits are around their loved ones, except we don't wear white suits! We are Hopkirk- deceased, except you can tune in a little bit by allowing us to blend your thoughts with our thoughts. But the others do not allow us to do this; they can only if they allow it. We can do this with your permission only. Again, it is cooperation between us that allows this.*

At this point I felt the energy change, and the group's energy came through.

Group: Once you allow and give your permission to us, the communication becomes frequent and is clearer and is as often as you allow it to be. The others (referring to Louise and Scott) do not allow this communication to come through, so we come through you only, at this time, but we would like to communicate with more people. It is also a privilege for us to communicate with you, as it is a privilege for you communicate with us. It is a two-way street: two-way cooperation. We see and hear you; we hear your thoughts and tune in. We don't always tune in because we have better things to do! We come when you allow us to, when you give us permission to come. The sensation that you feel is our energy blending with your energy. You are truly never blended completely. We are blessed you have come along this far and this quickly. You allow us to blend very easily, and we thank you for that and will blend more frequently.

We have many forms of energy, many depths of energy, from light to heavy. The light energy gives an easy floating sensation, and strong energy gives a lifting sensation. The lifting sensation brings you closer to our side. Neither is right or wrong. We can blend however we need to for the purpose of the communication. It is all spirit communication. We control the type of blending, what is appropriate each time when we blend or link into you. No harm will ever come to you, just a different blending is all. A loved one's energy is different to a healer's energy, which is different to a philosopher's energy and so forth. Just be aware that they are different.

This explained why the strength of the communications I experience is different. Spirit determines the degree of energy blended based on the learning experience required at that time. It has nothing to do with my wishful desires or control.

The Sun And The Moon

The moon is also a ball of energy that gives out new younger energy and brings it back in during the daytime. The moon has its role to play in the universe, peace, and harmony on the earth through its energy field of white light that is sends out. Just like the sun sends us rays to give life to the earth.

Everything is balance: the sun, the earth, and the sky, God and his children. We have balances on this side too: life and death; growth and shrinkage; happiness and sadness. Now I go on, but you get the picture here. Natural law takes control of all this, and we don't look at one side of the coin. Ask yourself what is the positive, and to balance it out, it has to be give and take.

Piece Of Elastic

Linda was on a piece of elastic attached to your mother, for when your Mum passed over that elastic was stretched. For you, you learned how to bring that elastic back to its normal length, but Linda's soul did not and could not do that. The elastic stretched so much that it was broken, and the soul had to be reconnected to your mother's soul again, which took place in Heaven. She couldn't live with this broken piece of elastic; it made a hole in her soul, in her energy, that could not heal and became bigger. It was her destiny to be together again with mother. They are together again now and are as natural as a piece of elastic that having been stretched returned to is pre-stretched size. They are relaxed again. They have a new stronger energy and are together on this side! The energy lights up all around them. They are happier than any earthly experience they could have had and are in a position to help those who they love when on earth in the physical form, and they do.

Their energy is so strong; they are easily able to come down and visit you, like one of those sparklers that light up. Sometimes they walk next to you and talk to you, and that is when thoughts or ideas come into your head. They travel in the car with you. Yes, they can travel in the car with you! Many times they are there. They—we—watch over you and protect you from any earthly situations that may occur.

Mum and Linda had expressed several times in their spirit communications to me how much Linda had suffered over mother's loss. With the Group explaining Mum and Linda's relationship and their bond in such detail, it helped me to understand even more the reason for Linda's passing. I felt contented knowing that they were together. And, it warmed my heart to know that they were with me and protecting me. As the Group left, I saw an image of the Native America Indian. He was sitting with his back up against a rock. He seemed to be part of a council of Indians who I sensed had opinions to share:

Many teachings I bring for mankind. Man lives in a world of self-absorption and does not step out to look at world. Nature is by far the most beautiful gift to mankind. Use wisely; do not corrupt. Mankind has much greed. There is no importance of responsibility to nature. Mankind will destroy natural resources if not protective of them.

Earth is God's school, his creation for mankind. God's earth is for humans to enjoy. God created the earth and gave it to the humans to love, to learn, and to grow their souls to a purer form of energy that is closer to God's energy. That is the key to all. Speak words of truth at all times, and you will be honest to yourselves and to God. He loves you all. That is the message today; no need to say more about that to anyone.

With those few words of wisdom the American Indian's energy left. The teachings did not blend with the information I received from the Group, Mum, or Linda. Often I found some theme amongst the communications, so I did not know what to make of this information. I decided to leave it in the book since he took the time to communicate with me.

Chapter 25: Heaven on Earth

Angie, this is Linda! Been doing lots of fun things here, even learning is fun! Who would have thought! Focus on your book now. Some great vibes coming now, so you will be able to sail through the book. More examples about Heaven today! Others, from the group are with me today, so here goes.

Heaven On Earth

Heaven is like the best of everything that you have on earth, but magnified thousands of times. Your happiest moments on earth, your happiest days, are like that every day here. You mix with people all day, and every moment has a sensational feeling. We talk about many topics, of course, especially philosophy, but also science and new technology, not just on earth but in our world too. We have new technology to keep up with the new energy that is created. Our scientists are very busy creating ideas to cure illnesses, invent sophisticated technology, then we plant it in the minds of the scientists, and they say they have come up with an idea or a solution to something, but the thought comes from us. Yes, we have laboratories set up, testing centers, similar to those you have on earth, but ours are more advanced, automated, and they never break down or malfunction. We have told you before about the different teams, departments, colors, etc. and how it works. We even experiment with plants, animals, etc., and decide the best combination of species that will benefit God's earth, God's creation. It is all a sophisticated replica of all species in Heaven that are on earth. They are duplicated on earth as it is in Heaven. Remember that phrase "as it is in Heaven" because Heaven was created first by God. God created Heaven on earth, not the other way around.

We do not need to prepare or cook food. You just visualize what you want and it appears like magic. It is your mind that has the power to create all things, whether you are in Heaven or on earth. In Heaven, because you do not have the physical body, you are not limited and your mind, your soul, and you can create anything from a meal, a simple thing, to a factory, where production and creation takes place. As long as it is for the good of mankind, your mind can create anything, even a camera. It may not look or feel the same way as a camera does on earth, but the end product is the same. It is an instrument that can take a picture.

You see, there are many things in Heaven you can do that are beyond the capability of human thoughts. If you open your mind to the vast world, the other world that exists out there, you will open up and see a full world with much more than you know. Hollywood has somewhat attempted to depict extraterrestrial life and always as smarter intelligence beings. Well, I must say, that is true; we are much smarter, intelligent beings. However, we are by no means aliens. We are human souls departed from Planet Earth and now in Planet Heaven. Yet, the earthly souls call their Heavenly souls aliens, and that is very funny to us. And yes, we have a sense of humor. We call you as many names on earth: "earthlings" comes to mind because you are attached to the earth, but there are many more!

We would like to communicate more with our earthly souls, but most human souls are limited in their acceptance of anything foreign to them. Yet we are not foreign; we are all one; we are your friends. We were earthly people ourselves—not all of us because some like it so much here they refuse to come down! The only benefit to the soul to come down is to learn the soul's lessons, which are much more intense, harder on earth, so souls can evolve quicker. But some prefer to stay and evolve at a slower rate because they prefer to stay in this magnificent world.

We ask that, while you are on the earth, you open up to the world of spirit and let us communicate with you in a way that will help you benefit mankind. That is what we want: to benefit and help mankind. We can help by developing your soul, making you aware of your life's purpose so as humans you don't waste this opportunity. We do have spaceships that come down. They are built to enable us to travel to your planet with ease, and with the best use of our energy, but again they are not like the UFOs depicted in Hollywood films. They are a sophisticated design of energy that travels in seconds from our planet to your planet.

We come only for special purpose to take samples from the earth's soil. We measure the chemicals in the atmosphere, the resources in the land, but we do not interfere with natural disasters or any catastrophic event. Human activity is responsible for the earth. We have told you this before, so there is no need to repeat that, but we want you to get the message out that the soul continues on after and before the physical body is created and departs the earth. That is all. We want you to enjoy your time on earth. We want to communicate with you, with loved ones, because it is like being in a different room, a different town, or country. We want to connect with you as we did on earth; that is all.

Heaven Made Up Of Energy

Next we want to talk about Heaven. We will take you on a ride now so you can see it. Fasten your seat belt—a little humor to remind you of your old days. (I used to be a stewardess.)

I go through a ring, like a ring of fire without flames, into a garden, like the one I went into before. There are people sitting around, some are standing. They are wearing white gowns or robes, which remind me of a Biblical scene. I see the big tree. It opens up and I see a lift shaft move, taking you up and along one of the floors with corridors. It is like a hallway with rooms off to the side. I enter a room and it is full of specific controls.

We want you to look down at the towns on earth and see the layer of energy. It is stronger in some places. That is where the spirit energies are, obviously, so they can be around loved ones. This is the lowest vibration field we go to: just as I am communicating with you now. Then imagine that field being another level when all earthly remains dissolve. At this point we don't think like humans. Our conscious minds are pulled to a higher place where there are more important aspects of life.

Energy Fields

We want you to learn about the energy fields: life is dependent on the energy fields. We use the energy fields to create all what we need on this side and put it into forms. We can create anything, such as creating a blanket with patterns on. We can do that. Our world is all energy, and our minds evolve tenfold and beyond that of the human mind, which is restricted in its ability to grow beyond their limits, which are put there by the human society. Mankind limits conscious thoughts, disabling them. Yet all they need to do is allow the mind to escape from the constraints of the body.

There is so much more to the world than Mother Earth. Each planet plays a role in the universe and is just as important as earth. Yes, we as spirits go to these other planets where there is also energy and also life. Other planets are learning schools for the soul, as is the earth planet. We can visit any planet in the same way we visit your planet earth. We want you to be aware of life on other planets because like earth they too make up the universe.

Don't you see? It is all Heaven! Heaven is the generic term for the afterlife which you humans are so interested in. Yet your life in Heaven, on those other planets, has a purpose based on their role in the universe and the energy level. The more energy you acquire, the further away from earth you can be. That is why loved ones are immediately around you because their energy field is only in the next vibration level to you. As you build up energy, your soul moves forward. Communication with earthlings helps build this energy and provides a springboard to the next level. It is the blending of those energies on earth when you first pass over that provides the greatest strength.

People hang around to speak with loved ones, but this often falls on deaf ears. When a loved one is able to recognize a spirit by scent or perfume, a connection is made, and the energy builds strength for that loved one. Your mother has developed a lot of energy because she is around you so much and, of course, Linda has also increased her energy.

Planet Heaven

Living in a place called Planet Heaven reminds Linda of a scientific campus, a university campus, living simultaneously with earth. If you put on your 3D glasses at the cinema, you can see characters appear in front of your face as though you are in the room with them. When you close your eyes and meditate, it is like putting on extra, extra x-ray vision 3D glasses; you see the world that lives amongst us.

Yes, they live amongst us. It is like taking a step outside your ethereal body and joining them. Your mind is a big ball of energy and is capable of doing many things. It can travel back and forward in time because your mind, without the human body, has no sense of time. That is how you can travel back and forth in time. Time continues to go by and continues to come.

It is another new world up here, yet we live and co-exist together; that is the most important piece of your research, your journey: to discover that the two worlds co-exist. You can step into our world any time, as we do step into yours all the time! We want you to progress your soul while on earth, so you will have less work over here to do; otherwise, you may say you wasted your time on earth.

Count your blessings and life will be good. Do not spend your life waiting for things to happen, and you see the world pass you by. Now is the time to take charge and do what you want. You are your own destiny; you create your own destiny. You have the power to do it; don't ask another human being, what will I be? What will I do? They only tell you what their guess is or what they think. (Referring to psychic readers) Often they misinterpret the information. The key is inside each one of you. Write down your goals, your dreams, and plot them out. "Seeing is believing" is the old but wise saying.

Once you see your dreams and goals on paper you will begin to imagine them, and they will become a reality. If you want a new job, write it down. If you want a new career, a new car, etc., write it down. Thoughts are energy. Anything can be created with energy. Remember that. I have given you enough for today, so go and plan your life, your book. Your book is part of it; tell the story.

It is an honor to speak to you today. Know that we see your thoughts and your dreams. We, the group, want to thank you for sitting with us today. Spring is here and brings new life.

Jesus

It was Easter weekend and, again, memories from the previous year came flooding back. It was the time Linda had her diagnosis, and we were hopeful that she would have radiotherapy. It was the time when the hospital staff was on vacation for the Easter holiday adding to the delay of treatment. It was the time Linda had a bleed on the brain and lost her mobility functions. It was a time I remembered, and it made me cry. I felt an urge to meditate and picked up my paper and pen. I was absolutely stunned and overwhelmed when I saw an image of Jesus.

I saw the back of a person's head. Although I could see the long, dark, shoulder-length hair, I knew it was a male and not a female. Then, I saw a crown of thorns. It was Jesus! As soon as I identified him he said, "Walk a mile in my shoes, and you will surely know pain and suffering. You need to experience pain and suffering before you can fulfill your life's purpose." I followed behind him on his walk along the path, and then I found myself standing behind him while on the cross. His head was tilted to the left and I felt my head tilt to the left. He said, "I would do it all over again. It was worth it when people follow my teachings."

When I came out of this meditation I did not know what to think or what to say or what to do. I just sat there on the settee in a state of bewilderment. It was only a short meditation, just thirty minutes long, compared to some of my three hour marathon sessions. Instinctively, I knew the meditation session had ended. I thought about Jesus and wondered what thoughts went through his mind as he carried the cross, as his imminent death drew near.

Chapter 26: Two Worlds

The month of May was approaching. It was soon to be the one year anniversary of Linda's passing. I no longer refer to the day as her death because I know she is alive in the afterworld. I wondered whether she would make some important communication in honor of her passing.

<u>Explore The World</u>

I see Linda to the left of me. Yes, Angie it is me. I love you, Angie, and I miss you so much. I am with you all the time. I want to thank you for taking care of me my whole life, not just when I was sick. My whole life you were my support, my guide, my helper while on earth, my guardian angel. You helped me to be happy in life. America was a wonderful time in my life, and that was thanks to you. You made it happen—my life, my home. In the end, you were the one who held my hand every day, who comforted me when the time was near. I was not afraid to go because you held my hand and believed so much in the afterlife that I knew I was going somewhere special, and that my life was not ending and that I would be alive in another world so when I passed I did not think of myself as dying. I knew I was going to a world where I would meet Mum and others, so I was not afraid at all. In fact, I wanted to go at the end, as my physical body was not what I wanted any more; it was not me.

Lying there unable to move was not a life I wanted. I did not want to be like that. My only regret was leaving all of you and the family. You were my life, and I knew I could not be in your lives anymore, and that made me very sad because I loved you all so much that it hurt me to see you all so sad. Believe me! I did not want to leave you! It was just my time to go. I am sorry it was so soon, but it had to be that way for all of you to grow and live your life's fulfillment and purpose. If I had lived your lives would be different now. You wanted to be with me, but I wanted to be with mother more than you know. I loved her more after she died, and my love pulled me toward her, so I am where I should be and you are where you should be.

I love you very much, my Angel—the perfect name for you. Mum gave you the right name, the angel in the family, for that is what you are now, the angel in the family to help them where I cannot—no longer in the physical way, but I can help them through the spiritual way, through my love for them.

Two Worlds

I want to talk about my life here. It is a wonderful life Angie. Just like the movie It's a Wonderful Life. *We come down to earth, dressed up in human form—like Clarence, if only for a minute in your life. (I know I use movie analogies all the time, but it makes it easier for me to explain to you.) You do not know it is us, but we do it more often than you realize. Then, there are some of you who come and visit us, but that number is very small since not all people want to know how to do that.*

You have been very fortunate to travel to our world, but you were always the fortunate ones—all those Jesus points I used to say you have. Now you should know what I mean. You have seen our world and you know much.

Mum and I are busy every day. We travel to many different places. In nanoseconds we travel to earth, the moon, to Pluto, to all the planets because we fulfill different needs at different times. We have told you that planets have different energy and vibrating levels and, depending on our lesson here, we travel to that planet to learn and build our energy. It is like building a database of resources and information from life on all planets that the spirit needs in order to develop and grow, and to move in higher spheres of the spirit world.

Our world is so vast that it is too much to know and explain. That is why there are so many accounts of the spirit world, which are mostly all true because people visit different parts of the spirit world. Just as you have difference experiences traveling to Africa, China, and Australia, there are different experiences within the spirit world. There are hospitals, schools, and houses here, but again, they are different in appearance and style depending on where you visit. You will visit a place that your soul is naturally drawn to because you are home again, in the place of comfort for your soul. Even in one country, city, or town, your life on earth is much different; so it is here, much different. We showed you part of the spirit world in a way that you could identify with, but we may choose to show it differently to another person because it is how they can understand the information in the way it is presented.

The work here is the same: helping souls evolve and adjust to the spirit world. There is a center for disease control where we work on solutions for earth's man-made diseases. Yes, they are man-made diseases. We look at technology, which helps today's world communicate efficiently, and at intermingled cultures so humans can learn from one another. We monitor earth very closely. It is after all, God's earth, God's creation, God's spirit world. It is just that in the spirit world we do the work of God all the time. One hundred percent of our lives are based on love: love the creator and mankind and all things of the Creator—the universe.

Extra terrestrials are not far off from how they are depicted by human imagination and real life experiences, for some have seen us. We have many shapes and forms so humans may see different forms of E.T. They are all true. We come to earth as part of our monitoring program, and it is only natural that from time to time we are seen.

Ghosts are a minute part of the spirit world with a few stragglers that have not completed their crossing and remain on the earth's sphere without a physical body. Sooner or later they cross over. We are not concerned because they come across eventually, and spirits work on this side to encourage them. These few souls, or lost souls, are few and far between, so we do not worry or direct unnecessary energy in their direction. We direct our energy for the good of mankind and the good of the universe. We are all part of the universe, God's universe. There is much to do here and much to learn. You have only seen the tip of the iceberg. Keep meditating and you will develop more

Make Life Happen

Make life happen! Life is precious—a gift—so don't waste it. No one should live a life without God's love. When you feel sad or lonely remember that God loves you; we love you. Do not be upset any longer. Life is a wonderful thing; don't waste it. I am repeating myself so you will understand the importance of it. Let no one or nothing stand in your way; life is yours to live as you choose. What you choose is up to you, no ifs, ands, or buts. You decide; you are in control of your destiny. It can be whatever you want it to be.

Life is full of challenges and chances sent your way to enrich your life. Make no mistake about that. Life is full of challenges and decisions. Make your life full of things you like to do and with people you like to be around. Life is full of opportunities, and it is up to you to take them. Seize the moment and take advantage of life's opportunities. Make all your choices count—stand up and be counted. Don't be led into situations you are not sure about and that you will regret later. What I mean is don't do something because someone wants you to do it. Ask yourself if it is what you want, and then make your decision based on that.

Focus on your life. Decide what you want and then plan it out. You are capable of making that happen. It is all within you, ready to unlock. What are your dreams? Write them out so you can see them. Life is only as good as you make it, so make your life full of dreams that you want, then you will feel fulfilled. Otherwise you live a life of existence, which is no way to live. Your life will be blessed once you take charge and own your life. Instead of waiting for things to happen, make them happen. Make them how you want them.

Linda's energy disappeared, and the meditation finished suddenly. As I came out of the meditation, I wondered if the time had come for me to stop writing down all the information that I received. Twelve months had passed marking the anniversary of Linda's passing. Should I stop now or continue on until July? July marked the one year anniversary of my first communication in San Francisco. I decided that since Mum and Linda had told me when to start writing, they would probably tell me when to stop. Since that was my decision, each time afterward, when I meditated, I wondered whether or not it would be my last communication with them. As if they were making the way for other energies to communicate with me instead of them, unexpectedly, days later, the American Indian re-appeared. He immediately began to speak.

Life Balance

Fire is a symbol of earth's power, the elements fire, water, air, earth. Opposite to fire will come, but need fire first to burn old ways, make way for the new. Can rebuild new way. Fire creates heat, warmth, but then comes the cold to balance. You have lived much in the fire; now will live in calm cool water to cool down and settle all basic and simple theology for you. Must get use to my style of writing. I am a warrior, a healer for many people. I fight for the cause, a pioneer for the truth.

Seek the truth, and you will find your path. Do not worry about both; they will be paved. If you dedicate life to spirit, then spirit will dedicate life to you. Your soul should be nourished and fed like your physical body so you are in balance. A soul that is not in balance only causes grief and anguish. Once you get used to looking after your soul first, your life will be happy, so simple. To learn of the afterlife, and live your physical life with this knowledge, is the best of both worlds. Knowing your purpose on earth, your life's purpose, and actually live it every day, is your truest happiness and most fulfilling life of all.

Life's purpose for all human beings is love and compassion. With love you have compassion; with love you have the unity of souls, unity of spirit, God's spirit, God's love. But humans choose to love in limited and small ways through their family and friends etc. But when you truly fill your heart with love, it will reach out and touch everyone and everything. Live your life with love, fill your life with love. Create love for all things, and you will truly be blessed. Let love flow through. Start now with your life. Do not hold back. Once you let love flow, unconditional love flow, your soul will be released of the burden it carries, day to day. Yes burden because it is weighed down by the lack of love that it has inside. Let the love go free. Stop limiting yourself with your thoughts. Listen and feel the love in your heart. Remember to make decision based on love, and you will be on the right track. Will visit again.

The following day he re-appeared.

Thoughts Of The Universe

Good day to you. No need to go fast. I like the slower pace. Want you to discuss life's importance to the world, the universe. Many times we live our lives without thoughts of the universe. It is wrong; we must think about universe. First, all things in universe are important to growth of soul, of spirit. Make time to learn such truth of the universe. Don't waste time on unimportant things. People find their way in life, must learn own lesson. Great Spirit hears all requests, all dreams on earth, and manages what dreams are needed for your growth, not dreams that are not needed or else spirit not evolved. All tried and tested. Will watch you progress to keep you on track. Will help you get what you need, not what you want. Follow spirit path and you will not go wrong.

That is all I have for today. A short message but profound.

Chapter 27: A Happy Soul

On a few occasions I have seen and communicated with my grandmother who passed over almost 30 years ago. I was excited when I sensed her energy. Instantly, I could see her sitting in her favorite armchair. She turned and smiled at me and said, *"Hello, Angie, life is not what it seems. Reach for your full potential."* In an instant she was gone. It was as though she came to reassure me that my family was around, watching over me. Then, the energy changed and to my surprise the monk appeared. I could see his robe. I had not received a communication from him in several weeks. I had begun to wonder whether he had moved on and that out time together had finished—apparently not!

<u>A Happy Soul</u>

There are no secrets to life that you do not know. You have discovered much during your journey. Of course, there are more details regarding that of what you see, but you have the overall picture of our world, which is suffice for now. Life is only as good as you understand life to be. Life is fulfilling once you have the ingredients, which you have been given. Life is measured by what you put into your life in order to get out of life what you want, what you enjoy. Life is what you make life to be. Remember that you create your own life by your words and your actions. There is no point saying or wishing something and not taking action to do it. That has no results. There cannot be any results, only nothing, because nothing is a result of no action.

Plan your destiny and take action. Plan to make it happen. What do I want? What shall I do? What can I do? All simple questions, but humans do not practice this little exercise, and they wonder why their lives are so frustrating and limiting. To reach your full potential is to do what you want to do. It is as easy as that. People do things to pay bills to get through in life, but I say to you, when you do something you enjoy, wealth will come in abundance to you. I am not talking of just material wealth; I am talking about the wealth of a happy soul. The true meaning of life is when your soul is happy, and you are in a place of love, a place where you love doing what you are doing, and you love others and yourself. It all goes together. Love who you are and what you do when you love others. Listen to what I say to you, and you will be truly happy. Happiness is the greatest emotion on earth that people strive for every day.

Don't waste this lesson. Take action now before it is too late or you will ask ten years from now, "Why didn't I do that?" You will be unhappy later if you don't act on your dreams. Dreams are what keep the human soul alive. Without dreams your life is empty. Dreams are connected with hope. Without hope, your life is empty. I want you to follow your dreams. I am telling you to follow your dreams.

Thank you for listening today. It has been a long time.

Your friend, the monk.

I saw the back of his robe and he disappeared. Instantly, I felt the group's energy building around me.

Love And Harmony

We wish you well today. We are here to continue your lesson. No names are needed or required. We want to tell you about life on earth today, how it mirrors our world very much— without all the hate and crime. Imagine a world with only love and joy and happiness, and you will have a glimpse of what the spirit world is like. It is a world where love and harmony exist because that is the key to life, the existence of the soul. The idea of earth is for this place, this school, to learn how to love so our worlds can be as one without the hate and crime. We have much work to do before that can happen because your world has many wars and much hate. If people loved more, the energy in the world would change, and there would not be all the problems that you see now caused by bad energy that circulates in the world causing natural and manmade disaster and ill treatment of people. Make life full of love, and your energy will circulate. That is all.

After these short messages I wanted to continue with my meditation, so I asked if I could travel to the spirit world. If this was not possible, then I asked for communication from Mum or Linda.

Explore Your World.

Linda came through. *What am I, the consolation prize? I don't think so! I have been waiting to speak to you, Angie. It has been a long time since we spoke. Mum and I have been on a holiday. You can explore other planets any time you want. Mum and I do a lot together—always off somewhere on little trips, just trying to get our bearings and to explore this world. It is so vast and so big; you can't imagine! There is so much to do here. Our days are full. We have been to other planets but always return to the earth plane to be near you and not far away*

I am smiling at you to let you know things will be all right. Life is too short to worry about the small details. Yes, they are small. Learn what you can from it and move on. Life is precious and each day should be treated as a gift from God. Build your world more; make it how you want it to be; plan it out then create it. Don't let time tick by any longer. Get on with your life. Get settled and focus on what you want. There is much to learn about and analyze. You can do whatever you want, as long as you create it. Make it fit. Work with what you have. Don't keep waiting for a magic cure. There is no magic cure. All the answers lie in your thoughts and in what you do and say. Create your own world. There are many hands to help—helping hands here to guide you—but you must put some effort into it. Make your life the way you want it to be.

Mum suddenly joined in and said:

Make Your Life Count

Mum: Been watching everything going on. Don't keep waiting and wishing, living your life that way. Learn from your mother. Get on with things and make the most of each day because life goes by so quickly. Stop looking at what you don't have and look at what you do have. That is the key to life: to work with the ingredients in your life and make it work each day. If you need more ingredients then add them slowly. Another important thing to remember is to live each day to the fullest. You will get the most out of life that way. People are there to learn to live life to the fullest and have no regrets. Don't stop yourself from doing what you want; you are your own worst enemy. You will make your life count if your help others. Remember that philosophy.

Will go now, love. Start your day. Remember, we love you and help you always.

Love Mum x

A Visit To Heaven

The following day, I did get my wish to travel to the spirit world. Initially, when I sat down to meditate I felt slightly restless and unsettled. I used my visualization technique and pictured a staircase. After several attempts, I began to see a bright staircase and, strangely, had the urge to ascend very quickly, which I did. At the top of the stairs I could see a bright light coming from a room at the end of the corridor. I hurried along the corridor and pushed open the door where the light shined brightly from behind. The door opened with just a little force. I could see clouds, white puffy clouds. I could easily walk through them.

When I came through to the other side, I could see people sitting around on benches; they were talking. They were people in another world, the spirit world. They wore robes, reminiscent of those worn in Biblical days. They were sitting around wooden picnic tables. I saw white plain clothes and multicolored clothes. I saw goats walking around. People were socializing and talking about their day. Some were reviewing their class notes; it was a study break. They see me looking at them. Some smiled but they knew I am not one of them. "Come and sit," one man said. There were mostly men here. I sat in between two of the men toward the end of the bench. They were eating fresh, juicy fruit out of a wooden bowl.

The Bowl Is Never Empty

A sermon begins: Life is simple and has an abundance of joy for all when you sit with nature and eat the fruit that God provided. We all get along because we all share in God's love and God's fruit. There are juicy peaches, blackberries, oranges, watermelons, and other succulent fruits today. Give fruit to the soul and enjoy the juice that squirts out of them: a simple pleasurable experience.

Message: to share your juices, bowls of fruit with all friends because there is plenty to go around. No need to save them all for you. More will come when the bowl is empty because the bowl is never empty of God's love, God's juice. A quick simple lesson for today: Eat well with fruit from God.

With those words I found myself transported back to the room at the end of the corridor. As I wondered what had happened to me I saw the image of Mother Mary.

Image Of Mother Mary:

I saw an image of Mother Mary with light shining around her head. I heard these words: Mother of all nature and nurture, who gives love to all. Mother Mary spoke, "Rise up and live your life with God's love and you can never be alone, for his love walks with you all day. Come into this love and your life will be happier. Walk with his love."

The image disappeared as quickly as it had appeared. It was gone in an instant. It was as if I had woken from a dream and, try as I might, I could not re-capture the dream. I tried to remain in a meditative state in hopes of receiving more images of Mother Mary. Like many people who awake from a dream, I could not go back and recapture it. After the meditation had ended I reread my notes several times to relive and savor the experience.

Chapter 28: Journey into the Light

I had often wondered what happens to you when you cross over to Heaven and the spirit world. What does the other world look like? Does it look like earth with flowers, trees, houses, and hospitals? Do spirits have a body? What do we look like? One day, I had a powerful communication from the group. I felt as if I had been lifted up out of my physical body on a journey into the light. Along the way the group spoke to me.

Journey Into The Light

Group: *Much to say today! Many here to help you get started on your journey. We will take you on a ride beyond your wildest dreams. Hold on tight! See the light! Go upward and follow the light! See the flowers that blow in the wind as we come up through the ground into the world of Heaven. Once you are here you can see all the wonderful things in our world. It is like going to the cinema. You can watch all that goes on in our world. First you can see the hospitals, which are very busy. They do not need equipment or tools because it is a place where we heal the souls when the soul may need a little adjustment when it returns home to our world. Always a busy place because loved ones want to visit and there are no visiting hours, so people come when they like and as often as they like! There is the convalescent home where people spend their time in the garden with the birds, bees, and flowers. They get adjusted. There are people who lived a sad life on earth and think they will have a sad life in this world. They forget to be happy or how to be happy. So we help them adjust to our world. It doesn't take long, since happiness is contagious.*

Then, they move into their new house. We have told you a little before about our houses. They are communities in the sky, which have houses and cottages, and communal centers where a person has his or her own room like the one your mother showed you in your dream. Then there are the cottages where your sister lives, next door to her husband. Yes, we showed you that before, so no need to repeat that information.

Once you are settled in your new life on this side, you study and develop and move to a different plane. We say different because you no longer need to see a physical house or building. Your mind creates your house, room, etc., all done by thought, by consciousness. We can take on any shape, form, vision, or image we see fit to take, in order to fit the circumstances that we need. We see only replicas of human physical things for the immediate time after passing over.

Then, as our soul develops, we no longer need to be reminded of earthly images, so they go away. The soul has evolved somewhat and it moves onto the next level. There are gatekeepers at every level. Call it the pearly gates at each level. They decide to let you through to the next level when the time is right and not until. When it is your time to go through the next level, which is a level within a level, you lose the images of earth and the image of your physical body. Many find this concept hard to understand. It is like shedding your body from your mind. You shed your physical body when you come home, and then, at this point, you have to shed the memory of the body so that what is left is only the soul. Your soul will return to its purest form closest to God. It will then be truly home.

But in the meantime you must learn to develop your soul without the earthly connections. For your mother and sister, they remember their earthly family and life and are around you. They choose to do this because they want to communicate with you, but, at some point, they will move on. Maybe sooner or later when all the family has joined them. Please don't think this holds them back in any way; it does not. It helps their souls to develop just as much as those souls who move on because in the next level they catch up. There are others in the next level who may choose to stay there a while longer, and so on, and so forth.

The next level is the learning school where souls are tested on their understanding of life, God's creation, the universe, and how their soul is part of the universe, as well as how all souls play a role in the growth of the universe. They start to think in a group and not individually as one—that is all. To think in a group loses the individual, and you think as one and what is best for all because you are all one. We communicate as one, which is why when you say it is the "group" that communicates with you it feels like one person speaking; collectively, it is all one.

Your group is talking to you now, Angie. We want to help you communicate to the world about the spirit world. That is our purpose, my friend. Once people understand the spirit world, they will adapt their human life on earth and their thought process to consider other people in their daily lives. That is what we want: for humans to love one another and love God. Let them not forget the purpose of their life on earth to love one another. That is all there is to learn about life: love one another as God loves you.

As the group returned me gently to my physical surroundings I felt Linda's energy surround me. Instantly she began to communicate with me.

I feel Linda's energy with me and suddenly I feel joy and happiness. She is so excited to come through. She wraps her arms around me and gives me a hug just like she used to do. *I am here, Angie. I am always here. Sometimes I hold myself back when you are getting all this information out about our world. The book is not so much about you, but about the information you received about spirit. I am not saying your life is not interesting, but those who are fascinated by the spirit world will enjoy reading all the meditations we have given you.*

There is much joy here, Angie. Our lives live on in the purest form you can ever imagine, only love and joy. That is all there is here, so don't believe that you will have pain or suffering because that is all left behind. Pain and suffering are the soul's learning lessons, which create a deep energy that is needed to evolve the soul. The deeper the energy level, the deeper the soul's experience and growth.

My love for you will never die, just like the title Love Never Dies. *Although you are separate from my world, my love is still on the earth as energy. Love is the greatest energy of all. As you know, the more love you create, the better your life will be. The more love energy you create, the higher the energy around you. It is hard to create this energy, and that is what makes it so rewarding: the greater the challenge, the greater the energy fields. The love will come back to you tenfold.*

If you look back through the book, you will see all the meditations have been regarding love and energy. That is the basic principle of life: love one another as Jesus said in the Bible. This is a basic teaching of Jesus, so powerful yet humans choose not to love one another as they criticize and blame others who are different. For example, they will feel strongly against the information in this book. There are those who feel strongly against homosexuals, people of color, people of different religions, and so on, so forth.

If all people chose to love and accept one another, then the level of energy created with this love will be strong enough to wipe out the destruction of earth and mankind. No more wars or fighting, but nations living in peace, accepting one another's way of life and embracing them as children of God. All people on earth are children of God.

Many find that concept difficult to accept and use other passages in the Bible or other religious books and doctrines to support their view of not loving all mankind. Remember that to love one another is a simple gesture and easy to do if prejudices are removed. People must not hide behind their principles in the name of God. For God loves all his children. The truth is simple.

Love is the energy that the soul feeds on and continues in this life. The more love sent to your loved ones in spirit, the more energy they can accumulate and share with the universe, nourishing and replenishing the universe and the world.

My love for you is greater than in the human form because now it is pure, pure love, given to you as a gift from spirit. All loved ones in spirit send love to their loved ones on earth. Your guardian angels are there to bring love to you all, which is their purpose.

Humans on earth do not create the level of love needed for energy levels to succeed on earth, so spirit brings love to feed the energy which supports life on earth. Without energy such life would not exist on earth. It is not money that makes the world go around but LOVE; the more love the more richness and the better quality of your life. Redirect your energy to see the good in life, and do not waste your energy on negative thoughts. That is all today, Linda.

The journey into the spirit world and the hug that my sister gave me are amongst the most important experiences that I cherish. My body felt as if it was physically in the spirit world. I experienced the sensation of being pulled upwards out of my body. I was not scared at all, rather excited by it. I felt safe. I could see the flowers swaying gently in the wind. Most important was the beautiful hug from Linda. It felt as real to me as any hug could feel. The next few days I took time off from meditating as I relished the memories of this experience. The next time I sat to meditate my mother came through and spoke about twin souls in the spirit world. Many times I have often wondered whether there was more to the little voice inside each of us, the voice that gives you a sense of knowing or a hunch about something. Could this be a twin soul?

We Are All Connected

Mum: You see, we are all connected to our ethereal bodies in the spirit world but people do not realize this connection. They believe they are on earth as a single living organism, a simple cell. I say to you, no; you only have part of your soul, your spirit, with you on earth. Your main soul is part of the big soul, the one spirit of God that remains on this side. I say to you, let people know that the rest of their soul lives life in the spirit world. If humans tap into their other soul as you are doing now it can bring them all that is missing in their lives and make their lives in the physical body worth living. Their twin soul is here in the spirit world and continues to grow but together their soul as one can grow even faster. People wait until they cross over to realize this, but, I say to you, know that while in the physical body today you can be connected consciously to your spirit soul in Heaven. No need to wait until your physical death. They can work in tandem while on earth.

Teach people the benefit of being in tune with their inner soul that lives here in the spirit world, and it will guide them through their lives. There are many things to learn more deeply than the Bible teaches, which is only a beginning. Life is much more than what it seems. Understanding life while in the human form is the key to the soul's development. We have given you many teachings about the soul, about life, about the universe, love, God's world, and God's creations. If one person understands this then that is one more than there is today my friend.

We are happy for you. Very happy and we want you to enjoy your life. We are with you without our physical form but we are here. Can't you tell that we are giving you all this love? We are around you very much. We want you to know that. That is the best we can do. We cannot be in the physical form but, remember, the physical form is only a temporary shell, which you shed. Your beautiful soul comes through, the real you. Your soul can communicate with our soul any time: a soul-to-soul communication is how it works. When you meditate like this you temporarily move out of your physical form that restricts and hinders the soul, making it impossible to communicate with us. But once you meditate and are in a trance state, you temporarily free yourself of the physical body and you allow your spirit, your soul, to communicate and join in the great soul, the great spirit of all souls.

We are all connected; your soul springs back to nearer the soul's core, the great soul of oneness. Once your soul travels back towards the center, core soul, you can link in with other souls, one consciousness, one soul; that is how it works. And we can share our thoughts, ideas, like a pipeline. When you meditate like this, you step into the edge of our spirit world that is all and we seize the moment and link in with you. There are many ways to explain it, but we hope this may help you understand it and explain to others. Our world is so exciting, Angie, and this is what makes it exciting: opening your mind and soul to spirit.

I will return. Bye, Angie. Love, Mum. The energy changed and the group began to speak

Group: Much joy and happiness. Linda is here saying that. She wants to pass along feelings of joy and happiness to you and the family. She is around you and them always. She and your mother do not want to move on because they have the best of both worlds. It is funny that humans talk about the best of both worlds, yet they deny the existence of the spirit world and believe only in the earthly world. So, which world do they mean? Many true words are said in jest because they are true.

A Harmonious World.

I see a picture of a line in a graph—like a heartbeat: many times, man beats to own drum. Listen to your heart and feel the rhythm. If it is in harmony then your life is harmony. When it is out of harmony your life is unbalanced, and you are going against the natural rhythm. Your spirit is in tune with all aspects of life of energy and when it is in harmony they go together like music, playing harmoniously. Feel how thing should be. If it feels right, then naturally flow with the energy like flowers gently blowing in the wind.

See the babbling water as it moves purposely along the brook in harmony. When you see the babbling brook, you know you are in sync. Make your life harmonious and it will flow. Roadblocks are because there is a blockage in the flow you came to. Stop and understand what is wrong, then see the energy flow along the river—watch it ebb. You have come a long way, learned more than most do in a lifetime, but don't think this is all, my friend. There is more to learn.

Our world existing is the most important thing to know. We want to bring love to our souls on earth; we see the pain and suffering caused by war and hate. War and hate will self-destruct the human race. Know that spirit world brings love to heal the earth. Love is the essence of our essence. Without love there would be no soul. Our world is where all that is imagined in the mind of the human mind is a reality in the spirit world.

When you dream at night, your thoughts are your soul experiences; have experiences. When you lose your physical body you continue to have these experiences in the spirit world. That is the best way to describe it. When you dream, your mind floats into our world, and you experience this knowing. Just like when you dream, your mind travels to a higher vibration level that is within your mind. There is no physical world that you visit. It is all done through consciousness, which are your thoughts. Your thoughts create new thoughts every second. Your thoughts remind you of past memories, so you, as a spirit being with a consciousness, have thoughts whether you are in a physical body or not.

When you communicate with spirit world, you are lifting your spirit, soul, thoughts, and consciousness to one great consciousness. At this point you link up with other minds, thoughts, and consciousness and, in turn, connect and experience a two-way communication. You may see pictures or images in your dreams. The floating sensation in your physical body is your soul reaching to the energy of your consciousness, drifting to a higher vibration, whether asleep or awake. But in your sleep, the human mind is not dictated by the left side of the brain. The right side of the brain is free to receive communication and free to drift and blend with energy of the spirit world. When doing this, the mind sees pictures and words. Whether spoken or written, words are energy, thoughts are energy, and the energy level rises in the world. We are all energy. Energy cannot be destroyed. You were created out of energy. Life on earth was created out of energy—

very powerful sources. This energy does not die, so you are part of one energy of life.

Energy is the physical and spirit world. All you need to do is tap into this great bank of energy, and you will be able to communicate with spirits in the human form, which you call telepathy or mind reading. If people open up their energy radars, it is easy to blend with each other. That is why women who work together have the same monthly cycle because their energy has naturally blended subconsciously, and they are in tune. So you can see it can happen regardless of whether or not to want it, regardless if you are aware of it or not. Energy blending happens.

We want you to be aware of the energy blending and know that spirit world is around you as well. You blend energy in and with both worlds. We want greater blending of energies as this will create harmony just like the natural ebb and flow of a river, like harmony of music. Right now, the physical world is not in harmony with the spirit world as the energy vibration on earth is so low caused by strife, grief, wars, and all that negative energy brings.

Our goal once again is to bring positive energy to the earth to make the earthly experience more harmonious. We want our world to be as one. We can only do this once. The vibration level of the earth rises. You as individual mediums can raise your vibration level and can receive communication with our world. But you are few in number. Word needs to spread to bring awareness of spirit world. That is where you can help us. Through your book, an awareness of our world and people will become intriguing and others will want to know more.

Chapter 29: Time

Sometimes I am fortunate to dream about Mum and Linda. I would like to share this particular dream with you because I remembered it so vividly when I awoke. A friend once told me that when you dream about your loved one and you remember the dream when you awake, then the dream is actually a visit from them. It is a nice thought.

Louise, Scott, and I were in a gift shop looking at the displays on the shelves. Suddenly, I felt Linda look over my shoulder. She pointed to a gift and said, "That's nice. Why don't you buy it?" I told her that I had enough knick-knacks in the house. Then, Linda went outside and sat on a concrete bench swinging her legs. Then, I heard a stranger's voice say, "She's still around to protect you. She won't leave you because she wanted to stay with you. She did not want to die. It was not her choice. It was her time to go. Now, she has the chance to be with you from this side and she does! She is not going to let her physical death stop that. She can be with you from this side. She has made an agreement to do this. It is the best of both worlds for her. She is able to be with her mother, and you all at the same time." Then, Scott told Louise and me to "Hurry up because the rain was coming." I heard Linda say that everything was okay and that she had an umbrella. Linda had a big smile on her face and she exclaimed, "I'm not going anywhere without you!"

Often in my meditations, Mum and Linda use titles of movies, songs and well-known phrases to communicate their message to me. To my surprise, this meditation had quite a few of them.

Mum: Life is like a box of chocolates; you never know what you are going to get. Remember that saying? It is important. There are many options available to you in your life, which is why psychics can tell you many different things. They read your energy. It does not always mean they can predict the future. Thoughts are energy, and they become the future unless you have new thoughts, and then the new thoughts can become the future.

When a psychic reads you, the psychic is taking a snapshot of your energy right there at the time, but tomorrow you can have a different energy and the psychic will read you differently. The only true message or prediction of the future comes from spirit communication.

Now, I have said that and explained that, I want to move on to spirit communication. Life is not what you think. Life is full of surprises and changes from day to day. You in the present can change the future. You can change your thoughts, actions, words, and you can create a new future each day. It is up to you to create what you want and not what other people assess for you.

You will find all the answers within you—remember that. Just see and think about what you want and it will come. Build your dreams and they will come, just like the movie Field of Dreams. *That is what you have to do. Dream what you want and your dreams will become a reality. Life is too short to wonder and wait. Say what it is that you want, and you will receive. There is no magic formula. Life is not a mystery. Life is how you design it. Yes, you design your life. If you want success, just send out your thoughts and the universe will respond. Linda is here and she wants to say hello.*

Linda: I miss you, Angie, very much and the others too. I love you all. You know that. That is why I came to you in your dream. I came to make you happy and to say hello. I have not forgotten you my sister, my friend. We are part of one piece of the master soul like a cluster of souls that make up and are part of a bigger soul. We are all pieces of each other's soul. We are connected through the bonds of love. Our love bonded us together for eternity, not just our physical bodies on earth but now in my world. I am so connected to you all that I am never far away. I am in your dreams. I put happy thoughts in your head, in all that you do. It is as though I am still there. Your dream was an important message because it is true. I am around you all protecting you from this side. I am with you all more than you know because it is where I want to be. I am with Mum, which is where I want to be. I am with you, Angie. Can't you see? Can't you see the smile on my face as I look at you now? You have come a long way with my help of course! But what are sisters for! I miss you so much.

Memories of our lives together are with me, although I do not feel sadness. I see your sadness, and I am aware of it. But I don't want you to be sad because I am around you. I love you always; remember that. That has not changed. Angie, please don't cry anymore. Just live your life and get the job done. Live your life each day. Time goes by so quickly. Mum and I are happy. I know I keep saying that, but I need you to understand and know that. We look forward to the day when we are reunited, but until that day, this is the best we can do: communicate with you as we are now. We send all our love and watch over you. It is such a phenomenon that I had no idea how it worked while on earth. I should have listened to you more and paid attention. I might have done some things differently like listen to my hunches and intuition more. Now I understand that they are God's spirit, God's love, speaking to you from Heaven.

Mum is here again, love. Linda came for a visit, but I am still here. I am around you also giving you hugs and love. You are developing very nicely while on earth, and you are fortunate to be able to do this while you are in the physical form. That is a gift, so remember that. You were always the sensitive one, which adds to your spiritual growth, showing compassion for all.

Compassion

Compassion is what matters in life. To live a compassionate life is the true meaning of your life's purpose. You cannot have compassion without love. You cannot have love without pain. You cannot have pain without suffering. They all go together. You cannot have one without the other.

More highly evolved souls are coming down to earth with the ability to feel compassion for their fellow man and the world. It is this new energy of compassion that will help drive the negative energy from the world. You will see a gradual shift coming and feel the compassion for your fellow man. New love energy will arise. The new love energy will change the negative energy in the world. Nations will be at peace. Nations will work together to create harmony and be at peace. Leaders will come together and decide a plan best suited to benefit mankind and not their own countries.

The children born will be full of love and bring love to the world. Love will increase for everyone. Happiness will increase. Health will increase. People will spend their days focusing on how they can best help others in their world, not just those in their lives. The energy is changing. We in the spirit world are making this change. We are sending down highly evolved souls full of love and God's light to heal the world. More will come. There are many more. There are many there already. Recent generations have highly evolved souls, but many more are needed.

This is a beginning of the change. More people would like to know about the spirit world, about life's purpose on earth. Why things happen in this world and that world. Yes, there is a higher force keeping track—keeping an eye on everything. Evolved souls are coming down which is a big sacrifice for them to experience the physical world. It is so much easier to stay in the spirit world where love is in abundance. It is endless and with love and is, of course, the happiness, the immense happiness, of all souls. For all souls are energy. A new movement, a new generation, is emerging. A phenomenon you see. People will become aware of this change.

That is all I have to say about that. I hope this has been helpful to you with your endeavor. When it is for the good of mankind we are here in full force!

This is what I believe is meant by the big change in 2012. It is a change in the energy level around the world that will bring positive change to the world. Children today are born with souls that radiate lots of love. Just look around you at the younger generation, and you will see a shift in positive energy that has begun.

Group: This is important work that you are doing for spirit, bringing awareness to the world where love and hope is needed for many. Our goal is to resurrect the movement to bring awareness of the afterlife, of the spirit world, to all souls on earth who will benefit from this connection—if they want to. I say "if they want to" for there are many who do not want. They choose to live their life in ignorance of the truth, but that is their decision, their choice, and God gave all his children freedom of choice to do and to act in what they believe. There are many of you who do seek truth, and we are happy to provide that connection, that communication, the truth to you.

Never forget the love and support of the spirit world. We are here to help you and all souls on the earth. Do not live a life of sadness but live a life of love, compassion, and joy of the realization and promise of future life in the spirit world. For you see, my friend, it is the greatest emotion that there is to feel joy and love. It is truly an emotional experience that often brings you to tears, but they are tears of joy and not tears of sadness. Try to concentrate on giving more time to spirit; just twenty minutes a day will help ground you in your life, for when you are not connected to spirit, you are out of kilter and thoughts of sadness enter your mind. So give spirit a try; use this slogan for your daily life. Try to connect with spirit every day, and keep on track with your life's purpose and your life's lessons. Many people forget to do this and wonder what is wrong in their lives. It isn't that anything is wrong; it is that they are out of touch with their soul and their spirit soul, that part of them that lives and remains in the spirit world. They only get in touch with their spirit soul in times of need and they dismiss the connection, the feeling as a hunch. But I say to you, it is not a hunch; it is more than that. It is God's spark to them for the divine spirit that is in all of us.

There are many people in this life who follow the wrong path while on earth. They think they are doing right by copying or following the paths that society has led for them, but I say to you, do not follow what society has laid down for you to do. Follow your own soul, your mind's purpose; that is why God gave you a mind to make your own decisions. Plan your life. Man has one purpose while on earth, one life; live it wisely and choose your destiny. Make your life. Do not wait for others to make it. Take charge.

Thank you for listening to me today. I will leave you now and make room for others to speak. Until next time, love to all mankind.

Instantly, the next communicator was there and ready to speak. To my surprise it was the Native American Indian, who I had communicated with on a few occasions before. He came with words of wisdom. They were in reference to the ego and I called this meditation "I am."

I Am

'I' is just one letter but powerful in its meaning. 'I' is a pronoun but 'I' is a being, larger than life. 'I' is often described as ego, the other part of your soul, or rather the part of you in your soul that raises it head now and again, often as a protection mechanism. "I am" is what Jesus said. Think about that 'I am.'

What did he mean when he said "I am"? He said it to recognize that which is within him. That state of being which is larger than life. Trick is to get it in harmony with whole being and not let it take over who you are.

Wise old Indian again here - to remind you that you are part of one Great Spirit, the spirit 'I am' which is in all of us. Sometimes we connect with this spirit in Heaven and we communicate with our inner being but don't imagine this to be greater than who you are. The trick is to just know that you are 'I am' and live your life with purpose and meaning and never let 'I am' become more than what you are. Let 'I am' be what it is. Don't let it become who you want it to be. Such riddle and confusion you say, but 'I am' is bigger than you and is not to be confused with you. It is the God within you, not you, so you can recognize it as a higher self than you and know that it is not 'you' in the human flesh but a spirit sense, then you will not have the ego problem that so often comes with this. Let no thing or another corrupt.

Many live their lives based on actions and thoughts of the ego. 'Look at me - see who I am.' That is the human part of the soul thinking it is better than their spiritual soul. It cannot be. It must not be for the spiritual soul is part of God. "I am" Jesus said, He is the spiritual soul of the Holy Spirit without the human soul. It is the human soul, which is the ego. When you become more spiritual - practice to live life in a spiritual way, so the human soul, the ego diminishes, and the spirit flourishes. Sometimes it takes a helping hand to do this like the loss of a child, spouse, parent, etc., but your job is to develop your spiritual soul with the added constraints of the human soul. This is why souls develop more rapidly, while on earth, due to all the distractions of the human soul.

Sometimes people cannot control the emotions of the human soul and they live a life of searching, wanting to satisfy the human soul, the ego. It is only when the spiritual soul is fed and nourished, allowed to blossom and develop, that the human soul will be in balance with the spiritual soul. You will become 'I am' once the human soul is controlled and the needs are met.

I hope I have given you an overview of the ego and the human soul - sufficiently to describe to people the difference. Again it is the reader who is important to this book. To reach as many readers as possible to get them to understand in layman's terms how the soul-spirit works. Once people understand the importance of the soul, the connection with their spirit soul will keep their life in balance and in harmony with life and the world, their surroundings. Such a simple concept for people to understand. Once they understand they can fulfill their life's purpose.

Time

Time has no meaning in our world but time means everything in your world. "Time is on Your Side," as the song suggests, is one song influenced by spirit. Many songs are influenced more than the artists are willing to acknowledge. Time is a precious commodity while on earth; your physical body has only a certain number of years, a certain amount of time to fulfill its life's purpose. Don't waste your time on frivolous activities that do not contribute to the better of mankind. This should be your aim every day. How can I better mankind today? For you see, when you better mankind you better yourself and your soul.

Many have come to learn, but many do not learn. They leave their physical bodies without development of the soul. Their souls do not grow and they waste time on earth. Yes, they may think they have all led beautiful lives, but it is only based on physical needs and desire. What have they gained on earth they cannot take with them when they come home. Yet, people do not understand this basic concept. Please remember to remind people of their purpose and place in the universe. Your mother asked me to say "place," that word in particular. She says it is a private joke between you two and that it will bring a smile to your face as it has done. So, there is no more to be said about that.

Let me continue. Your place on earth is chosen for you, with you, before you depart to the great school which earth is. You choose your parents, you choose your friends, your choose all that is in your life, but once you are on the earth you fine tune your choices. So, you will finely choose your actual friends and workplace. Once you are there, you are given the freedom while in the physical form to make choices. So you see, you set the framework from this side, then you finely tune it while on earth, so you can mix and match what it is you have in your life.

Many forget that they have chosen certain professions or friends or family, so they go through life not appreciating the lesson that each one brings. For you see, it is the lessons that teach the soul. Once you have learned your lesson, your soul moves onto another new friend, a new job, and a new adventure. Your life on earth is an adventure, an incredible journey to discover your soul.

The word commitment is a strong word that many humans do not understand the importance of. Commitment is answering to a higher self. Commitment is your word. Your word is your character. Your character is your soul. Your soul is everything. It is important to understand that the destiny of the soul is to fulfill its life's purpose by assisting others. Only through assisting others does the soul truly develop.

Thank you for sitting with me today. I will be back another time when it is appropriate for me to come. Know that we are friends, and we come in peace with much love from our world to your world. Go, my friend, and fulfill your life's purpose.

These were wise words from the Native American Indian: a reminder of the purpose of life, the soul's development, and life's lessons. When you wonder what life is all about, re-read these words.

Chapter 30: Tree of Knowledge

Sometimes when I communicated with Mum or Linda the energy changed during the meditation. At first, I would have a strong sense of whether it was either Mum or Linda, but then I felt a change in the energy as it blended with a different energy. This meditation started out with a communication from Linda and then blended with the group until it became completely the group.

Linda: My life was not in vain. My life was meaningful and purposeful. My life was precisely what I wanted it to be: loving others and caring for others. That is what I wanted, and that is what I did. No life is wasted when you give love to others; that is the most rewarding part and aspect of human life, and the purpose of existence. So, if you love just one person, you have fulfilled your life's obligation, your prophecy.

As Linda communicated with me I felt the blending energy of the group.

Group: Your message today is to love mankind and you will be fulfilled as a human. When your soul is fulfilled, you will live a contented happy life: one leads to another. It is the only way you can truly be happy to love one another as Jesus loved you. Our master Jesus came down to teach the world to love one another as he loved you. There is no more spiritual message than this. Love one another. That is all and you will be truly blessed. Child of God, we are all children of God.

Angels Amongst Us

I see an image of angels. I hear the group say, *Look at the angels in their beautiful wings. They float around your loved ones, embracing them, welcoming them to their new home in Heaven. There are many beautiful places in Heaven. Let us start with the garden. It is full of colorful flowers, bright luminous color beyond the imagination of any flowers on earth. Your loved ones stop to pick some flowers, and they carry them in their hands, for one day they will give them to you when you join them in Heaven. They have many friends. The angels lead them on the path to the field where their friends and family are around them. It is so joyous. People walk up to them, shake hands, embrace, and welcome them to their new life. They mingle amongst the many that they know and the many that they do not know. For in Heaven, we are friends of family to everyone, to each other.*

Heaven sings. Sounds of beautiful music fill the air. Harmonious voices sing songs that fill the soul with love. All the songs are full of loving, sharing, compassion. The songs welcome you to Heaven, much like giving a concert or a theater. You are surrounded by the beautiful voice of the angels singing harmoniously to make you feel part of Heaven, which your loved ones are now. Angels serenade you along the path as you explore your new world. Angels guide you through the maze of Heavens, which is never ending, so you will never be able to see or experience all of Heaven—only the first level when you cross over

Angels walk amongst us. It is not necessary for you to meet them. For when it is your time to meet them, you will. They will be there and speak to you as is needed, as God's will permits. He can talk to many and all or just one. Jesus is omnipresent, allowing him to be with all his children. He welcomes you home when you return. We cherish the work of the angels who help in your adjustment. The angels are so full of love that you cannot help but feel happiness to be in Heaven again, in the kingdom of Heaven. Earth is but a school where you have to love and create relationships and friendships. When you return home, we celebrate; you are home again. We are pleased. Your pain and suffering has ended. You are alive and free, free to explore all that you did not on earth. You say you want to learn about consciousness. Well, that is all there is on our side of the world, so there is plenty of time to learn this. Our souls are energy and have a center with intelligence that gives us our thoughts. We are no more than souls without the human body. Your thoughts continue on our side. Your mind is still there, except now it is free. It is free to explore the world.

We have touched on a little, but there is much more to learn. Try and spend time to decide your life. Life is wonderful when you think of life outside the limitations of your body. That is the purpose of today's lesson for you, to think of the possibilities and to learn how to apply them in your life. Life is precious. The physical experience is just temporary; so don't waste it.

Love

All you need is love. When you have found love, you have the power to create your world. Love is the main ingredient of life, but people do not know what it is, and they go through life searching for it. Once they have found it—and I say truly found it—then life begins. It is the peace and knowing inside that you have awakened and tapped into. When you feel this, this is when you know you have found love. You no longer just feel it; it is who you are. You become love. You radiate love; everything you do becomes based on love and your life becomes fulfilled. Many go through life and do not find love because they seek something other than love—that which they think is love—so they are never contented. Love is not a feeling or a sense of how you feel. It is an inner sense of just being: a completeness. There is no high or no low. It is a state of being. When you have found that state, you have found love and the secret of life.

Love is an act of giving and receiving the yin and the yang. When they are in harmony, they come together as one. That is how your love has become between you and mother and sister. You discovered the meaning of life: giving and receiving for the benefit of each other. Loving acts of kindness, loving acts of compassion: it is these acts that create love. Once these senses have been enlightened, you will understand that the love that is so called when you meet someone is only a state of euphoria like you get when you take a drug; it is not sustainable love. The love that is sustainable is that which grows out of compassion—the deepest kind, not a temporary "in love" moment.

Take Control Of Your Life

Finish your book soon. Your book is very intriguing to others who will be fascinated about your journey and your writings. Some people will not believe, but that is their choice, their decision. It will bring comfort to those in grief and knowledge to those who want to learn about the spirit world. You have opened them up to our world and for that we are truly grateful.

There is so much more to learn about our world that will help people on your earth. Yes, there are other books that have been written, but they are old now. We need new writers today who can talk about it from their own experiences, so people can ask them questions about their experience, their knowledge on the subject matter; that is what we want. We want to educate people about our world through people like you who will write from your own experiences with communication with spirit. It will cause controversy amongst the non-believers but that is to be expected, so don't let that stop you. Always be aware of it when talking about Spirit to other people; their opinions are valued by them, so remember that it is not a case of right or wrong. It is a case of educating those who are open to the truth: the truth that the spirit world does exist. It is our Heaven and your Heaven once you cross over, that is all.

Our world is vast with so much to learn. Cannot learn all in one book. We are your friends and helping you as much as we can from this side. We are here to encourage you and assist the best we can, but it is up to you to write the book as obviously that is a human function to do. We can only provide you with the information, so it is up to you how and what you do with the information. Do we make it clear for you? I hope so. Linda is saying, "You need to spell it out for her because she does not always see the whole picture like she did, and does now: 'what are you like'" she keeps saying. That must be a private joke between you too—a sisterly joke it seems nonetheless. (Linda teasingly used this rhetorical question when I didn't understand something that she thought I should know!)

Take control of earthy wants and desires, so they don't take control of you. If you want something then take the steps toward it. That is all. Take the steps. You have to put effort into what you want. It does not get handed to you on a silver platter. You create your own silver platter. After all, it is only a metaphor: symbolic of what you want and get in life. So you see what you want you can have, if you create your own silver platter and stop waiting for people to give it to you. Give yourself your own silver platter, and you can have it all. It is called the law of attraction; that you already know about, so create what you want, and you will receive. Most people do not know what they want, and they do not receive. They ask why they do not receive—so simple. The basic truth of life is to ask and you will receive. You need to put some effort into the equation that is all we ask.

I hope I have described it well for you today. Go in peace, my child.

Your friends, the group.

One Year Of Sprit Communication Draws Near

It was one year since I had first communicated with Linda. On this day, as I sat for my meditation session with pen and paper in hand, I saw an image of Jesus. I froze in the moment as I saw his face with piercing blue eyes looking directly at me.

I see a water fountain in a garden. I can hear the water trickling down over the edges. I look up and see Jesus. He speaks: *"My child, I am pleased with your progress so far. More teaching to follow but for now this will suffice. Follow my path to righteousness; it is a simple path but not always easy. Tread lightly; one thing at a time. No need to rush. All will come. Time will tell."* I see his feet. He is wearing sandals. *"They protect all I need to protect. Remember to have all you need and not more, it is wasteful."*

The vision of Jesus disappeared. As I continued my meditation, I was transported to another world.

I see people in a black and white image, like a negative of a photograph. They speak to me. *We are spirits that are highly evolved and travel to different planets. We do not come down to earth; we send helpers to get information. These helpers can appear as aliens or human-like. They will not appear in the human form, so make no mistake. They come down for a purpose to make an adjustment to the earth to keep it balanced.*

We want to take you to the blue room. This room is the biggest and the busiest. You can see it like a production room. We are figuring out ways to advance technology on earth. You see, eventually we need earth to have a high level of energy so we can visit more readily and freely in a way that will become normal to the earthly form. The worlds co-exist, yet earthly forms pretend they do not. They don't believe. But when we adjust earth's energy, it will make it easier for the earthly forms to communicate with us as you are doing now. It will take a change of consciousness, a change of energy for the human world to move closer to our world. That is what they are working on in the blue room: a way to change the energy force in conscious form.

They take me to a red room. The red room is monitoring for now—retesting things. It is not as important as the blue room. Responsibility does change with need. They show me the yellow room. The yellow room is busy making ideas for the blue room. The blue room takes the ideas and tests them out; they all work together you see. They explain the brown room: they like to write about the new ideas and compare them to past ideas, analyze them, etc. This is the intellect where they assess and grade.

I don't think we told you about the pink room. The pink room is full of love; that is all you need to know. Souls often come here to release and soak up all the love in the room. The love is sent to the humans on earth because there is plenty here to share. It appears in the hearts of those who need love on this side or your side. Love is universal. We all share love. It is probably the most favorite and popular place.

I go through a white light and see people in white robes wearing sandals like Jesus. We have come full circle. They wear simple white robes because that is all they need. When you walk in the Garden of Eden, you only need simple things. The Tree of Knowledge is always there. You can tap into it when you can and need to. The Tree of Knowledge is the Tree of Life in this world and your world. Just tap into it. That is the secret, which you have discovered.

As in previous meditations when I had visited the spirit world I was brought back to my surroundings in an abrupt instance and without warning. I can only assume that I had seen all that I needed to see at that time. Still feeling as if I was in a meditative-state, I remained seated with my eyes closed. My meditation session had not finished. I felt the energies of both Mum and Linda surround me.

I see Linda and I am smiling. I have an overwhelming sense to smile from cheek to cheek, from ear to ear. She speaks: *So good to be with you today! There is much work to be done. First, learn all you can about consciousness. I repeat consciousness, different levels, many levels, which is the key to our world. You have been given much knowledge on the different levels of energy fields; now start to look at the big picture in your mind. It is like taking a lift, or an elevator, to different floors and looking around, learning and seeing what is on each floor, fulfilling one's work on that floor, one's obligation, and moving to another floor. It all depends on what your need is or what your obligation is for that day.*

Her Work Is Done

I want to make you laugh today and bring a smile to your face. I am very happy. I want to make your life happier for you as well. Always do the right thing and you will be rewarded. That's all, Angie; no more stories today. I feel like I am drifting away from you because you don't need me anymore. I will visit you from time to time, but not like before with all these sermons. I have done my work, Angie, and feel so happy we were able to connect like this. I can't keep doing this forever; I have work to do! However, I promise that I will come and I will be around you when you need me. I send my love to everyone. You can help them now; you are ready to do that. I have given you the insight to life and insight on living a full happy life. Teach others, and they will live one too.

I will go now, Angie. This is your sister. I see her smile as she waves goodbye.

After Linda told me our communication was near the end I felt sad; it was as if I was losing her all over again. As Linda waved goodbye, Mum appeared with words of comfort.

It is me love, Mum. I am here. I will always be here. You are my darling daughter, so I can never leave you. Linda has done her work, but I will be around longer for you to get you launched on this path for good. I don't want you to give up or forget what you are supposed to do, so I will help you stay on track. My love will never die, will never leave you, and will never go. We are one soul, part of the same soul, cut from the same cloth you and I. We will always be with one another. We are lucky that our souls are entwined. You found that out during my life with you. From an early age, you comforted me and I comforted you. Our love was so strong that we naturally bonded it was easy. I don't want to say I loved you more or that I loved the others less because that is not true; I mean that our souls were the same; they were compatible, and that made our lives, our relationship, easy and so loving. I want to help you with your book now. Keep writing it, Angie. You will do fine. Write as you think. Look at other books and learn from them, like everything I told you in life. Learn from the experience. You will do the right thing.

Your Inner Guide

I know you miss me, but I am always here. Such love we have cannot be broken, remember that. I love you my darling daughter; I will always love you. That is all you need to know to keep you and to sustain you in your life. A mother's love is never broken, not from the physical to the non-physical form. I want to help you on your path. You will be amazed what will happen, what will be if you follow the path. Just do what you think is right, what feels right, and let that be your guide. It is your guide; the feeling you get is your guide speaking, so remember that. Make all decisions based on what feels right. Remember I said that. It will be important one day. You have nothing to fear, so just do the best you can and you will live all your life well. I will go now. Just a quick hello today. You are doing fine, so carry on love.

I will go now. I love you, Angie.

Chapter 31: Full Circle

Group: My dear, what more can we say than what has been told to you already? You have been given much information for your book, and now it is time to complete this step, the first step in the process. Finish the book my child; we are pleased. Our work has served its purpose. Write your conclusion on what you have found and discovered about the spirit world. What did you expect to find? Did you find it? Are all your questions answered for now? More questions will arise as you develop more. Do you understand the meaning of life? Do you understand the purpose of life? Do you understand that you did not lose your mother's love and that it is still there my child, child of God? Love cannot be broken, cannot disappear. Love is energy. Energy cannot be destroyed as Einstein so correctly surmised.

Thoughts are energy, and it was these thoughts, these determined thoughts, that created the energy necessary to communicate and blend with spirit energy making it easier for your energy and spirit world energy to blend. You created such a strong energy through your thoughts, through your desire to communicate with loved ones in spirit, that you created the ability to make it happen.

We are pleased that you have chosen to communicate with our world; there is much to learn and write about. We want to congratulate you on your progress these last twelve months. You have come a long way and embraced our world as your world, which it is. It is every human being's world, but not all humans embrace it as you have.

You mother and sister are well pleased. They knew you would and could do it. They are sorry that their deaths, their loss, were the key, the catalyst, to put you on this path. But don't you see that it is the natural law of progression. Their loss pushed you in this direction. I am not saying that it was a deliberate thing to lose *your mother and sister to spirit in order for you to discover our world that could not be further from the truth. The truth is, their deaths were their natural progressions in their journeys. You and you determined what you did after their deaths alone. You were naturally drawn to our world, their world, because you followed their love, followed the chain that connected you, and now you have achieved much in the way of knowledge that will help you and others who not only are in grief, but those who want to know about the other world, for humans are curious about our world and have been since the dawn of time.*

Look at the Egyptians and their pyramids. All those magnificent treasures they stored in hopes of a better life in our world, but they did not know that earthly treasures are not needed in our world, only treasures of the soul. Love and truth are all you need, which you have been taught in our lessons many times these last twelve months. No need to repeat the lessons as they are there to be read and reread by all. We have merely given them to you to pass along to all who wish to see the light, the light of truth and the light of love, God's love.

My dear child, you have come far and we are pleased. No more needed for this book; you are finished with this book. Make good use of the knowledge, and use it wisely. Help others who need help. We ask that of you. Our time is finished for now, my child. May God's love fill your heart and bless you and all you meet.

Go in peace. God bless you.

As the group's energy disappeared and I felt my mother's energy surround me.

Mum: My love for you is stronger now than ever. You have come a long way and I am pleased—we are pleased. This is your Mum and Linda speaking today. We are proud of you and want you to know that. We knew you could do it, Angie. I knew you could do it. You just needed a little encouragement and guidance from us, and we have done that. We want you to do well. You represent our lives in the spirit world, and you keep our love alive and foremost in the minds of the world. You have been given valuable lessons to share with humanity and mankind. Do your best to get the book finished as soon as you can. Your book will bring happiness to people who need some uplifting and comforting. That is all.

You will receive negative feedback; that is to be expected. Don't let that upset you or offend you. Keep focused on your book. It is full of love, full of the truth about life. It is there for all who want to know, and already there are those of you wanting to know the truth. It will be a book that is used again and again. Not a novel or a quick read. People will be curious about it and will dissect each page, each paragraph. They want something that appeals to them, and that is meaningful to them. May your life be blessed, blessed with the love and joy of knowing the truth. How you choose to live your life will be up to you. We have given you the information to follow: a blueprint for life. Follow your dreams. Dreams are your soul talking to you. All dreams keep HOPE alive. Without HOPE there is no happiness. Always have a dream; your life will be full.

I felt mother's energy fade. As her energy faded I could see crusaders on their horses. They look magnificent riding through the street. The horses rode very quickly with such force. I stood on the side of the dirt road as they rode by. On the other side of the road, I could see someone fall into the street. The crusaders do not stop. It is my sister, Linda. She is killed by the crusaders in the street. She did not want to watch them in the first place and now she is dead. Oh no, what I have done? It is my fault that she was there. She never believed in the crusaders' mission and now she has been killed by the crusaders in the name of religion. I rush to her side and pick her up. She is dying but tells me she loves me and will be in my life many more times for we have many to live.

This image was like watching a scene out of a movie except that my sister and I were in it. The significance of what my sister is about to reveal helps me to understand our relationship in this lifetime.

Linda: *You are lucky in this life because it is the first time you have recognized and acknowledged our lives together; the purpose of our lives together was so that I would die of my own free will and not in an accident that you believed was your fault. I came down to earth again to free you of that guilt. You paid me back in this lifetime by your kind generosity and love. I lived a happy life because of you, and I died of my own free will, which had nothing to do with you. Now you are free of that burden of that obligation in this lifetime.*

Think of it as a wonderful gift for your development on earth. Remember we come back to earth, the learning school, to pay debts owed in other lifetimes. This emotional debt has cleared. You are free to live your life with freedom and with no guilt. Live your life with freedom now. You have paid your debt to me and to mankind. I am now your guardian angel, which is why you can see me with wings, your fairy Godmother. You saved me in this lifetime—don't you see that, Angie? I lived a life of mundane existence—by giving me a life of joy in America where I had the love for Harvey, my precious cat. It was the happiest time of my life and the best thing that happened to me. Harvey was my treasure, my joy. I am happy now. Harvey is with me; I don't go anywhere without him. Mum likes him too. Although she was never an animal lover, she does love Harvey. He is our companion. Everyone comes to see him. He is "Top Cat." Shane, the dog, is a little jealous in a fun way but he doesn't mind. After all, he says, Harvey is just a cat and not a dog! Linda is smiling at me.

I can't believe you figured it all out while you are on earth. Usually, these things are discovered when we all get back home, here in Heaven. But you have discovered a way to do it now. You were always the clever one, figuring out ways to do the impossible. But as you know, nothing is impossible while in the earthly form. The answers are all within. All you need to do is tune in as you do! It is a wonderful gift you have discovered. Keep on communicating, and you will be surprised what you learn about yourself.

God bless you, Angie. We are pleased. Go and finish the book. God bless, we are going now. Love, Mum and Linda, your guardian angels.

As Mum and Linda said their goodbyes I saw the judge-like figure whom I had seen before. He was the same judge who came to me in the very beginning, and now he leaves me with these parting words:

Judge: *Your mother and sister are proud of your development. They had no doubt in your ability. I have none. I am the judge who you met in the beginning. So you see, you have indeed come full circle. I stamp my hammer again because you have completed or finished this part of your life. We will go now and plan your next steps in your development. We take this seriously because this is part of your precious life on earth, and we have to ensure that the time is well spent. Your mother has presented you well. She is very proud of you. You are her protégé, her child. You are fortunate to have her as your guide. She is helping you every step of the way just to make sure you stay on track and don't get distracted that is all. I will go now.*

The courtroom was empty. I stood up to leave. Mum gave me a hug and left the room. Linda ran after her while yelling to me: *"Bye Angie. I knew you could do it! My savior! Remember that. All is well now, Angie. Don't let anything drag you down. You are free, free to spread your wings and fly; fly, Angie, fly,"* and with those parting words she was gone.

Afterward

When you will something so much anything is possible. I was a desperate soul in search of hope. Without hope, my life was empty. In my search for the truth, I found that life does continue beyond the grave in a place called Heaven, the Afterlife, and the Spirit World. With this profound knowledge came hope. I followed my mother's and sister's love that I thought was taken from me by their physical death because I knew in my heart that our love was so strong that it could not die. By refusing to accept or believe that our love was gone, I was determined to find it and to never let it go. Through my will and determination, I found it. I have it. It is with me all the time. All I have to do is to think about them and their love is there. I can feel it. Love never dies.

Eventually God brings all his children home, and that is where Mum and Linda have gone. They went home. I know because they took me there. They opened my eyes and my mind to their world. They communicated with me so I could understand what happened to them after their souls left their physical body. They did not die; they only lost their physical bodies for their souls live on in Heaven. I feel their love around me, especially when I meditate; it is such a strong emotion that often it makes me cry. I know they are happy and that one day we will be together in God's kingdom, in Heaven. God loves us all.

My journey has taken me to places beyond my imagination and dreams. I found a world full of love. It is a place where we return home to God, our Creator. It is a world that encompasses our world, and I know that our planet earth is protected by a greater force, our creator, God. Through my journey, I have learned the purpose and meaning of life: to love one another and to have compassion. Beyond this, I have learned God's purpose for creation and his love for mankind. I discovered that love is the positive energy force and the bond that connects our two worlds together where they co-exist as one, for our loved ones are around us. I found that the bonds of love can never be broken and that they never disappear. Love is an energy that cannot be destroyed and that losing the physical body does not destroy the love.

Although we suffer the loss of our loved ones, I know that they watch over us and send their love. They comfort us in our grief and in our sorrow. I finish my journey knowing that they want to communicate with us. If I had not experienced it myself, I would not have believed it. I know that is a strange thing to say, but I had no idea that the spirit world could communicate with me and I with them. I found that Spirit wants to communicate with all human beings and, because I was a willing soul, we were able to form a two-way communication.

There maybe some of you reading this book who may follow my path and communicate with loved ones, and I hope that you do. There is nothing more healing than experiencing this phenomenon. There are those of you who may be comforted in your grief by reading my story and can relate to my pain. I hope that you feel some comfort. There are others who may appreciate the information regarding philosophy and what Heaven is like and find it fascinating, as I did. Then, there are those who will strongly disagree with most of the information in this book, and I respect your right to disagree.

At the end of the day, I still remain a person who misses her Mum and sister every day and would give anything to have them physically in my life again. My meditation sessions have been the next best thing to having them physically with me and in my life. I take these experiences and know that they were a special gift—from Mum and Linda. They have opened my eyes to the existence of the spirit world. Do I want to spend the rest of my life meditating for hours each and every day? Probably not, because I will miss out on my earthly experiences.

I hope my story has helped you in some way; it has certainly helped me. If I have opened your mind to the possibility of the afterlife and the existence of the spirit world then I am truly pleased. Remember your loved ones; they have not gone. They are here with you and they send their love.

God bless you all.

CPSIA information can be obtained at www.ICGtesting.com
Printed in the USA
BVOW07s1519180914

366579BV00014B/7/P